PRICK WITH A FORK

PRICK
WITH
A
FORK

The world's worst
waitress spills the beans

LARISSA DUBECKI

ALLEN&UNWIN
SYDNEY·MELBOURNE·AUCKLAND·LONDON

Author's note

Each breakout in the text comes via fellow hospitality travellers, talking about their own waiter experiences in anonymous restaurants. Elsewhere, some names have been changed for obvious legal reasons. But it all happened.

First published in 2015

Allen & Unwin
83 Alexander Street
Crows Nest NSW 2065
Australia
Phone: (61 2) 8425 0100

Email: info@allenandunwin.com
Web: www.allenandunwin.com

Cataloguing-in-Publication details are available
from the National Library of Australia
www.trove.nla.gov.au

ISBN 978 1 92526 605 4

Internal design by Kate Frances Design

Set in 11/17 pt Sabon by Midland Typesetters, Australia

Printed and bound in Australia by Griffin Press

10 9 8 7 6 5 4 3 2

MIX
Paper from
responsible sources
FSC® C009448

The paper in this book is FSC® certified. FSC® promotes environmentally responsible, socially beneficial and economically viable management of the world's forests.

For Ben, of course

Contents

Foreword

There's a Kurt Vonnegut line that reminds me of the decade I spent waiting tables for a living. It's from *Slaughterhouse Five*, which seems appropriate given the clear parallels—the firebombing of Dresden, the alien abduction, the pervasive air of unease and existential distress. But amid all that fuss and bother it's a remarkably gentle little thing: 'Here we are . . . trapped in the amber of this moment.' For me it evokes the soft, late-afternoon cottony hush before service starts. A precious hour, maybe an hour-and-a-half, this is the grown-up equivalent of Quiet Time for toddlers at crèche—an enforced period of golden calm before the clang and the haste of the dinner rush. Optimism hangs in the air. Tonight will be easy; as smooth as that butter you're taking out of the fridge to soften so it doesn't tear the bread. A slow ease into the evening, a casual kick into first gear to warm the engine: setting tables, rearranging chairs, filling water jugs. Sweet, sweet busywork without the annoyance of those people who can make the job such a pain in the arse.

Oh yes. Customers.

By 7 p.m. it's a different place altogether. The dockets are coming in like artillery fire; a dozen of them bristle angrily across the pass. The chefs are screaming, the diners are restless and the boss, a dyspeptic alcoholic with kidney stones and abandonment issues, is chain-smoking at the bar and fixing his specially patented Death Stare on any staff member who stops moving for more than half a second. Yessir, Charlie's in the bushes.

I don't think anyone sets out to become a career waiter. If that's a rude hand gesture to the industry that kept me fed for more than ten years, I apologise. It's just that I grapple with the idea of someone being naturally endowed with the urge to serve others. At the very least such a lofty ideal is rather priestly, and hey—we all know where *that* winds up, don't we?

I'm sure being a waiter was once a noble calling with its own arcane procedures and rituals. Now, however, it's a default position. Even the lowliest chef can claim to feel a vocational pull, but the people running the food from kitchen to table are, nine times out of ten, simple economic tourists, doing the job as a means to an end. All biding their time until real life begins, driven by no more than the mantra of youth: there for a good time, not a long time. Blissfully unaware that if you don't exercise due caution, not a long time can turn out to be quite a sometime.

Me, you ask? No more than a garden-variety service drone, never aiming for anything higher than finishing my shift and necking down a knock-off beer, maybe two if the boss wasn't looking. Management? Get outta here. I'll be gone soon, off to the land of the professionals with my briefcase and skirt-suit, my packed lunch and serious hair. But then you look up from folding napkins, polishing cutlery and de-scuzzing tables and ten years have passed. Ten years. Until that point, a third of my life. Seriously, the number of blameless people's nights out I must have sabotaged, either through boredom or indifference or pure evil intent. It's chastening, although in the hotly contested title of World's Worst

Waiter, I could probably lay a decent case. Believe me, I was bad. But 'worst' sounds boastful. And was I really that bad? Or was I just another piece of flotsam floating in a vast sea of mediocrity?

There was my friend Belinda, for instance, who took the job title literally and mounted a spirited argument to her first boss that she had signed up only to take orders and carry food. Cleaning the bar when things were quiet? Restocking the fridge? No, no, no, if you would kindly read the job description . . . Fired from that one. At her next gig she grew tired one night of reciting the specials to each separate table, and announced to the room, 'Listen up, everyone. I'm only going to do this once . . .' Fired from that one, too. Or Andrea, who didn't even make it through a single night thanks to a teensy spot of docket mis-scribing that was only picked up after the kitchen had freshly shucked twelve dozen oysters instead of twelve.

And that's just two former housemates. The competition is heating up. The field is wide open. The petty thieves, drunks, druggies, liars, princesses, comedians, charlatans, misanthropes and assorted oddbodies I called my co-workers are champing at the bit. Finally, a chance to excel.

You know what I did like about being a waiter? The way each new shift erases the previous one. You're only as good as your last spin on the floor. In that way it's a bit like writing for newspapers, where I unexpectedly ended up after performing the career equivalent of a reverse four-and-a-half somersault pike from the 3-metre board and became a restaurant critic. *Me*, sitting in judgement of *them*. The universe does indeed have a sense of humour.

Hospitality is a marvellous industry, really. Never a dull moment. Well, plenty of dull moments, but with the potential for something hilarious or amazing or horrifying always hovering tantalisingly nearby in a way it does not, I would imagine, if you were a console operator or a quantity surveyor.

The real professionals of the industry have my undying respect. I've had the privilege of working with a few and witnessed many more in action from my seat at the best table in the house. Being a good waiter is hard enough. Being a great waiter is something I couldn't dream of achieving if I had twenty lives instead of one. Good and great waiters alike may well sneer at my pathetic dabblings in a serious business. What would I know about the art—the *art*, dammit!—of being a waiter? The other 99 per cent? Game on.

DON'T BOGART THAT ROACH

Consider the pizza. A cold and lonely slice orphaned on a clunky white plate, surrounded by the detritus of gluttony—masticated olive pits, half-eaten crusts, a limp crescent of over-marinated capsicum. It's destined for the bin, you would think, a sign of another satiated customer who crumpled their napkin and performed the internationally recognised hand gesture of an imaginary pen on paper that means 'bring me the bill'.

However. Consider you're a waiter. You've just spent the past four hours serving food to thankless idiots after pulling a double shift the previous day with vodka-based refreshments to follow. You woke late, with only enough time to do the minimal gesture to social civility of the dry shower—a quick spritz of deodorant over yesterday's clothes—before fronting up to work again. The gnaw in your stomach has gone from insistent to hostile. Blood sugar levels have plummeted to dangerous lows yet to be fully understood by medical science.

You're bottoming out. The law of diminishing returns means the odd cigarette break, snatched in the rear laneway on an upended milk crate, is no longer enough to quell the pangs of hunger. It's still two-and-a-bit hours until staff meals will be ready. Anyway, the kitchen has been going through a phase where they let the first-year apprentice experiment with his avant-garde food ideas as a sick joke on the waiters, regarded in this particular establishment (and in many others) as a sub-class of humans not unlike the Morlocks in H.G. Wells's *The Time Machine*. Unbeknown to table six, lingering innocently over their tiramisu, there is a very real danger of this turning into a hostage situation.

And there's that pizza, abandoned on a table, ready to be collected and thrown in the bin without a second's thought where it will fester among a decaying food gravy of scraps and offcuts and eventually make its way to a stinking landfill. Would you eat it?

You spy your chance. The chefs are preoccupied by a spirited intellectual discussion ('Britney's *hot*; Christina's a dog, man'), the floor manager has disappeared to places unknown, and there's a blind spot near the dish pig where you'd be able to squeeze into a corner, between the bin and the ice machine, and stuff that bad boy down.

Let's call it Il Crappo Italiano. One of those Lygon Street restaurants doing for the reputation of Italian food what the captain of the *Costa Concordia* did for cruise liners. Forget the nation's proud regionalism, its produce obsession, its *Denominazione di Origine Protetta* swagger. Il Crappo is a swamp, a veritable red-sauce sea of shoddy ingredients with red and white checked tablecloths and, for that extra frisson of Latin authenticity, candles jammed into Chianti bottles. You might have been there. If you haven't, you've likely been to one of the thousands upon thousands of places exactly like it dotted across the world. You know them: there's a spruiker out the front, bellowing about the 'REAL, OAR-THEN-TIC ITALIAN FOOD' and screaming 'CIAO BELLA!' in the face of every female under the age of ninety on the assumption that women need only be told they're beautiful by a glib arsehole in a waistcoat to think 'Goodness, I really feel like lasagne'.

You don't need experience to work at Il Crappo. Who sold you that idea? Sure, they advertised the job like this: 'Fun, Energetic, Vibrant, Proactive, Experienced Waiter/Waitress Wanted for Quality Italian restaurant.' ('Hey, that's me!' thinks the morose, lazy, dull, reactive dolt in desperate need of some quick coin to pay this month's rent. 'How do I convince them I'm their man?') But here's the thing you will quickly realise. Il Crappo is bullshitting just as much as you are. Working here is the hospitality equivalent of going down the salt mines. They churn through staff here like a logger going at a Tasmanian old-growth forest. Six months is considered a damned good innings. You'll either be fired or— better still—muster the self-respect to walk out and never return.

Il Crappo doesn't really need to see a CV when you front up for what passes for an 'interview', although it will expect you to bullshit up a several-page litany of half-truths and outright lies. No one's going to be calling your references. It doesn't need to see a pathetic little certificate in hospitality ('Bar, Coffee and Floor') from trade school, a gold rosette stamped pompously on the masthead.

Anyone can become a waiter at Il Crappo. That means you. Yes, you. And me.

And why, you may be asking yourself, did I desire to work at Il Crappo when it was so clearly, so patently, awful? Simple. Cool people were waiters. And I was neither. This abject story opens on a gormless nineteen-year-old working casual shifts in a Well-Known Australian Fashion Store. A retail assistant. A fashion adviser. Basically I was being paid for my ability to lie to middle-aged women that a sequined bomber jacket is a fabulous investment piece that can be dressed up or down.

Waitressing has its downsides, certainly, but fashion retail is a living death. Far nobler to operate a checkout in a supermarket, calling for a price check on cat food. Better to work on a production line screwing smaller bolts onto bigger bolts for eight hours a day, willing the rhythm of the action to dull the acuteness of time. Selling clothes is nothing more than a grand illusion that involves projecting the appearance of busyness while waiting for the next victim—known in the trade as a 'customer'—to wander into the web of well-dressed despair. There are no positives to speak of—apart from, in my case, a sweet little scam that involved buying clothes with the 50 per cent staff discount and returning them to a Large, Well-Known Department Store for a full-priced refund. Until they twigged and started demanding receipts it really boosted the discretionary spending fund, but that's pretty much all I have to recommend for three years' worth of telling people their bum didn't look big in that.

Alternatively, I could blame the weather. This fateful day, during summer break from university where I was diligently failing both law and arts, the light on Collins Street was flattened in the heat and a thick northerly blew a hail of city grit along the tram tracks. Inside the Well-Known AFS it was fridge-cool but deserted. Melbourne was practically tipping on its axis with all the inhabitants running for the beach. Nothing to do aside from listen to my bubble-headed co-worker talk about her dentist boyfriend and all the ways he was treating her mean. I'd tuned her out. Instead I was contemplating gnawing my right arm off in boredom. And maybe it was the thought of listening to Prince's *Diamonds and Pearls* one more time, maybe it was the company directive to 'engage each customer in conversation that does not solicit a yes or no answer', or perhaps it was simply that an old high school friend ventured by at exactly the same moment I had thrown a stack of T-shirts on the floor in order to have something to do on the long, slow crawl to 6 p.m.

Donna didn't say anything. She didn't have to. You could have cut my desperation with a knife. She fixed me with the considered look that translated as 'Wa-hey, girlfriend! What the fuck?'. It was the same look that had seen her catapulted to McDonald's shift manager while still in Year 11 before heading off to a proper restaurant where—impressively—she had to wear a waistcoat and tie. Donna was one of those preternaturally mature people already on their path in life, ticking boxes, being responsible. (We'll discuss fast-food outlets later, but let's get their great lie out of the way: boys and girls, working in one of these places is not the stepping stone to CEO of a multinational corporation. Swallow that line and the best you can hope for is employee of the month.)

'Why don't you do something a little more . . . er . . . structured?' she said.

'And interesting,' she added. 'Like waitressing. It's fun. And you get fed.'

Working in a retail coffin where the highlight of our day was the brief visit of Dom the flirtatious delivery driver, waiting tables seemed hopelessly dynamic. It seemed tantalisingly, sparklingly real. There was a beguiling kernel of honesty in providing an essential service. Everyone eats and drinks, but not everyone does so in a sequined bomber jacket. There was an innocent practicality in asking 'Would you like to order?' as opposed to 'Don't you love the colour of those jeans?' and then realising you'd just broken company policy by soliciting a yes or no response. Serving the world coffee instead of wrapping it in the lies of fashion? I was in.

We held a boot camp. The one thing they would ask, Donna sagely advised, once they'd ascertained I had my own teeth and no face tattoos, was if I could carry three plates at a time. It didn't matter if I could only *sort of* carry three plates, and then only if they were empty, and then only if there were no sharp turns, or in fact any turns at all. That wasn't the kind of detail Il Crappo would be interested in. Not one bit. They had to be seen to be taking their professionalism seriously; I needed to be seen to be pretending to be professional. It was a two-way street of pretence.

In regards to the plates, the truth is there's really not much to it. For a right-hander, pick up one plate in the left hand; use the thumb and forearm as a flat surface on which to balance plate number two; third plate in the right hand. Not to be tried as an amateur with soup, which typically comes with a base plate and bowl and is therefore excruciatingly heavy with an extremely high potential for mishap dovetailing spectacularly with an equal and opposite potential for full-thickness burns. The better guys can zip around with three plates on one arm and two in the other, but best leave that stuff to the professionals. The secret's in the ballast—keep the feet low to the ground to minimise jolting, and activate the hip swivel so you glide between tables like Torvill, or even Dean. Smooth. You gotta be smooth.

For anyone with the unenviable task of hiring waiters, sifting through the human flotsam can be a full-time job in itself. Hospitality is an industry that attracts more than its fair share of miscreants, thieves, liars, university students, psychopaths, druggies, borderline personality disorders and Danish backpackers. It's a long, slogging, thankless, shitful task of trying to divine the human being lurking behind the eager face at the interview. It's Murphy's Law. Get a good one and they'll soon be off to that ashram in India for a year-long spiritual retreat. Get a complete nuffy and they'll be hanging around like a fart in a car. Crucial stuff, though. Restaurants don't just sell food, they sell hospitality, and whomsoever slips through the net will become its appointed representative on the floor.

Oh yes. That was me.

Of course I got the job. Of course they figured out pretty much instantaneously that I had no clues whatsoever, although if they had challenged me to walk in a straight line carrying two empty plates on one arm, I could have just about managed it. They might have grumbled among themselves but the owners—snivelly little Paulo who kept a stack of Men's Gallery vouchers by the till for his favourite male customers, and huge, impassive Antonio, his neck chains glinting like buried treasure under an impressive thatch of chest hair—were desperate or indifferent enough not to make a big issue of it.

The food was like a copy of a copy of a copy: a faded facsimile of one of the world's greatest cuisines. Bad food is bad food, but there's something about bad Italian food that really makes me sad. The 'our famous veal parmigiana' was anything but. Even its own mother wouldn't have recognised it. The osso bucco was like a joke played on the natives of Lombardy, who had grounds for demanding its arrest for crimes against regional pride. To wit: a lump of meat so overcooked it collapsed into a soggy pile of fibres at the merest threat of a utensil, a mound of risotto that managed to be simultaneously both gluggy and undercooked, and more of the smoothly sweet red sauce that ran through the place like blood through an artery.

I've given Il Crappo a bum steer in one matter only. Standards were not so high that eating customers' rejects was frowned upon. In fact, management tacitly encouraged it as a way of reducing the cost of staff meals. The only rule was that it couldn't be done in sight of the dining room. Everyone knew that as soon as you hit the fire extinguisher halfway down the run, the contents of that plate were fair game.

Oysters were the big currency at this joint. They were the filthy lucre, sent back to the kitchen with such regularity that they were obviously not the sparkling, ocean-fresh creatures of briny loveliness that are the mark of a truly great oyster. I know plenty of places where sending an oyster back to the kitchen would induce mass weeping and possibly ritual suicide from the chef who allowed them through quality control. Here it was a case of bottoms-up.

Nino the general manager loved them. '*Mio caro*, come to papa!' he'd croon over the suspect bivalves instead of actually doing his job and trotting out to ask the customers why they didn't eat them. Nino was one of those guys who come in fifty-two flavours. A moody bastard, in other words. Gay with a side order of misogyny. This was a man who, when asked by a plump female customer what the gnocchi gorgonzola was like, replied, 'The gnocchi is amazing, madam. But you are not the one who should be eating it.'

Il Crappo was a place where management flounced about in their invisible 'Italians do it better' T-shirts, as insufferable as Madonna in her 'Papa Don't Preach' era. As if we'd all been whisked back to the social mores of the first Roman Empire, anyone who wasn't Italian was a second-class citizen, and if you were from the subcontinent then you weren't even a third-class citizen, you were an actual slave. That was where the dish pig came into it.

The French have a good word for the dish pig—*plongeur*. *Plongeur* derives from the word for a submariner—a bit of Froggy humour for you there, folks—but in Australia it almost goes without saying that the dish pig is Indian. The Nepalese community has got a bit of a foothold as well, and a few Pakistanis, too, but young men from the subcontinent have become the sherpas of the Australian restaurant world. They are to Australian restaurants as Mexicans are to the kitchens of the United States. The entire industry would collapse if they were to turn to each other one day, say 'What the hell are we doing this for?' and walk out. A bunch of white people would be left looking at each other helplessly, shrugging and saying 'Nah, mate, not my job.'

Our dish-wallahs work incredible hours for incredibly low pay, little thanks, and often outright abuse. They finish after everyone else then schlep home on public transport where the threat of physical violence from some drunk yobbo is a very real and immediate danger, before arriving at some cheap outer-suburban accommodation where they bunk in, four to a bedroom.

You'd think they deserve a break, but Nino treated Il Crappo's dish pig like his own guilty conscience. His favourite trick was to hurl a massive stack of plates into the sink so Vijay, a silent young man from the Punjab, would be covered in a tidal wave of gunge-slicked hot water. I can't remember any occasion I walked into Il Crappo's kitchen and Vijay wasn't there, slaving at his Sisyphean task in order to save enough money so he could go home and get married and bring his new bride back to Australia to chase the dream of a better life. He copped it endlessly from Il Crappo's Italians-do-it-better. The monkey gags, the shoving, the swearing, the sharp knives being thrown in the hope he'd reflexively catch them, the hot pans thrust into his bare hands. Vijay copped it and copped it and copped it. Plenty of the waiters silently willed him to bite back but there was a

GILLIAN

One of the waiters walked out of the men's toilets.
He'd gone ghost-white. I asked him what was wrong
and he just pointed. So I go in there and the first
thing that hits me is the smell. The rankest smell.
And I went into the cubicle and someone had done
a drawing on the wall using compacted shit. It must
have been from a colostomy bag, that's the only
explanation we could come up with. It was even
signed—it had the initials SJ inside a circle of shit.
When Brian the cleaner came in after service that
night, I gave him a hug and said, 'I'm sorry.' He
walked into the toilet and I heard him scream. He
later said that in seventeen years of cleaning he'd
never seen anything like it.

gulf between us, a bunch of middle-class white kids lying about our
income to get Austudy, and him, working because his life depended
on it. He never snapped, never grabbed Nino by the throat and
threatened him with something deliciously violent, making his
persecutor wet his pants just a little. Life is rarely so satisfying. But
sometimes things just happen more quietly.

One day, for example, Nino's car keys went missing. Sure,
there's a possibility he misplaced them, but he always—*always*—
kept them on a hook next to his bag. Then they vanished. Just like
that. Never to be found again. It cost him a bomb to have the locks
replaced, and that was after he got a parking ticket because he
couldn't move the thing when the road he was parked on turned
into a clearway at 5 o'clock every afternoon. Nino was rampaging

around the joint in a scarlet fury and I caught a brief look on Vijay's face of pure, absolute satisfaction before his protective mask went up again. It was lovely.

From a purely selfish point of view, the dish pig is a valuable ally. He can be your eyes and ears in the kitchen. The dish pig flies under the radar so he can be a great source of kitchen gossip. No one notices him, so other staff don't think to censor what they say in his presence. But in the end it doesn't matter if he can do nothing for you. Being nice to this person is your duty. Every time someone is mean to the dish pig, a fairy dies.

∿

I couldn't bring myself to eat the returned oysters, those rejected gobs of sea snot. But I ate the pizza, and the chips—chips being an authentic Italian staple invented by Garibaldi, if I remember my history correctly. No matter that those leftover chips could have been on the floor. They could have been sucked on by a toddler. They could have been coughed over, spat on, used as props in a re-enactment of the Battle of the Somme, for all I know. But eat them I did. It was an early lesson in how quickly the standards of the group reset your own personal compass.

There were moments to make me question the wisdom of the herd. An entire table of sixteen staged a dramatic walk-out one night. Just after their meals arrived they stood up en masse and left, leaving a table that heaved with oysters and veal, spaghetti bolognese and eggplant parmigiana. Was it a political statement about bad Italian food? Was it performance art? Their cult-like silence was bewildering until the last person pointed to the culprit: a fat brown cockroach baked into capricciosa pizza. It could have passed for an olive if not for the legs sticking feebly out of the congealed mire.

Il Crappo closed for good only a few weeks after the cockroach incident. You're probably assuming it was the health department but I assure you it wasn't. All commercial kitchens have cockroaches. Most domestic kitchens have cockroaches—except yours, of course, of course—although the human inhabitants are usually unaware of the nocturnal activities taking place in the pantry and underneath the fridge. Before going into the waitering game, I once read with a thrill of horror that at any given moment a person is likely to be no more than a metre away from a spider. Such statistics no longer hold any fear. Try rats. Try rats the size of chihuahuas, their obscene little pink feet scurrying for the dark when the storeroom light goes on. Rats in a commercial kitchen? Of course it happens. Especially in the inner city, where half the kitchens back onto alleyways. Rats were accepted as a part of life in the nineteenth century when those alleyways were laid. The problem still exists, it's just gone underground.

For our creepy-crawly friends, commercial kitchens are equipped with the self-same attractions of the domestic kitchen, only supersized into a carnival of fun. Can you imagine being an everyday, self-respecting cockroach accustomed to scavenging on the often-scant offerings of nature, stumbling into a restaurant kitchen? It must be like Columbus discovering the Americas. Of course they're going to jump on the blower to share the good news. Send more ships! Life is great over here! Come on down!

Deal with it. Discreet visits, always conducted out-of-hours, make the exterminator the restaurant world's answer to the mistress. He comes armed with synthetic pyrethroids instead of petroleum-based jelly, but he is the industry's best-kept secret. Anyway, it takes more than a single incident like the cockroach pizza to be closed down by the clipboard brigade. It requires concentrated effort: a flowering of filth, nurtured over time.

RICCARDO

A man called me over, a few minutes after I'd put his mussel and saffron risotto in front of him, and quietly showed me a metal bolt he'd found in it. I apologised profusely and asked what I could get him to replace it. He said he'd simply like another risotto, minus the bolt. I raced back to the kitchen like John Cleese in *Fawlty Towers* and requested they make a fresh risotto, pronto. A couple of minutes after I served him the second risotto with another round of grovelling apologies, the customer called me over and showed me the metal spring he'd found in it. It turned out the mixer had blown, sending internal shrapnel all over the kitchen.

That greasy takeaway on the corner that's regularly closed 'for renovations'? I promise you, it's trying really, really hard to cultivate a bacterium hitherto unknown to mankind.

The real story behind the restaurant's end was just as timeless. Il Crappo was going down the gurgler and like plenty of desperate owners before them, Antonio and Paulo were looking for their way out. Their not-so-cunning plan was simply to slink away, leaving a trail of bad debt. It happens all the time. Liquidate the operation, shuffle the directors and hey presto—a new dawn. Creditors and employees get more or less legally screwed.

But the kitchen got wind of it when Paulo left a loan application on the fax machine. They were planning to open a new place, in an area they touted enthusiastically to the bank as having lots of brothels and therefore a ready-made clientele. What can

I say? They were classy guys. Chris, the head chef, showed me the incriminating evidence just before he and his entire kitchen brigade walked out, precipitating Il Crappo's premature demise.

'Look at what these fuckers are doing!' he yelled, flapping the papers in his hand. 'Taking us all for a fucking ride!'

That was another lesson that stayed with me. A restaurant is habitually referred to in the singular. In reality it's a complex organism of individuals, ideally acting as one cohesive whole working towards the common good (as in a beehive, or an ant colony) but in the breach more like a flock of seagulls, each one grabbing for the chip while a couple of the wilier ones look for sympathy by pulling the old fake broken leg stunt. Judging by the exalted places I've worked in, the average restaurant is a mutually exclusive bunch of individuals whose self-interests only occasionally overlap, and then on a strictly accidental basis. So call it the first commandment of hospitality—if you think a place is shaky, make sure you get paid after every shift, or just get the hell out.

Still, I felt guilty for a while. That cockroach? It was my table.

I escaped a major bollocking that night when Antonio decided to go for the pizza chef instead, the hapless guy who'd let an unfortunate member of *Blatella germanica*, the German cockroach, meet its maker in a wood-fired pizza oven. He was only my age, a skinny little thing, being verbally eviscerated by a fifty-year-old man-mountain who stank of stale cigarettes. A hail of spit splattered his face as he cowered in his sauce-stained jacket. Behind him, in the blind spot between the bin and the ice machine, two waiters were shovelling down oysters as if their lives depended on it.

— 2 —
THE BARE NAKED TRUTH

There are kids these days who are restaurant connoisseurs. Truly. Ten-year-olds who visit high-end restaurants, order the spanner crab *velouté* followed by the pork belly with onion marmalade, then blog about it. Their classmates go to Little League on Saturdays. They go to farmers' markets. Their classmates love improbable cartoons about talking penguins. They love improbable TV chef Rick Stein. Their classmates love fries. They love friands.

This is a new breed of youngster—when the marketers get their hands on them they'll be called something like iChild, or Kid 2.0— that simply didn't exist a decade ago. Not even a wicked glint in that nice Jamie Oliver's eye. I guess the reason they engender confusion, wariness, even horror, in other people is because they don't conform to the norms of childhood. They're more like grown-ups trapped in pre-pubescent bodies. All their parents have to do in the face of insolence is turn off *Junior MasterChef* and keep them from viewing other like-minded children weeping over a soufflé that just didn't try hard enough. It's way too easy.

When you've had kids of your own, you tend to stop judging. The minute you pop that baby out you're bathed in the great truth that parenting is a long, hard slog, that we're all in this together and that everyone's choices have to be respected. On the other hand, self-evidently these children are precocious, over-entitled brats whose parents really ought to send them for an emergency session in the sandpit. No one under the age of consent should be conversant in the difference between the summer and winter truffle. ('As I said to Mama the other day, the summer truffle is just expensive dirt,' such a child might say in the seconds before I strangle her to death with a piping bag.) These children, not to mention the families that condone such grossly antisocial behaviours, ought to take a good, hard look at their screwed-up priorities.

Fluency in restaurants is something that ought to develop slowly, like a fossil, or a baby elephant, or a taste for prog-rock. Just as the grit creates the pearl, it is a process embedded in friction. The normal child will be tortured in a restaurant ('restaurant' in this case excluding anywhere that uses the phrase 'meal deal' and has seats bolted into the ground). To the normal under-ten set, a restaurant with linen, soft lighting and expected manners is Guantanamo Bay.

Those kiddie food bloggers who collect restaurant bragging rights in the same way their classmates collect footy cards are an inversion of nature. It's a lot like babies who skip the crawling stage and go straight to walking. They might give their mothers a thrill. Playground bragging rights count for plenty in this world.

But they also risk having an appointment at the therapist's office a few years down the track, thanks to missing out on an important development milestone. Back you go, kiddo: down on all fours to fill in the neural gaps.

Ditto the mini-gourmand. Adolescents don't bond over their fabulous, foie gras-filled childhoods. They don't find friends by talking about friands, or artisanal bread, or first-press olive oil. They need pain. They require suffering. It is the parent's sworn duty to give it to them. There is nothing wrong, for instance, with the McDonald's party. It's a rite of passage no less significant than discovering masturbation; double points if the Happy Meal is regurgitated on the playground after a spin in one of those whirly-gig contraptions built (I suspect) for that express purpose. Forget the Lego spaceship or the Star Wars light sabre with built-in sound-effects. *This* will be the gift that keeps on giving. That twirling vomitorium will be your child's failsafe conversation-starter for years to come.

                       ~

By way of a control mechanism in this socio-gustatory exploration, let's food-map my disturbingly typical Australian suburban child-hood of the 1970s.

CHINESE HAPPY DRAGON PALACE

I think it was called the Chinese Happy Dragon Palace. Maybe it was the Happy Chinese Palace Dragon, or the Royal Dragon Chinese Happiness. Whatever it was called, the jewel in the crown of Main Street, Heidelberg, was indistinguishable from every other mid-sized, putatively Cantonese restaurant in Australian suburbia where prawn crackers come as a complimentary appetiser. You know the deal: Chinoiserie, lazy Susans, carved screens, red walls, dense carpet and a soundtrack that displayed the astonishing depth and breadth of the Richard Clayderman back-catalogue. It goes without saying that the air-conditioning was turned to Arctic. Here's a tip: always take a jacket when you're eating at a Chinese restaurant. You'll be thankful when frostbite starts to attack your extremities sometime around the arrival of the beef in black-bean sauce. On which subject, please note that involuntary physical responses aren't always due to the temperature. A Happy Dragon family favourite was the minced pork balls: battered deliciousness in a pink, gelatinous sweet-and-sour sauce that made everyone at the table cough uncontrollably. Who said MSG couldn't be fun?

IL TEMPIO

Il Tempio in (then) outer-suburban Bulleen was blessed with the soft, humid fug of all good pizza parlours. It's a devastatingly evocative scent that always makes me want to curl up in a gently leavening ball of dough and fall asleep under a coddling blanket of sugo. Seriously, someone ought to bottle it and sell it as cologne— they'd make a killing. I remember the smell of happiness, the windows condensing with a fragrant fog, the comforting thump of the electric oven door. Il Tempio, with its rather poor mural of the first pizza being made in Naples in the 1600s, fixed my neural pathways early. I make my lasagne béchamel with white wine, extol the margherita over all other pizzas, and it remains the optimal temperature to which I heat my house, meaning the owners of Il Tempio, which still exists to this day, owe me the equivalent of Monaco's GDP in gas bills.

THE *SEA PRINCESS*

A two-week P&O cruise around the South Pacific, stopping at various picturesque tropical ports to allow passengers to stock up on shell necklaces, synthetic grass skirts and cheap electronics. There's a photo of my parents looking improbably young and glamorous at dinner, smiling at each other across a curved booth in the turquoise-carpeted dining room. They look like 1950s movie stars snapped by a society photographer. They look happy and relaxed. That's because my sister and I are not there. My sister and I would have been watching bad Japanese dinosaur films in the cinema or trying to smother each other to death beneath beanbags in Kids' Club. No wonder the parentals look so happy. That photo represents a sweet respite from the foul progeny who turned those two weeks of tropical bliss into hell on the high seas in a cabin that measured four square metres. Credit must go to our Fijian-Indian waiter who quickly remembered the breakfast peccadilloes of a couple of sulky Australian girls and would bring yoghurt and white toast posthaste each morning. My life-long love of individually wrapped butter portions began here.

CAFFE SPORT

Note the early use of the double 'f'. Classy. Caffe Sport was the real-deal Italian before the whole dark-timber-mood-lighting-ciao-bella thing was flat-packed and sold at restaurant supply stores. It was on Lygon Street, back before Melbourne's Little Italy became a cautionary tale. It was the only grown-up restaurant I remember visiting as a child, and I always—always—spilled my hot chocolate at the end of the night, which the waiters would smoothly insist wasn't a problem at all while whisking away the sodden linen with the practised efficiency of the Ferrari pit-crew. Caffe Sport and the way it suddenly disappeared from our lives was symptomatic of modern parenting. My folks had hung grimly in there for a few years, pretending that everything was business as usual after having children, but after one too many spilled hot chocolates and tantrums over who got the cassata and who got stuck with the tartufo, they had to admit they were now the unpaid handmaidens to a couple of ravening wolverines and that life as they knew it was O-V-E-R.

BANYULE FISH AND CHIPS

Fish and chip shops do not have waiters and table service, I grant you, usually because they do not have tables. Yet any straw poll will show the fish and chip shop punches above its weight in providing early positive examples of hospitality to impressionable young minds. Why? The simple act of throwing in extra potato cakes for free. At Banyule it was a given, thanks to the kind-hearted Greek owners. Cue scenes of delight when the steaming paper package was torn open in front of *Wide World of Disney* on a Sunday night. Happy days.

PIZZA HUT

Not strictly from my childhood but illustrative nonetheless. An early date with my first boyfriend to Pizza Hut during its short-lived all-you-can-eat phase. Adam went a little crazy, as eighteen-year-old boy-men tend to do when computing the brain-snapping definition of limitless food. He was a machine, shovelling in slices of Super-Supreme like it was his last meal before attempting to row the Atlantic. The dessert bar tipped him over the edge. All that soft-serve ice-cream with chocolate sprinkles. He had to duck into

TREVOR

The chef was a psycho. I told him to fuck off back to
his kitchen so he head-butted me and broke my nose.

a doorway on Bourke Street on the way home to vomit up $15.99
worth of food. I'm ashamed to admit he still got lucky that night.
We dated for another year.

～～

If you're wondering what my point is—well, it is this: it is a
cardinal sin to waste the impressionable early years on fine
dining. The more—ahem—'interesting' dining experiences will set
youngsters on the road to resilience. The ability to recover from
incredible setbacks cannot be underestimated if ever they have
to face the hospitality jungle as a prospective employee. To use
an analogy, it's like exposing a child to bacteria. Too much and
you wind up with meningitis or something similarly horrible, but
the regulation doses of colds, flu and communicable diseases will
do their immune systems good. Smother kids in an antibacterial
fog and you wind up with weaklings. That's the explanation my
mother gave, anyway, when she locked me overnight in a room
with my chicken-pocked sister. Or maybe it was a cold-hearted act
of revenge for the *Sea Princess*.

So yes, it's important to keep an open mind if you're thinking
of being a waiter. Sounds like something you'd hear in the porn
industry, doesn't it? Banish the thought—porn pays far better and
comes with discount hair-removal. Junior Gourmand isn't going
to be interested in the skin business—not from a professional point

of view, although he may turn out to be a dedicated consumer of its wares. But he does say he'd love to run a restaurant one day, or simply work the floor while he studies for a double degree majoring in commerce and taxation law ('Thank god,' thinks Junior Gourmand's mother). And for that, despite the many, many hours his privileged little bottom has spent perched on the suppleness of soft leather banquettes, he will be entirely ill-equipped.

Even the straightforward indignities of the trial shift are guaranteed to send him running for the comfort of Daddy's trust fund. The unpaid trial shift is a necessary evil. Everyone does it. It's also illegal. As your attorney, I advise that an employer can only justify not paying a trialee if he or she is engaged in an active demonstration of skill. Translation: get someone to make a few coffees, okay; stick someone on the coffee machine for a few hours, not okay. But really, who's checking? Cry to the Fair Work Ombudsman all you like, the reality is you either suck it up or go home.

I've done a few trial shifts in my time. Okay, more than a few. A significant number of trial shifts. The collective noun: an embarrassment of trial shifts.

It wasn't like the door to the cloistered world of fine dining swung open for me after Il Crappo. Quite the opposite, in fact. The only way was down. I remained a bottom feeder, chasing job after job but always being trumped by the candidate who had a slightly better reference than the one written by Paulo where he praised my 'punctiality' but noted in a rare fit of honesty that I could only carry two plates. Bastard.

The trial shift is always a gamble. You're hoping the people who are trialling you have a modicum of sympathy and a legitimate opening in their workforce. You're hoping they aren't simply exploiting a free, disposable pool of labour. And, if indeed they

---

MATT

This young guy in his twenties was having dinner with his parents and it didn't look like it was going very well. We decided he must be coming out to them because the dad kept going outside to smoke cigarettes and pace up and down, and the poor kid just looked stricken. Their mains arrived while the dad was outside so I went to tell him the food was on the table. He came back in, took a big swig of red wine then threw the whole glass at his son, who did a defensive move so it smashed into his hands and wrists. There were shards of glass sticking out of him and blood spurting everywhere. The mum was just screaming and we were trying to stop him pulling out the glass in case it made it worse. The parents went home separately and we put him in a taxi to go to hospital. We had to paint the walls to get rid of the bloodstains.

---

aren't just riding the gravy train, they're hoping for someone with the skills to pay the bills.

It typically proceeds in the following fashion. The phone call, always genial, saying thanks for the job application, we'd like to get you in for a trial. Enough enthusiasm to make you do a little inward woohoo! This one, you think—this could be the one.

You arrive five minutes early, and the moment you step in the door the maître d'—yes, this place has a real-life maître d'—clocks you with the practised eyebrow raise of the true professional. Somehow, he knows. He sees right into your soul—your hopes, your fears, your empty bank account. You are a walking X-ray of incompetence. It's nothing you say, although your voice has the slightly wobbly cadence of a pubescent boy who's just discovered bum fluff on his chin. It's nothing that you do—not exactly, although your well-practised confident smile betrays your lack of confidence. But your fear? He can smell it as if it's stuck to the bottom of your shoe.

You're assigned to running plates. That means no meaningful interaction with the diners, simply delivering food and clearing empties. They don't always guess at your lowly status. Some ask questions you can't answer. The veal is from where? You'll—erm—ask the chef! Is the bread baked in-house? You'll find out! You look over to where the maître d' is standing at the bar, staring over at you with an expression that makes you wonder if he just smelled a fart. He summons you over with a twitch of his finger. You're ordered out the back, past the rugby forward line of chefs, to a cheerless alcove set up with two steel buckets and a mountain of cutlery that's just come steaming out of the dishwasher. Your job for the next four hours will be to polish these babies until they shine. And polish you do.

You're ignored while the other waiters have their staff meals around you, bitching and laughing about the night's customers—the guy with the bad hairpiece on table ten, the hot mama on six. You polish and polish like your life depends on it, because you really, really, need this job, and when the mountain finally disappears and you are left sitting there alone, utterly spent and surrounded by limp polishing rags, you go wandering through the now-deserted kitchen to find the maître d', who is laughing with a waiter over knock-off drinks at the bar. You interrupt him and nervously stammer something like, 'Is there anything else you want me to do?' and he looks like another fart just wafted through the room, and says something along the lines of, 'I have to do the roster but if there's any work I'll call next week,' and you know—and he knows that you know, which is precisely the effect he was hoping to telegraph—that he won't call.

You take the hour-long tram ride home, collapse on the couch where your housemates are engaged in a PlayStation marathon fuelled by a packet of chopped-up Sudafed, and feel a part of you die inside.

But onwards you go. There's an ad in the university employment office, which adds an ivy-clad veneer of credibility to the unskilled vacancies for cleaners, babysitters and mail sorters. Surely it must be less the hunting ground of exploiters and more a proper, bona fide pool of gainful employment for the professionals of tomorrow.

The ad is for waiting staff at a city gastropub. Gastropubs are the big new thing. Pubs with decent food, or decent-enough food. They've recently taken off as the latest last word in food fashion. I'm not really an expert on the subject of food fashion—at this time I consider it a rare thrill when 2-Minute Noodles launch a new flavour—but I'm vaguely aware that the gastropub is something of an allergic reaction to nouvelle cuisine, the oft-derided big-plate-small-food movement of the 1970s that saw restaurants charge a lot of money for teeny-tiny bits of food on enormous white plates, which was followed by the knee-jerk abundance of the tall food era in which dishes reached for the sky, thanks to the guiding principle 'the higher the plate, the closer to God', and the fusion movement—philosophically inclusive but more often than not a big, incoherent mess—running interference. Gastropubs are meant to be all about reclaiming the honesty of a bygone era when the tweed-wearing working classes could get an honest pie that wasn't a mass-produced thing made from snouts, anuses and additive codes. Young men in flat caps stolen from their grandfathers are rediscovering the joys of corned beef and mash in unprecedented numbers.

If there was any truth to the English language, 'food fashion' should be an oxymoron. Our ancestors were so busy trying not to starve to death they simply didn't have time to invent edible 'dirt' and spherified peas made from peas turned into gel to resemble peas. Now that everyone's dead bored with the novelty of being able to eat whatever and whenever we want, like capricious monarchs surrounded by sycophantic courtiers, we're allowing unspeakable things to happen to food in the name of art. I think it's important to remember that most food fashion falls into the category of 'stuff you queue up for two hours to eat now that you'll fall about laughing at in two years' time'. Or as I like to say: today's paleo is tomorrow's punchline.

Looking back it's hard not to get all misty-eyed for the beautifully uncomplicated nature of the gastropub. A pub! A pub that serves food you don't want to regurgitate! How incredible! The gastropub was never as high-concept as the acres of press coverage would suggest but, hey, it was the early 90s. We'd only just recovered from the sun-dried tomato craze.

'You look nervous,' says the young guy behind the bar when I front up for an interview, his hair neatly parted on the side like the past thirty years never happened. He's dressed like an extra from a Dean Martin film. White shirt, black bow tie, black pants, shiny shoes. It's reassuring that this is the sort of place that trusses young people up in outfits their grandmothers would love. 'Have a drink while you wait.'

Why thank you, clean-cut young man. It's not a good look, potentially, but Gary the manager is nowhere to be seen and it might calm the nerves. A vodka tonic, thanks.

'Don't worry,' smiles my new friend. His name is Julian. I can almost smell the private school on him. 'You'll be fine.'

Gary finally appears. He's your typical ex-footballer prototype

—tall and well-built but running to seed. He seems distracted, engages in perfunctory chit-chat for a few minutes, then asks if I can start a trial shift right away. Yes, my hoped-for future employer, yes I can.

And it goes well. It goes exceedingly well. Table after table of identikit businessmen in their grey suits and red power ties would attest that I don't drop things, mess up orders, or ruin their power lunch by spilling a single precious drop of the McLaren Vale cabernet. It goes so well that Gary gives me the thumbs-up as he dashes out the front door and says Felicity is going to have a chat to me before I go home.

Yay-hey.

But Felicity is apologetic. Felicity, a pretty redhead with freckles and sparkly earrings, makes me think I'm about to get the old don't-call-us-we'll-call-you routine. The routine that says the past five hours of my life have been for nothing except to chip away a little bit more at my rapidly diminishing stock of self-esteem. Not exactly. Turns out Felicity is concerned about something else. 'Sorry about this,' she says, biting her bottom lip, 'but Gary says your skirt needs to be shorter. He was too scared to tell you himself.'

'My skirt?' My skirt is probably 6 inches above the knee. I'm no seamstress, but I'm pretty certain the technical term for this is 'short enough'. Felicity indicates, however, that it could stand to have another 4 inches lopped off.

Right.

While I'm computing my skirt's impending diet, she starts on the positives. There's lots of work available. I can expect some decent shifts each week. In fact, why don't I stick around for a private function that evening? Trial over. They'll pay me.

Still percolating the disjunction between the Rat Pack-styled bar staff and my shrinking uniform, I do. The function begins well enough. It's some college old-boys' football club reunion. Mate. *Maaaate*. The first hour is taken up with hauling trays of Carlton Draught through the crowd. I'm called 'love' too many times to count. Occasionally one of the guests will murmur in my ear that he needs a light beer, as if scared he's going to be called out as a purse-carrying nancy boy by his full-strength buddies. Occasionally a hand brushes my bum, although it's impossible to tell if it's due to malice aforethought or the closeness of the crowd. Whatever. It's no worse than the 96 tram in peak hour.

Across the room I spy my new pal Julian pulling the blinds down on all the windows. Curious, I think. It's very un-gastropub to have blackout shades. It's not like it's World War Two or anything. Julian turns and gives a nod to Gary, who's appeared behind the bar. Gary grins and flips a switch and the lights dim low and 'Rhythm Is a Dancer' comes blaring through the PA system. I hate 'Rhythm Is a Dancer'. The lyrics are nonsensical (what the hell is a 'source companion'?) and it rhymes 'dancer' with 'cancer'. Obviously the work of semi-literate German Eurodance idiots, but my little digression is arrested when three women burst through the bar doors and start performing a sort of high-stepping cheerleader routine, only with no clothes on.

And this is the precise moment when my skirt realises its insignificance in the wider scheme of things. My skirt doesn't need to sweat the small stuff. These men don't care if my skirt is 2 inches or 10 inches above the knee. They don't care if my skirt is made of expensive silk or cheap polyester. All eyes are on the three pairs of impressively fake tits cavorting with their owners on the bar.

The inner dialogue has plenty to say in such a situation. In fact it's babbling incoherently. 'And you call yourself a feminist!' 'But I need the money.' 'It's degrading and these men smell like cheap cologne.' 'Why didn't the ad say I needed to be open-minded? Isn't that code for strippers?' 'Can't stripping be an empowering act?' 'Oh god, what would Germaine Greer do?'

While the men cheer an objectively impressive display of flexibility—one of the women touches her toes as if she's hinged at the waist—I decide Germaine would stick it out for the rest of the shift. Even feminists need to pay their rent. I'll get tonight's pay, go home and call an emergency meeting of the sisterhood to discuss the problem in depth.

Performance over, the beaming crowd of men trudge up three flights of stairs to the function room, where tables are laid out for their power dinner: rib-eye, the steak of choice for the red-blooded bogan, and many, many more of the second-cheapest bottles of cabernet. They eat. They drink. There are speeches and awards. *Maaaate.* Then the lights once again go low, and a song booms through the audio (Bobby Brown's 'Humpin' Around', which makes much more sense thematically) and—*quelle surprise!*—three different near-naked women bounce out like the presenters of *Nude Aerobics Oz Style*. 'Why do they need new strippers?' Felicity whispers as she passes with a tower of gravy-smeared plates. 'Were the other ones broken?'

Captivating though the floorshow is, there's work to be done. Schlepping trays up and down stairs to the ground-floor kitchen is pretty aerobic in itself. It's exhausting, sweaty work, which perhaps explains why I lose concentration for a nano-second—just long enough for an opportunistic steak knife to break free from the urgent cluster of silverware heaped clumsily on my tray. It slithers to the edge and—I swear this all happens in slow motion while I struggle desperately to prevent another two dozen following it in sympathy—takes a suicide leap over the balustrade. It spears downwards at a terrifying angle, and after what feels like an eternity I hear it clattering on the terracotta tiles three floors below. The sound echoes up the stairwell, hideously amplified for everyone in the building, and quite possibly the greater central business district, to hear. So does the female voice, pitched upwards by shock. 'Oh. My. Fucking. God!'

And that's how I lost my second, short-lived waiter's job, when I nearly killed a half-naked stripper with a sharp knife. True story.

— 3 —
DOWN MEXICO WAY

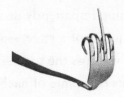

Six easy folds are all that stand between a 20 × 20 centimetre two-ply napkin and a graceful paper swan. I could go into more detail but the sun appears to be setting on the origami serviette. Once a staple of the restaurant dining table, it's now sighted only rarely, usually staging brave guerilla skirmishes alongside the single pink carnation in outer-suburban Chinese restaurants.

The first job of the evening was to arrange the swans—in red, green and white, the colours of the Mexican flag, *olé!*—in wineglasses; not delicate crystal but clunky things cunningly designed to withstand dropping on hard surfaces, temperatures of up to 500 degrees and all-out nuclear Armageddon. If the bomb ever dropped on Melbourne, the only things left standing would be cockroaches and the Mexican Casa's stemware.

You know how Mexican food has become hotter than a jalapeno, the cuisine du jour for a certain demographic with their beards and tattoos and deep, almost subterranean irony that no one else can really understand, man?

No. Not like that.

The Mexican Casa was so old-school it made franchise chain Taco Bill's look like the final word in cutting-edge cool. It pre-dated the fashionable new-wave Mexican by several thousand light years. In terms of gustatory fashion, it was pre-Columbian. Actually, that's not going back far enough. It was positively pre-Lapsarian, although there's room to argue that diners carving their initials and the odd expletive into the wooden placemats were an early precursor to the social media revolution. But truth is, if there was ever a crowd mooching impatiently around outside this joint on a weird retail non sequitur of a street—a mechanic next door; an office stationery supply across the road—it was because the fire alarm had gone off thanks to a plate of nachos catching fire in the dodgy oven.

To its customers it was the Mexican Casa but to its disaffected band of novice waiters it was more commonly known as the High Enchilada. Susie, another high school friend, got me the job with the promise that inexperience in Mexican food was no barrier to employment here. Right she was, too. The hiring process was based on a completely different set of criteria. Only in hindsight did I detect a certain pattern in the gender of the floor staff. All female. No exceptions. The policy can be traced in a direct line to one half of the owners, a porcine slob named Bruce with a weak chin, a massive gut barely corralled by his trademark striped polo shirts and a fondness for the genial sexism of the middle-aged man.

'You know why men like to hold doors open for women?' he'd ask while holding the door open and looking skin-crawlingly pleased with himself (quite an impressive feat, incidentally, while wearing Stubbies shorts). 'So we can look at your bottoms when you walk in front of us. You don't think men are so stupid to do something for nothing, do you?'

Listening to Bruce's proselytising was an unspoken part of the job. Bruce had plenty of wisdom to share, most of it revolving around the tortured age-old questions of male–female relations and why women are far happier when fulfilling the noble role of homemaker, even if they don't realise it thanks to the lies of feminism. Creepy, yes, but pathetic, more. You quickly got the feeling he wasn't the kind of guy who was listened to unless he had a captive audience being paid ten bucks an hour under the table, no questions asked. He was snatching his moment in the sun—a sexist sensei teaching the ways of the world to a bunch of post-adolescent girls.

Women's bottoms aside, Bruce's main topic of conversation was his infant son. I can't remember the boy's name, mostly because Bruce habitually referred to him as 'the little fella'. It was a sweet-sounding verbal idiosyncrasy—in fact, it seemed the only thing going in Bruce's favour until it was pointed out that no one had ever met Mrs Bruce or Bruce Junior. This added weight to Susie's theory that when Bruce talked incessantly about 'my little fella' he was in fact referring to his dick.

'My little fella's just amazing,' Bruce would announce apropos of nothing while slicing the top off a 10-kilo bag of pre-shredded yellow cheese. 'My little fella's growing up fast,' while stacking caterers' tubs of sour cream. Or, horrifyingly, 'Gosh, you should have seen my little fella this morning.'

Bruce had gone into business with a fellow named Trevor. Bruce made Trevor look only moderately offensive. Trevor was a mouse of a man with a silken blond moustache left over from the set of *Semen Demons 4* and big, weepy blue eyes. He was the guy who had sand kicked in his face at the beach by the guy who had sand kicked in his face by the other guys.

Their background had nothing to do with hospitality. Bruce had been an advertising rep; Trevor was a teacher. In a similar vein to the three-year-old who announces she wants to be a hairdresser in outer space, they decided it would be a brilliant idea to open a restaurant.

It was the usual story. They wanted to be the captains of their own destiny. To break free from the shackles of the wage-slave working in a corporate chain gang and waiting anxiously for payday every second Thursday. In reality, they shared a fate similar to many restaurateurs in that they essentially bought themselves a job. A seven-day-a-week job of unsociable hours and the ineradicable perfume of stale nachos. The High Enchilada turned out not to be the road to riches but the unsaleable coffin of two men's dreams of a better, self-actualised life. They might have thought they were being clever by opting for Mexican—essentially, a bunch of pre-prepared components thrown into the oven to heat, melt and generally deliquesce into protein-and-cheese pap— meaning they needed no actual chef. Instead they ended up being tied to a tiny, overheated, unventilated kitchen hardly bigger than a double fridge.

Clearly the marriage wasn't working out. The tension between the two was palpable. Bruce and his impressive gut lorded it over Trevor, who only inflamed the situation by responding with the affronted dignity of a 1950s housewife whose husband hasn't come home straight after the game. Front of house it remained the same desultory joint serving the same desultory slop; backstage it was like the *Kramer vs Kramer* theme restaurant. It was a relief to everyone when they stopped working together, taking a financial hit they could barely afford, doing one night on, one night off, and each prodding the waitresses for gossip about the other while pretending not to care.

෴

Like childbirth, waiting tables is one of those activities that's meant to come naturally. You get people food and drinks and you clear everything away when they're finished and it's just so freaking obvious, isn't it? Except it's not. Expecting people to know exactly what to do the minute they pick up an apron is like expecting a *Lord of the Rings* fan to know what to do in case of orc attack or someone who once watched *Grey's Anatomy* to perform a tracheotomy using a Stanley knife and the tube from a ballpoint pen. You don't pick up this stuff by osmosis. Despite the extensive experience I boasted about to Bruce and Trevor at what passed for an interview (Bruce looking at my bum; Trevor looking like he was about to burst into tears), I still had my L-plates on. I made ridiculous towers of plates and served from the left and leaned across people and interrupted conversations and started clearing before everyone at the table was finished. No one tells you not to do that stuff. Not at the places where I worked, anyway. And not that it mattered at the High Enchilada, where an evening's service was considered a success if no one was maimed.

VINCENT

It was a really busy Friday night when one of the men's toilets stopped working and I had to investigate. I found a pair of boxers stuffed in the cistern. Someone had shat themselves and instead of going home they'd ditched their undies and gone back out to drink at the bar.

Another important thing for the junior waiter to learn—you have to decide early on what type of waiter you're going to be. It's as crucial as it is urgent. The concrete is setting. You'll be frozen in that attitude forever. Fixed as if by superglue. I tried the sassy bartender: 'Wad'll it be?' I tried the blowsy American diner waitress: 'Want some more coffee, hon?' But the truth is even less glamorous than imitating a twice-divorced bottle-blonde named Valerie.

There is a modern school of thought that having to be nice in the line of duty has become the exclusive domain of the less privileged. Mandatory smiling is a sign of the underclass. Service industries that expect their employees to put on a veneer of friendliness force people to sell their very humanity; it's yet another one of capitalism's little jokes on poor people. But tempting though it is to wrap myself in the comforts of that philosophy, the truth is closer to the German notion of *schadenfreude*—otherwise known as taking pleasure from other people's misery (the classic example involves seeing a new-model Mercedes reverse into a pole). The default setting for waiters like myself flips that concept into *freudenschade*—taking misery from other people's pleasure. Sad and pathetic though it may be, I'm the sort of person who bitterly counts down the days until friends return from holiday. They're jumping on a plane right now; economy class; it's going to be hell, I think with satisfaction after spending two weeks torturing myself with images of my loved ones lying on deck chairs never more than a few metres away from the nearest cocktail. With an attitude like that, what chance did any of my customers stand when they decided to treat themselves to a nice meal out?

And even though it was willing to hire someone with virtually zero experience, a place like the Mexican Casa, with its idiot bosses and schlubby diners, was a dangerous place for someone with a naturally glass-half-empty disposition.

The concrete set. And as a waiter I was stuck in a *freudenschade* attitude forever more. Frozen, like the Little Match Girl, minus the sweetness and the sympathy.

I'd never experienced the joys of putatively 'Mexican' cuisine before I started working at the High Enchilada. I was bewildered by the plates of variegated slop, beans barely distinguishable from meat and everything striped with the tri-colour of salsa, sour cream and guacamole. With my two decades' worth of wisdom, I figured the customers would be, too. My line when delivering food to tables, until Susie overheard and made me promise never to repeat it again, was 'I know it doesn't look very good but it tastes okay'. Hindsight reveals I might not have been scaling the heights of customer service, but standards weren't so high in a place where diners were known to request cravats of water.

Back in those days Mexican food really meant Tex-Mex, which translates as something no Mexican national would recognise as a food substance. Like nachos. You know the story about nachos? In 1943 a bunch of American army wives arrived at a hotel in the Mexican town of Piedras Negras, just over the US border, after the restaurant had closed for the day. The considerate manager, Ignacio 'Nacho' Anaya, threw together what he found in the kitchen that day: tortilla chips, cheese and jalapenos. He cut the tortillas into triangles, grilled the cheese on top, and added the jalapenos. Hey presto, a legend was born.

It's quite possibly apocryphal, but I like this story. I like the way a supposedly 'authentic' Mexican dish came about through a few kitchen offcuts being thrown together for a bunch of cultural outsiders who didn't know any better. It's an accident of a dish. More

Texican than Mexican. An edible car crash. If Ignacio really did go on to open his own restaurant, I hope he laughed all the way to the bank.

Nachos sold their socks off at the Mexican Casa. We even planted a little paper Mexican flag on a toothpick in the top, just to drive the whole authenticity thing home. I lost my taste for them pretty quickly. If you've ever had time to observe the consumption of nachos, and I had ample opportunity, they are in the title-fight for the world's most disgusting dish. The problem is that they're meant to be shared, and nine out of ten people faced with a plate of nachos will go in with fingers rather than cutlery. This is fine on the first layer, where you can pick off individual corn chips without too much trouble. But excavate down to the second layer and you quickly run into a primordial swill of cheese and salsa, with guacamole and sour cream making their own contribution to the toddlers' pool gloop. What people generally do when eating through this stage is dip their digits into the gunge, rummage around, tear off some fast-collapsing corn chip, then lick their fingers before they go in again. Dip, dip. Lick, lick. It's an epidemical crisis just waiting to happen, and I'm not willing to be Patient Zero.

Nachos aside, the menu soon revealed an easy to grasp pattern. Tacos were fried corn tortillas filled with beef, beans or chicken. Taquitos were rolled, fried corn tortillas filled with beef, beans or chicken. A tostada was a flat, fried corn tortilla covered in beef, beans or chicken. An enchilada was a soft corn tortilla rolled around beef, beans or chicken. A burrito was a super-sized enchilada. Fillings? Beef, beans or chicken.

When UNESCO added Mexican food to its list of the 'intangible culture of humanity' in 2010, it was not thinking of the Mexican Casa's menu.

Nonetheless, authenticity—or a simulacrum thereof—was a big thing for Trevor, who eventually bought Bruce out of his share for the price of a second-hand family sedan. A great relief all round. 'More time for Bruce to play with his little fella,' Susie snorted. The upshot of it was that Trevor now manned the kitchen alone seven nights a week and his big, weepy blue eyes were weepier than ever.

This was a man who had never heard of a *mole*, and would have simply looked confused and weepy at the notion of putting chocolate into a savoury dish. As far as I could tell, the kitchen had never come into contact with chipotle, the smoked chilli that gives so much Mexican food its thrilling, smoky backbeat. Trevor's version of authenticity was to repaint the dining room in pale pastels the colour of nausea. Festive sombreros were hung from the ceiling. To drink there was Mexican punch, which was equal parts raspberry cordial to pineapple juice with lemon slices floating on top. Margarita glasses came crusted in sugar instead of salt. Mexican rice was dotted with red and green capsicum. Dessert was Mexican crème caramel, made with Kahlua. Mexican coffee—with a splash of Kahlua, naturally—was made in one of those drip-filter numbers that were big in the 1970s, until Trevor finally splashed out on a domestic espresso machine and celebrated by pasting 'Now . . . with Cup-of-Cino!' signs around the dining room.

The place owned two CDs: the Gipsy Kings' self-titled album and the *Pretty Woman* soundtrack. The Gipsy Kings were for the busy period. A bit of 'Bamboléo' action: make people eat faster, drink more, keep the mood upbeat. 'Psychology,' Trevor would nod sagely as though he was at the cutting edge of behavioural research. *Pretty Woman* was for pack-down, when the mood was getting sleepy and you just wanted the last of the nacho bandits to get the fuck out and let you go home. Roxette's 'It Must Have Been Love' was just the ticket.

Like I said, authentic. While never having visited Mexico, Trevor was the proud owner of a Mexican-themed windcheater that he'd pull on before heading out to do the old customer meet-and-greet. To put it politely, it had seen better days. Indelible sauce stains merged with the Aztec writing; the cuffs were a delicate shade of greige. 'I really hope he doesn't put that on just for us,' a woman sniffed witheringly one night after Trevor had done the rounds with all the self-importance of a three-star chef-patron.

For a while after Bruce left, Trevor was like the sole survivor of a shipwreck in a slowly sinking lifeboat. I had no respect for the man but it wasn't enjoyable. It was like watching your fourth-favourite cat suffer from scrofula. But then Trevor made the decision that saved him. He decided to employ an apprentice. It was a cruel move, really, to pay measly first-year apprentice wages for a seventy-hour week, with no tangible educational benefit that would put the victim-candidate on the path to fine dining. But along came Felipe, the Chilean soccer fanatic. Even aside from the fact that something about the cast of his mouth made him look endearingly like a Mexican walking fish, he was a shoo-in for the job. Mexico and Chile are separated by 7300 kilometres and entirely different food cultures, but that wasn't going to stop Trevor bragging to the regulars about his authentic South American chef.

If Trevor represented a black hole of entropy, Felipe filled the vacuum in the High Enchilada kitchen. Maybe it was a male presence that the waitresses could talk to without gagging, maybe it was his fiancée, a sweet young thing called Mariana, who'd turn up from her own waitressing gig at the end of each night to perch at the end of the counter and swap war stories, maybe it was just that he was such a gosh-darn nice young guy who bubbled with enthusiasm for everything from soccer to sci-fi and gently chided me for smoking. He proved a rallying-point for a disparate group of individuals, from Lana the eternally cheerful cyclist to Helen the cheesecloth-wearing hippy and Julie, who spent most of her work time flogging Mary Kay cosmetics. Felipe whisked us all post-work to smoky Latin clubs on Johnston Street that felt like being transported to Santiago circa 1950. Swarthy men swung sequined women around the dance floor and the air was thick with transcontinental longing.

Surprisingly, I learned a thing or two at the Enchilada that proved to have lasting value. One evening I took a phone call from a man claiming his take-out had induced a technicolour bout of food poisoning. I knew him immediately; a table of eight guys the previous night, hunkering down near the kitchen and making half-hearted passes at me and Daisy, the little blonde waitress young enough to be flattered by their Neanderthal attentions. The only things making them sick were the bucket bongs they'd sucked down before getting the munchies. Seriously—who leaves $10 as a tip for a takeaway order if they're not on drugs?

Food poisoning complaints are not uncommon. It's understandable: it's only human to want revenge as you hurl your guts up for the fifth time in an hour, and the first thing you think of is naturally going to be the last thing you ate. Notwithstanding the visceral element to food poisoning complaints (which means you should immediately distrust anyone willing to accept the offer of free food as compensation: clearly they're frauds), it's important to remain scientific.

So here's the deal: if someone complains of food poisoning it's best to adopt the brisk, no-nonsense manner of a librarian or school principal. The words 'stool sample' are difficult to say without sniggering, but it's imperative that the utmost seriousness be observed during the transaction or you risk provoking the aggrieved customer.

The stool sample (don't smirk) should be collected in a dry, sterile, screw-top container. Try not to collect urine or toilet water along with the stool; to this purpose, it's best to urinate first before spreading plastic wrap over the toilet seat so as to catch the specimen. Once the stool sample is safely inside the sterile container, seal it then label it: your name, the date and your date of birth. Put it in the fridge wrapped in a plastic bag before taking it to your local GP for analysis at the first opportunity.

In my experience the customer will have hung up by the time you get to 'toilet water'.

The best times at the High Enchilada were when Trevor took the rare night off to give his Mexican windcheater a rest. We could relax a little, put a different CD on the stereo. Felipe would be a whirlwind of energy at the end of the shift, making takeaway bags for all the staff to take home, hunters after the kill. Each of us would become, however briefly, the most popular person in our share house. Nachos all round! Depending on the level of poverty that week, grateful housemates might even cross your name off the cleaning roster. A symbolic act, on the whole, but a thoughtful one.

ROISIN

We needed to restock the wine shelves before
service one night. There had been a delivery and we
had the invoice but couldn't find the wine. I looked
everywhere and finally turned to the kitchen,
wondering if it had been mistakenly put in there.
The head chef told me to look in the cold room so
I did. While I was looking up and down the shelves
he followed me in, locked the door and put his hand
up my skirt. I told him to remove it or his wife would
know about it very quickly. It worked.

Things ended up going awry, as things tend to do when you're in your twenties, with the unfathomable possibilities of life making your synapses zing with distress. Mariana started waitressing at some hippy cafe, fell in with a whole new crowd and dumped Felipe just before their wedding. He was inconsolable. It's one thing to lose your first love, quite another to lose her to the dark forces of veganism. But things got worse for poor Felipe—much worse—when his now ex-best man took him away to Queensland. The idea was the age-old prescription for recovering from a bad break-up: a bit of sun, a bit of golf, a bit of consolatory action with persons of the female persuasion. Visiting a scenic lookout, the ex-best man took a step backwards to take a photo and fell to his death from a cliff top, Felipe looking on in horror and no doubt wanting to follow him over.

All the High Enchilada crew drifted away after that. The next floating population of pimple-faced waitresses arrived to investigate the ancient art of turning paper napkins into swans and the industrial adhesive properties of high-fat cheese. I ran into Lana more than a decade later. She didn't remember me, by which I mean not only did she have absolutely no recollection of my name or face, she had no memory of the restaurant itself. Talk about eternal sunshine of the spotless mind. Maybe the High Enchilada era was so bad for her she simply had to blot it out in order to continue on the trajectory known as living. Maybe she's just got a bad memory.

Don't let me romanticise it: the High Enchilada was no picnic. But for a short while we were a happy little gang—one of those de facto urban families you read about in the weekend supplements, brought together by temporary circumstance but making the most of our fellowship at a crappy little suburban joint before life spooled out in different directions. Until this day I've never been able to listen to the Gipsy Kings without a stab of nostalgia, and the phantom scent of stale nachos lingering in the air.

— 4 —

LA GRANDE ILLUSION

My friend Marcus got into the waiter game for all the wrong reasons. Marcus got into the waiter game because he loves food. For him, every meal is a cause for rejoicing. Each step in the shopping, preparing, serving and eating is a quasi-religious act of homage to the thing that injects his life with its colour and elan. He savours wine like a Trappist monk who has lovingly tended the vines in the scorching heat and the freezing wind. He can spend a blissful hour in a cheesemonger, imbibing the dank aromas, the nostril-slapping barnyard essence of a really good Trou du Cru. He emerges from farmers' markets looking like he has just witnessed The Rapture. His dinner parties—at which it is not uncommon for the food to emerge at midnight thanks to Marcus lovingly cutting the vegetables for a sofrito in a perfect brunoise and attaining the desired consistency for his curry paste only after two solid hours of mortar and pestle work—are pure torture.

Marcus wanted to work with food.

Marcus wanted to work in a restaurant that loved food as much as he did. And so he found work at a brand-new gastropub that was getting good reviews and seemed the kind of place that would be sympathetic to a young man travelling life's highway with a washed-rind cheese in one hand and a ciabatta in the other.

It was a casual process of disabusement. Nothing fatal in itself; just small factual paper cuts that revealed the fiction behind the romantic facade of the restaurant industry. The chef did not make the gnocchi lovingly but, depending on the day, hastily, angrily or homicidally. The specials list was inspired less by what had just come in from the market and more by what was about to go off. The biggest-selling winter dessert was summer berry pudding.

Then one day there was an incident. I mean An Incident. And Marcus was never quite the same again.

It was the tail end of an otherwise uneventful lunch service. The dining room, one of the first to embrace the open kitchen (this being the 1990s and all—history relates that Everything But The Girl's breakthrough album *Amplified Heart* was playing on the stereo), was empty save for one last table that was starting on coffee. Marcus was left manning the floor alone while the sole chef left on duty began a cleaning frenzy ('quite out of character', the record notes). The four remaining diners, all expensively dressed, were sitting at a table nestled underneath a broad ledge created when a hole was punched through the wall separating the rear of the dining room from the kitchen. As well as providing a then-novel insight into the workings of a commercial kitchen, it also provided a handy shelf for corks, wineglasses, and the olive oil kept for drizzling on pizza and salads (remember this was the 90s—drizzling was *de rigueur*).

Perhaps inevitably during the chef's uncharacteristic cleaning frenzy a bottle of this olive oil was tipped over Expensively Dressed Woman No. 1. Perhaps just as inevitably, she was extremely distressed at the re-creation of the *Exxon Valdez* disaster on her white silk top.

The chef activated his emergency plan and pulled a swift disappearing act, leaving Marcus to deal with the fallout. And being a young man who appreciated good food, he tried to placate the woman in the only way he knew how.

'When I saw the green tinge I knew it wasn't any old olive oil—it was extra-virgin olive oil, the greener the better as we considered at the time, which we used to drizzle on everything,' he recounts sadly. 'So I tried to draw attention to the fact that we were a quality establishment and that if we're going to spill anything on our customers, at least it's the real deal. And here's the rub: I say something about how her white silk top really allowed the quality of the oil to shine through; she should have been glad it happened. Now she knows we don't skimp on ingredients. You know? It's not that bad . . .

'Anyway, she's outraged and demands to see the manager. I wish. None to be found. So I give her a business card and promise we'll sort everything. It turned out she was pretty high up working

RICHIE

I was standing at the counter one night and an incredibly good-looking woman sashayed out of the toilets and came up to me. She was totally hot. Supermodel hot. And she asked me, 'Are you the manager?' and when I said yes she started stroking my face really gently and looking at me with come-fuck-me eyes. I'm just standing there like an idiot, but like I said, she was hot. And finally she stuck her index finger in my mouth and said in a really sexy voice, 'I'd just like to tell you there's no soap in the women's bathroom.'

for the premier of Victoria and she wrote to my boss on state parliament letterhead demanding that he sack me. And he wanted to sack me, of course. He was furious about having to pay for this woman to buy a new top, which wasn't my fault in the first place, and he was furious about having this well-placed woman pissed off with the whole establishment. I kept my job in the end—I guess because it would have been too much effort to find a replacement, but to this day I feel like I was thrown under a bus. I guess my main solace is remembering that she obviously didn't like food that much. Her loss.'

A sorry tale, is it not? One man's soft-focus view of the restaurant world, destroyed by callous indifference towards its worker bees. Do take heed. There are lessons to be learned.

A forensic examination reveals Marcus was unwittingly caught in a classic pincer movement between the chef, who refused to own up to his mistake, and the owner, who valued his chef above his waiter. Surprised? Don't be. If the workforce of a typical restaurant can be considered a pyramid, then chefs are at the tip while waiters comprise the huddled masses at its base.

Or imagine the workings of a restaurant as a game of chess. The owner would be the king, the chef the queen, the sous and pastry chefs rooks, the sommelier and floor manager bishops, the waiters a whole pathetic bunch of expendable pawns. They come, they go. They're more or less interchangeable. A good waiter— not quite up to the standards of a maître d' but a professional journeyman nonetheless—might reach the status of a knight in our chess analogy, but knights are easily harassed and destroyed by pawns. Go figure that one out and get back to me.

Waiting tables during the good times can be extremely rewarding for the lover of food, as Marcus discovered. When time is ample and customers appreciative, one's knowledge of sourdough culture, *fleur de sel* sea-salt and the taste benefits of hanger steak over the more celebrated eye fillet are a delight to share. A good waiter will concoct a little conspiracy with the customers in which they giggle over the deliciously fattening triple-cream cheese like school kids who have just heard the word 'tits'. When times are good, a waiter will woo, and be wooed in return.

When the atmosphere is stressed, the customers hostile and time a rare commodity, it is the wise waiter who operates under the assumption an invisible target is painted on his back. This target might as well be painted in luminol (the chemical compound that glows blue in the presence of blood; you've seen it on *CSI*) because if there is blood to be spilled it is the waiter's. Does it matter if he was the person responsible for the lost order docket, the forgotten martini or the steak that was rare instead of medium-rare? No, it does not. In the bastardised game of pass-the-parcel that constitutes the average dinner service, the music always stops on the waiter.

When something punishable by sacking has occurred, the owner's mind will be a frenzy of rationalisation. He's itching to sack someone, if only to assert his authority over the staff, to SHOW THEM WHO'S BOSS, but who will it be? A chef? Where is he going to find another chef at short notice? He could always call an agency, but agencies are expensive and they're typically staffed by chefs whose anger management and substance abuse problems prevent them holding down a regular job. Anyway, it was all the waiter's fault. Yes, yes, it was definitely the waiter's fault. Sack the fucker!

The problem leeches directly from the fact that, unlike the chef, the waiter requires no formal training. This breeds contempt. 'That waiter . . .' thinks the owner, 'that waiter is fucking useless. My five-year-old could do the job just as well. No, my five-year-old could do the job BETTER.' It's yet another example of a valuable skill-set being reduced to the possession of two arms, two legs and a beating heart.

Despite this sorry state of affairs, waiters such as my friend Marcus are in thrall. Good food and fine wine for the many, many others like him start out as a hobby and quickly degenerate into a chemical imbalance. Such waiters enjoy a fatal symbiosis with the industry that employs them. In their time off they're likely to be found spending all their spare dough, then dipping into their rent money, on lushing out over lunch and dinner and quite possibly brunch and supper as well.

It's hard not to be sympathetic. It's an injustice to possess a tourist visa to the world of food without the funds to actually live there. The push-pull between desire and means is acutely painful. Anyone paid to watch people wash down pristine oysters with French fizz inevitably thinks, 'Hey, that looks good. I must get me some of that.' It's human nature.

George Orwell had a bit to say on this matter. It's no coincidence that *Down and Out in Paris and London*, an account of his year living with the downtrodden—in, yes, Paris and London—features a lengthy episode in which he toiled as a dish pig in a hotel restaurant. The view from the sink was not good for old George. He was rancorous towards waiters transported by the spectacle of the dining room. He was poisonous towards anyone deriving pleasure by proxy. In Orwell's eyes the chef was a bastard—fair enough—but the waiters were no more than restaurant Uncle Toms. They were the worst of the worst: sycophantic house slaves in awe of their masters.

Over to you, George:

The moral is, never be sorry for a waiter. Sometimes when you sit in a restaurant, still stuffing yourself half an hour after closing time, you feel that the tired waiter at your side must

surely be despising you. But he is not. He is not thinking as
he looks at you, 'What an overfed lout'; he is thinking, 'One
day, when I have saved enough money, I shall be able to
imitate that man.' He is ministering to a kind of pleasure he
thoroughly understands and admires . . . They are snobs, and
they find the servile nature of their work rather congenial.

NO! No, no, no, no, no! All due respect to the man who gifted the world *1984* and clocks striking thirteen and all that—but to suggest a waiter watching diners stuff themselves after closing time is simply admiring the cut of their jib is patently false. That waiter is not thinking fondly of the fine meals he will enjoy one day, God or Lotto permitting. He is full of bitter, pustular hatred towards the people who are not only keeping him from his knock-off drink but have also exposed him to the wrath of the chef by bullying him into taking the order with the classic line, 'We're friends of the owner.'

And so what if the waiter occasionally likes to reward himself with a little foie gras, a little Châteauneuf-du-Pape? To stick to terms Orwell might appreciate politically, let's reconfigure it as 'equal restaurant rights for all'. Up the revolution.

Finding a place of employment that does away with the problematic matter of chefs altogether is a Pyrrhic victory. It means joining the waiter sub-class better known as fast-food workers. A direct route to oblivion. The minute you pin on that name badge you cease to exist as an individual. A paradox, you say? Submit your complaint on company form 12A.3 to the human resources department. If you haven't heard back from us by the end of next year, feel free to follow up with a phone call.

It is said that a frog won't notice if the heat is gradually turned up on a pot of water. If you pop the unfortunate amphibian into hot water it will hop straight out. But if you start it in cold water and then put it on heat, it will remain blissfully oblivious that it's about to become the famous French dish known as *cuisses de grenouille*. By this stage of my 'career' I was a boiling frog. Next stop on the slow descent to despair: the rather grandly named La Ritz Cafe, encased in the morbid retail environment of a huge, airless shopping centre and cursed by an amorous Indian chef with little understanding of local mores.

Let's call him John, because that wasn't his name.

'I'd like to say you're looking very sexy today,' John says as I walk past with a tray of red wine hidden in coffee cups for the department store girls who were forbidden to drink booze during work hours. 'Your legs appear to be very fine in that skirt,' John says as I scrape the brown bilge of his *vitello tonnato* into the bin.

'That's inappropriate,' I say in an attempt to appease the Anglo-Indian relations that have become increasingly frosty since John began trying out his Flirting 101 coursework on the female floor staff. 'You can't really tell girls you work with they're attractive. That's harassment. You might get in trouble.'

'And may I share with you the news that I am able to see your bosom as you bend over the rubbish bin,' John says brightly.

La Ritz is largely lost to the fog of memory. They weren't good times, they weren't bad times, they were just . . . times. The customers were mostly men forced to accompany girlfriends and spouses on shopping trips. Glum bag-carriers, one and all. My biggest mistake was forgetting to put in the order from a famous ex-cricketer. He waited more than an hour before inquiring after his omelette's welfare in the manner of a person asking about the failing health of an elderly distant relative. And I tipped a glass of red wine all over a woman when I was startled by the shopping centre's dancing promotional lion. But my usual litany of disaster was cut prematurely short when everyone fronting up to work one day found the doors closed and chained. The owner was going into legal battle with the shopping centre management over projected earnings. He said they lied. They said he just wasn't running a good enough business. He hadn't been able to warn the staff they were about to lose their jobs, he explained without a glimmer of apology to half a dozen waiters mentally calculating if they'd be able to pay next month's rent, because he needed the element of surprise. At least he splashed out on a Spumante toast to his future legal victory. Half a glass for everyone!

Word got out that John had taken over a greasy-spoon cafe on Swanston Street and was spending the next day interviewing. La Ritz waitresses who had waged a long and bitter war over his admiration for their legs sat grimly holding their CVs, waiting for their audience with the new pontiff. He sat enthroned on a twirly office chair raised to its highest point so each job supplicant was forced to look up at him. Power clearly didn't agree with John. 'I would like to inform you that the pay will be nine dollars an hour, not a penny more,' he said with a satisfied smile, which is the politest way I've ever heard someone tell me I was about to be screwed. And then with an impressive grasp of the local vernacular he added: 'Take it or leave it, sweetheart.'

It was a breakthrough moment. It was the first time I thought, simply, 'No. I will not subject myself to this. I will not kiss this man's ring each day. I will not.'

Such rigorous principles are why I came to be wearing regulation black polyester trousers with a white polo shirt and a baseball cap, both emblazoned with a lime green logo that looked like the upchuck of the Incredible Hulk.

It is 31 August 1997. Princess Diana is meeting her maker in a Parisian road tunnel. I am descending into the more worldly hell of a subterranean juice bar housed in the sportswear basement of a large department store.

My new manager Katie is a friend of a friend. Katie is blonde, athletic and heartbroken. Not only has she just been dumped by her boyfriend, a young man who sells sports gear in the very same basement, but the premature death of Princess Di represents a tragic waste of all those hours spent at the gym.

That first day is spent consoling her over the double bereavement. Travis and Di. Di and Travis. In my head, an unstable English aristocrat and a third-year osteopathy student living with his parents in Sandringham will be linked forevermore. 'I really like you,' Katie says at the end of the day. 'It's weird, because you're a Sagittarian. I normally hate Sagittarians.'

I normally hate people who believe in star signs, but on this occasion I am prepared to turn a blind eye. The day's conversation has revealed Katie's relationship is the victim of a Montague-and-Capulet-style prejudice between the sportswear salespeople, a bunch of bronzed athletic types who look like they're about to be drafted by the AFL, and the Juice Out employees, who are generally regarded as untouchables. It wasn't difficult to grasp the basis of this social apartheid—they generally looked like they were glowing with lean muscle mass, whereas we were usually covered in a compostable spray of vegetable fibre. Katie was effectively dating up. Travis couldn't handle the pressure. It, too, was a tragedy.

～

TIMOTHY

He was a pretty famous chef and restaurant owner
and he fell in love with a waitress. Nothing unusual
there. However, once the two partnered up, the
young waitress began throwing her weight around.
Over the next few months the couple effectively
formed a team of two that terrorised the rest of us
and on top of it all; unbeknown to the chef-owner,
his girlfriend began skimming the tips pool. On
one particular Saturday night with a full restaurant
we all decided to confront her about it. At first she
denied it but then, with the boyfriend blissfully
unaware of the pending firestorm, she explained
that they were the partnership that drove the
restaurant and that it wouldn't have all its awards if
it wasn't for them. We all promptly downed tools in
the middle of service and walked out, leading to the
premature end of their relationship.

The fast-food industry is a slippery customer. I'm not talking
only about all those sad broccoli sticks decaying in the fridge at
McDonald's, but the way the whole behemoth constantly shape-
shifts, always probing for the soft, vulnerable underbelly of
consumer guilt. This was the era when the exponential growth
of juice bars was based on the Great Lie that a shot of pulverised
wheatgrass is the equivalent of 1 kilogram of green leafy vegetables.
This claim is the juice industry's equivalent of the Immaculate
Conception or the September 11 One World Government conspiracy. It's been thoroughly debunked—a shot of wheatgrass is

the equivalent of a shot of broccoli or spinach or other naturally occurring green substance. Quite possibly a shot of lawn clippings will do as much for you.

But plenty of people still base the 'healthy' component of their diet on juices, which is kind of like basing your calcium intake on ice-cream. Juicing fruit and veg means you can kiss most of their fibre goodbye. On an unrelated note, drinking a whole heap of juice also means lots of trips to the toilet. This was a deliberate strategy of Juice Out employees, who were allowed to consume as much juice as humanly possible. To a bunch of impoverished uni students this was tantamount to saying, 'Hey, try and consume all your B and C vitamins in your work hours so you can subsist on convenience-store crap for the rest of the week.' The added bonus was that each trip to the toilet—'Please, Katie, please, I'm busting!'—meant an impromptu five-minute break. For a while there we amused ourselves guzzling beetroot juice to turn our urine red. Kind of gross, but fun: 'Oh my god, get in here, I'm dying!' Let's just say it was a job with a lot of back-end appeal.

I didn't mind working the juicer, an industrial monster that could have disposed of a whole dismembered body quite easily. The body I would really have enjoyed grinding into oblivion belonged to Georgia, a Geelong blonde disturbingly vocal in her support of Pauline Hanson and One Nation. 'Well, she's saying what a lot of people are thinking. The Abos have it easy,' was her take on indigenous relations. I wasn't sorry in the slightest when her expensive mountain bike was liberated from a street post out front.

If Katie wasn't around, Georgia always left early. She'd grab her bag, drawl a nonchalant 'See ya' and brazenly walk out with a smirk on her stupid, One Nation-loving face. This meant she usually left me to mop a cocktail of chemicals onto the black non-slip matting. Mopping is a bullshit exercise. You're simply making dirt wet, then moving it around. And they were toxic, those chemicals. A thin, evil vapour rose off them. The cancerous gunge would eat through the rubber soles of our regulation black canvas sports shoes in a matter of weeks. Katie told me not to breathe it in but it was impossible not to. As I mopped and coughed, I sometimes imagined Georgia stuffed inside one of the chemical containers, a pink mist rising as her body slowly dissolved.

Have you ever noticed how smash-it-out food corporations have a weird obsession with the mental state of their workforce? Apparently it's not enough for an employee to front up to work each day, do their hours and go home. It's a classic abusive relationship based on startlingly unequal power. They want your heart. They want your mind. Not only do they want to hear the words 'I love you', they want you to mean it.

Maybe it's to make the inhabitants of the mahogany-lined executive suites feel better that the minions are content to be earning minimum wage while working for an entity that reduces everyone to a number. Any workplace that refers to itself as a 'family' deserves contempt. A corporation can be a family only in the bastardised way of the Mansons or the Jonestown cult. Gather round for the Kool-Aid, children.

The Juice Out, ruled remotely from a city far, far away, was part of one such corporate family. Life went on peacefully enough in our forgotten corner of the empire, but every so often head office would remember we existed and, like a matriarch ordering her grown children home for the holidays, announce a team meeting. 'A fun way for you all to get to know each other,' said the notice that also sweetly informed us attendance was compulsory under pain of sacking.

Thing is, we already knew each other. We just didn't really *like* each other. There was Caitlin, ambitious second-in-charge to Katie, so transparent her thought processes were telegraphed in neon above her head: *One day this juice bar will be mine! All mine!* Sandra harboured dreams of owning her own cafe but had fallen into a depression when her choice of business name, How the Foccaccia, was knocked back by Consumer Affairs for failing to meet community standards. Sara was a medical student who thought she was a rare intellect beyond the ken of her co-workers. (Sample conversation: 'What are you reading, Sara?' 'It's a novel by a Russian writer called Bulgakov. You won't have heard of him.')

Contrary to what the literature says, team meetings are breeding grounds of resentment. I'll grant you there's no 'I' in team—as team leaders like to say—but there's certainly a 'me'. These corporate group jerk-offs are basically a bunch of individuals sitting around a table, each quietly furious that they have to indulge in inane psychobabble to stop their file being flagged 'uncooperative'. And, just to rub salt into the wound then squeeze lemon juice all over it, it's unpaid. That's what happens when you let human resources teams loose onto an otherwise perfectly happy dysfunctional business. It's ugly.

It was quiet in the basement once the jock salesmen had gone home and the lights had been turned off. There's something eerie about a department store after hours. Sepulchral. It could have been the scene for a modern adaptation of *Romeo and Juliet*, the tragic tomb scene played out among moody rows of Nike three-quarter high-performance training pants.

The last trip to the toilet—the day's final juice had been kiwi and strawberry—was unsettling in the half-light. All those racks of sports clothes longing for a home, facing down their night terrors of being abandoned to the stocktake sale. They were the perfect hiding spot for a crazed customer armed with a knife and a burning sense of injustice at the lay-by policy. Turning a corner I gave an involuntary shriek on bumping straight into Waleed, the night security guard. Waleed let out a little cry as well, although that could have been from the tube of wasabi he kept in his pocket to shock him awake on his lonely night patrol. Smart man, Waleed— it was the healthier, cheaper alternative to amphetamines.

The senior-manager-slash-team-leader was named Daniel. Daniel had flown in from Sydney just for us. 'Just for you,' he beamed benevolently. He had the forced jocular tone of the bachelor uncle assigned to look after the kids for two hours. He said 'folks' a lot. He handed out a photocopy, printed in Comic Sans, headed FRUIT SLAM. It was an acronymn: you know, F—Fun at work!; R—R you being the best employee you can be?; U—Understanding the juice process! Despite the near-fatal levels of eye rolling from the rest of us, Waleed loitered in the background, grateful to be soaking up the human company by osmosis.

The last Comic Sans module (M—Magnificent new juices!) invited us to propose exciting new flavour combinations. 'Celery, apple and kiwi—green power!' chirped Katie, fully aware she was the only one among us who, in the eyes of senior management, possessed a name as well as a number.

'Garlic. And ginger. Together,' offered a resentful Georgia.

'I've got one for you folks—banana juice!' grinned Daniel, unaware it was a joke we'd heard a thousand times already from smart-arse eight-year-olds.

'Hold on, folks, just one last thing,' he announced over the flurry of a dozen irritable people grabbing their bags, assuming it was get-out-of-jail time. He wheeled out a television and inserted a video in the VHS player. 'You know what, though, folks? At the end of the day it's good to realise what the most important things in life really are.'

The screen flickered into life. There was a bright blue sky. The sun shining on a typical Australian playground. Monkey bars and swings and a wooden fort being clambered over by small children. Children with Down syndrome. Children with Down syndrome being subjected to a synthesised Muzak version of 'What a Wonderful World'. Pling-pling-pling-pling-pling-pling . . . pling-pling-pling-pling-pliiiiiing-pling.

It went on for a full ten minutes and I guess it did achieve the desired effect, because the staff really were moved. Georgia sat shaking with suppressed laughter that made her look like a late-stage Parkinson's sufferer. It figures—One Nation has never been known for its compassion towards the lesser-abled. Sara looked outraged, as if a bird had just shat in her mouth. Even Waleed, so desperate for human contact, quickly vanished into the shadows of male swimwear. Katie simply looked embarrassed to be associated, however tenuously, with such champions of new-age corporate leadership. She kept shooting sympathetic looks across the table. They were looks that said: 'I'm with you guys. Not with them. Please, please don't punish me for this moral outrage with increased toilet breaks and lacklustre mopping.' Ironically, that was the only time the Juice Out staff displayed any solidarity at all.

— 5 —

BEST
SERVED
STEAMING
COLD

The woman and her three lovely daughters have arrived at the Juice Out like the Four Horsemen of the Apocalypse or something similarly biblical. Like locusts. Or boils.

The four very hungry, very irritable Horsemen of the Apocalypse have just ridden through the gates of hell, also known as the department store stocktake sale. They are emotionally, physically and spiritually spent after their morning battling other Boxing Day bargain-hunters for heavily discounted netball skirts, tennis socks and high-tech watches that will chart their calorific output in a handy algorithm altogether unnecessary for their ectomorphic body types. All four are accompanied by the grassy whiff of pony club—their bearing carries the distinct suggestion of saddlery—but the sportswear department on its busiest day of the year is not their natural habitat. The jagged, staccato nature of their conversation indicates morale is flagging.

'No, Mother!' hisses one lovely daughter through a clenched set of private-school teeth that cost more than my car. 'I said *caramel* milkshake not *chocolate*!'

Mother places her order while I stare transfixed at her bob, a cumulonimbus cloud of immovable blondeness. The temptation to touch it is overwhelming. 'And we'll be sitting over there,' she finishes in the manner of a countess claiming her regular table at the Wolseley.

'No table service,' I say, flicking a thumb at the sign on the counter that says 'No table service'.

A fairly conclusive parry, I would have thought, but no. Just as the laws of physics do not apply to this woman's hair, the laws of the Juice Out do not apply to her person.

'We'll be sitting over there,' she repeats, slightly louder and slightly slower, in the manner of someone accustomed to donning a white cotton glove to show the housemaid where her dusting needs to improve.

'Sorry, there's no table service,' I say again, in the manner of someone telling small children they are absolutely not getting another five minutes of television even if they hold their breath for a really, really long time.

The woman attempts to stare me down as I glower at her from beneath my Juice Out baseball cap. She's good, but she obviously didn't get the memo about picking fights with disaffected juice bar employees forced to wear a lime-green logo that looks like nasal discharge. This is fast turning into the National Stare-a-thon Championships. The knock-down round. I wonder if we're still going to be standing here tomorrow, retinas combusting from their own heat while a crowd barracks around us.

'Her,' the woman says, breaking off and turning to Caitlin. She means me. 'She's not very good.'

She stalks off to join her three lovely daughters at their table while Caitlin rolls her eyes at me with a mixture of sympathy and bemusement. 'Suck it up, honey.'

I leave the salad greens in the sandwich when I slam it into the press so they collapse into a whimper, depleted of even the memory of moisture. I stick the steam wand in the milk for so long the steel pot is near smelting point. I put so much caramel flavouring in the milkshake the recipient is in danger of developing Type 2 diabetes on contact. I deliver the order to the table, but this concession is not enough for Outraged of Brighton. She demands to see a receipt before handing over her money. Back to the counter. Print. Back to the table. She watches with smug satisfaction that I have bent to her will, while the lengthy Boxing Day queue shifts restively. 'Why does that table get special treatment?' says the thought bubble above their heads. 'Why not us?' Violent revolution has been fomented on far less.

But Outraged has unwittingly exposed herself. She has handed over a $100 note. A serious tactical error. Why, you ask? Because it makes it all too easy to short-change her. Not with the intention of getting away with it, mind you. That would be stealing, and I don't steal—well, not except for that wheel of cheese incident, which I can explain. I'm playing to a longer revenge script. A script that begins with feigning amnesia.

Feigning amnesia is the one all-purpose tactic I can thoroughly recommend to any waiter. It's remarkably useful. Cast your eye over any arena of power, from parliament to the courts, and you'll see it being used daily for a dazzling array of purposes. Misused your parliamentary car? Facing a broad-ranging inquiry into the media's abuse of power? Accused of corporate fraud? I forget,

I forget, I forget. Feigning amnesia is like donning a cloak of innocence, size XXL.

When feigning amnesia it helps to become very, very polite and apologetic. Obscenely, obsequiously polite. So polite that no one could possibly point the finger of blame at you. Except, of course, your victim, who knows exactly what's going on BUT CANNOT PROVE A THING in the face of your barrage of niceness.

True to form, Outraged has calmly and respectfully reported her short-changing to the relevant authorities—actually, she stands up and screeches, 'You! You! Young lady come back here this instant!' Her daughters squirm in embarrassment, which is excellent: already you're accruing bonus points for collateral damage. This is your cue to tell her, so very sweetly: 'I'm really sorry but I think you gave me a fifty, not a hundred. I mean, I'm sure of it.'

There are plenty of super-snazzy, eye-wateringly expensive till systems on the market. They're not actually called tills anymore; they're point-of-sale solutions, which is about as sexy as a till can ever hope to be. But however many bells and whistles they come with, they're only as good as their human operators. If you don't record how much money goes in, it's ridiculously easy to create an unholy accounting mess.

Of course Juice Out staff were meant to record how much money went in. Company policy and all that. But when it was busy, those three extra seconds on the till meant more furious glares from the line. Everyone dropped the ball from time to time, even the managers. That's the golden rule about long-form revenge: keep your story believable.

By now Outraged is feeling the sting coming. She's being politely but implicitly accused of attempted theft. She bites. Rants about incompetent staff, puts on a full matinee of eye-rolling theatrics. 'So you cannot take my word for it that I paid with a $100 bill?' she asks Caitlin who has hurried over to investigate. It's rhetorical. She means that in a situation of her word against mine, the unspoken laws relating to age, money and power means that she must win. Without it, her world collapses into meaninglessness.

Breaking down a till is a time-consuming process. Do it after service when it's quiet and calm and it takes a good half-hour. Do it in peak hour when there are a couple of dozen people waiting to be served and myriad other distractions and it could feasibly take triple that. Every cent in that till has to be counted, down to the five-cent pieces and the foreign coins that slipped through the currency defences. It's satisfying work, knowing that you're keeping your victim from doing whatever she likes to do in her spare time—smiting the poor, or sucking the blood of the international students detailing her car. But wait, there's more. Counting the till means the Juice Out is down a person. Not only have you succeeded in further outraging Outraged, you've also managed to hobble the Good Ship Enterprise on its busiest day of the year. You look up and note with satisfaction that it resembles a war zone, where the enemy attacked mercilessly with pineapple chunks and watermelon rind and no one survived to tell the tale.

The taste of victory is sadly short-lived, however. You might win the battle, but you will not win the war.

Revenge tactics are a necessary part of the modern waiter's armoury. As well as remembering to upsell mineral water and pronounce 'zabaglione' correctly, it's imperative to have at least one sure-fire method to redress the power imbalance between server and served. Let me repeat: imperative. The health of your psyche depends on it.

I know what you're thinking. So what if one over-entitled woman wants me to walk 20 metres to her table in defiance of the no-table-service policy? Why get so steamed up about it? What's the big deal, sugar-chunks?

Well, here's the deal.

It's a bit like the story of the Native American tribes who believed photographing them would steal their soul. Only in this case it's for real. Some diners will suck your soul right out through your ears if you let them. They'll then burrow into the soul-sized hole and set up an internal dialogue on loop. An internal dialogue that stealthily assumes the sound of your own voice. This voice will accuse you of being somehow less than the people you're serving. A fetch-and-carry girl. A table-swabber. A loser.

The reason this voice gets away with it is because it knows, and you know, that waiters are direct descendants of the servant class. The window-dressing has been modernised, to be sure: there's probably an open kitchen and air-conditioning and a *Chill Out Session* playing on the stereo, but the standard uniform remains a maid-like black and white, and a tinkling bell is still used in most places to summon staff to the kitchen. Except for the chicken vindaloo pizza on the menu, the Dyson Airblades in the bathrooms and the notable absence of Maggie Smith, it might as well be an episode of *Downton Abbey*.

The worst kind of diner responds in kind to the fact that he or she—arsehole-dom is an equal opportunity employer—suddenly finds him-or-herself in brief possession of servants. For two hours, three hours, the restaurant provides the perfect forum to play lord of the manor. These are the kind of people who enjoy their meal more knowing others are hungry. I don't mean to *j'accuse* the majority of diners, who are well mannered and appreciative and abide by the unspoken rules of social engagement. It's a highly visible minority who make the acid build up in your stomach. The man who clicks his fingers to get your attention. The woman who answers her phone when you're halfway through reciting the evening's specials, then becomes irritated when you walk away instead of waiting for her to finish. The simple yet significant verbal dereliction of saying 'Get me . . .' instead of 'May I have . . .'

I have an as-yet unproven theory that people who are rude to waiters are predisposed to road rage. Road-ragers are a special breed of emotional narcissists and control freaks who live by the dictum 'Me right—everyone else wrong'. The sealed bubble of the car mostly quarantines their antisocial excesses. It allows the rest of the world to see them as red-faced idiots madly gesticulating and swearing soundlessly behind double-thickness glass. The restaurant is the unfortunate venue for letting that aggression off the leash, into the real world and onto real people forbidden by the terms of their employment to fight back. Tally ho!

There's something known as the Waiter Rule that originated in the United States via a corporate titan named William Swanson. He proposed it in *Swanson's Unwritten Rules of Management* thusly:

PAUL

It was an award-winning restaurant run by a couple of chefs who put out an equally award-winning cookbook. It was amazing how often people would come in carrying a copy, point to a recipe and say, 'We'll have this.' Umm, we have a menu?

'A person who is nice to you but rude to the waiter, or to others, is not a nice person.'

Being on the top rung of the corporate ladder, Swanson was accustomed to people being deferentially nice to him. But he noticed that sometimes his dining companions would be less than nice to the people serving them. He called it a 'situational value system'. 'Watch out for people . . . who can turn the charm on and off depending on the status of the person they are interacting with,' he wrote. 'Be especially wary of those who are rude to people perceived to be in subordinate roles.'

Swanson was at the time CEO of Raytheon, a giant defence contractor that manufactures the Patriot and Cruise missiles, among other cuddly things. He was later busted by the *New York Times* for copying large chunks of his *Unwritten Rules* from other sources. The inconvenient facts of plagiarism and weapons of mass destruction did not fatally injure his thesis, however. On the contrary, other bigwigs followed Swanson's lead and jumped on the let's-be-nice-to-waiters bandwagon. They were falling over each other to display their man-of-the-people credentials. For example, former CEO of corporate empire Office Depot, Steve Odland, revealed to *USA Today* how, as a teenage waiter before becoming America's King of Stationery, he once dumped purple sorbet all over a diner in a fancy French restaurant.

So there's another lesson for any wannabe dining room despot: that waiter you're calling an imbecile might one day be a Fortune 500 CEO able to fire your arse ten times over.

It's probably important not to overlook another elephant in Swanson's room: if anyone earning several million dollars a year is still so cantankerous they need to push around a waiter, they deserve to be sectioned under the *Mental Health Act*. But still. It's nice to know he cares.

A wise restaurant elder not dissimilar to Pat Morita in *The Karate Kid* once told me there's nothing servile about serving. He was absolutely right, of course. Waiting is an art form. Never more so than right at this exact moment in history, when the erstwhile ideal of the stuffed-shirt 'Yes, sir; very good, sir' waiter has gone the way of the landline. Expectations are so much higher. Good waiters these days must be informed yet informal; conversational without being chatty; telepathic yet discreet. Think of a cross between Marcel Marceau, the Dalai Lama and Batman's valet Alfred.

At the end of the exhaustive list of expected waiter-ly traits, the best waiters also need to have emotional resilience. Meaning: they can let people aim their shit at them without taking it personally.

I've witnessed many times over how the best operators do it. Whichever way they choose to personalise the job—the cheeky type, or the subtle flirt; cool with a flicker of wry amusement, or garden-variety cheerful—they always approach the craft with a Zen-like denial of the self. Don't make the mistake of confusing that with low self-esteem. In fact, it's anything but. Their sense of self is unimpeachable because they refuse to let any angry, small-minded, petty dickhead ruin their vibe. They know they're performing a valuable community service that falls somewhere between priest, therapist, psychiatrist and boot camp commando. It's not *me*, these well-balanced individuals think when confronted with a finger-clicking misanthrope complaining that the crusty bread hurts his mouth; it's *you*. Plus they know any behaviour deficit will be put to good use later that night at knock-off drinks. One of the principles of any martial art is harnessing your opponent's energy and using it against them. That's precisely what a good waiter does.

Even those not born a great waiter—and I honestly think being a really great waiter has something to do with DNA; genome sequencing will reveal all in due course—can hope with application and perseverance to become one, in time. But the vast majority have waitering thrust upon them and they, I promise, are going to chip away at the joy of your evening until you realise you would have had a better time sitting at home eating burnt chops and watching a re-run of *Taggart*.

How does a restaurant owner expose these Waiter Undead who walk among us, cunningly disguised as normal people? All the Myers-Briggs-type personality tests in the world won't reveal even half as much as sticking someone on a dining room floor in the heat of service for precisely one hour. Maybe the Rorschach blot gets closest to the truth: do you look at Outraged of Brighton and see someone stretched to the absolute ends of human endurance by the tyranny of a stocktake sale and the pressure of maintaining a lacquered bob in humid conditions? Or do you see a pampered woman whose sense of self feeds upon the relentless assertion of her desires at the expense of all others?

You should be fairly clear by now where I sit on the temperament scale. If a bad attitude could be subject to copyright, my ten years as a waiter would have left me obscenely wealthy. Working the floor, I was the Kerry Packer of passive aggression. Sullen insolence was my personal trademark, diligently honed and perfected over time. For a long list of perceived diner slights—ranging from ordering the tomato sauce separately to the fries, to calling me 'dear'—I could perform a Jekyll and Hyde switch into the most perfunctory, robotic and joyless server the world has ever seen. If I didn't like a group of people I would endeavour to do my very best to ensure that the only thing left of their night was a cold, dry husk. That I regularly used something I privately referred to as the 'Dead Eyes' should reveal plenty.

Whatever gets you through the shift, right? When talking about job satisfaction, however, nothing can beat a real, honest-to-god act of revenge.

First, a disclaimer: a waiter's revenge is rarely sweet. A waiter's revenge is, by necessity, curdled and sour. Why? Because the victim needs to be none the wiser. A customer aware they have been bettered in an unspoken game of wit and skill—that's a one-way ticket to Unemployment Town.

I know, I know. Where's the fun? It certainly raises an important philosophical question—something along the lines of the proverbial tree falling in the forest with no one to hear it. If an arsehole diner doesn't know they've been one-upped, did it ever happen?

In a word: yes.

The temptation is to be Jamie Foxx in *Django Unchained* and orchestrate a gleeful massacre in which all the bad guys are shot to pieces. But let me assure you, you really want to be Kevin Spacey in *The Usual Suspects*. Remember the tag line? 'The greatest trick the Devil ever pulled was convincing the world he didn't exist.'

Nothing good ever came from exposing yourself. Be secret, my friends. Be safe.

~

It is a truth universally acknowledged that 'CONFIRMED: POO IN ICE-CREAM' is not a desirable headline for anyone in the restaurant game. Following the edict that revenge is a dish best served cold, a family enjoying an afternoon at Sydney's Coogee Bay Hotel in 2008 were served a complimentary dessert after complaining they couldn't hear the NRL grand final over loud music. Shortly afterwards, mother of three Jessica Whyte discovered in the worst possible way that the chocolate gelato in the bottom of the dish was not, in fact, chocolate gelato.

It was a field day for the media, which ran polls ('Would you eat ice-cream at the Coogee Bay Hotel?), streamed video ('Watch the moment unfold on CCTV'), and published everything from laboratory documents ('See scientific analysis that proves it's poo') to special sections ('Full coverage of the Coogee poo scandal').

As the *Daily Telegraph* opined, 'The only question remains: who put poo in the gelato and why?' Sadly, we will never know. The settlement, which saw the hotel pay $50,000 compensation to the Whytes, gagged all parties. Tish-boom.

One can safely assume, however, that more heads rolled over the incident than Madame Defarge witnessed during an afternoon's knitting at the guillotine. Messing around with faecal matter turns revenge into an extreme sport. Extreme sports attract extreme consequences. To any disaffected kitchen or floor staff inspired by this incident out there, may I politely suggest that winding up on the nightly news is not the best way to make your point.

Popular culture prefers stories of waiters spitting in the food but, honestly, I've never seen it. I haven't seen chefs spitting in food, either. A good thing all round. There's a certain gaucheness to the act. No one wins points for subtlety, sophistication or sheer sinister effect by gobbing on the steak. If it does happen, it's the restaurant equivalent of slipping on a banana peel to get a laugh. Totally old-hat.

There are other ways a bad customer gets their come-uppance. Think about it next time you've been snippy with the service staff. There'll be plenty of time to think about it, because everything will have curiously slowed to a glacial pace. In fact, the polar ice-cap might have melted before you get your dirty martini. Your food order? Oops, forgot to give it to the kitchen. So sorry. So terribly sorry.

And even though restaurants are packing their tables closer and closer these days, it's uncanny how often your chair leg is being kicked. Every time the server passes through; an inconsequential little tap-tap-tap that develops into a kind of Chinese water torture effect. How unusual.

Look around the room. Are other tables enjoying prompt service, a steady flow of food and drinks, and no accidental chair kicking? Has a sluggish vortex descended on your table alone? Now look inside. Tell me the truth: is it your fault?

There once was a young woman who never looked inside herself to discover why it's so hard to get good service in restaurants these days. Her name was Hector's Girlfriend. Hector was a restaurant regular with a revolving door of female companions. There was no point getting to know their names as they were: a) more or less interchangeable, and b) likely to have the shelf life of a Jennifer Aniston movie. Anyway, this particular version of Hector's Girlfriend was a piece of work. A stripper—not that there's anything wrong with that—used to having men falling over themselves for her long boots and short shorts, her swish of blonde hair and her come-fuck-me attitude. Let's just say she wasn't a girl's girl. She was the sort of woman who views all other women as competition for a scarce resource—the scarce resource being in this case complete idiots like Hector. Her raging sense of entitlement, her inability to say 'please' or 'thank you', her sneering contempt, managed to alienate the waitresses pretty comprehensively, but she wasn't bright enough to figure out why her bourbon and Coke never materialised with the other drinks. It was almost endearing, the way she'd sit there surrounded by her adoring man-crowd, her mouth hanging open in shock that it had happened yet again. Gosh, what are the odds?

It's not quite as kaleidoscopic as serving up shit, certainly, yet there's a gentle beauty to undermining people in ways they will best

VANESSA

I was a first-year medical student working at a bistro when one night a middle-aged man started choking on his steak. His wife was screaming for help and the guy was going blue and the other waiters started yelling for me to help him. I'd only been studying medicine for three months, but I had to grab him from behind and appease the crowd with a vague approximation of the Heimlich manoeuvre. The steak popped out and he started breathing again. I couldn't believe it when they left a fifty-cent tip. Fifty cents for saving a guy's life?

understand—in Hector's Girlfriend's case, simply being ignored was enough to torture her look-at-me sense of self. Even so, it's still only paddling in the shallows of possibility. The following are all things I witnessed first-hand, at various fine establishments. May the record note that I would categorically refuse to testify about these in a court of law. In fact, I'd feign amnesia before I reveal the true identities behind these gunslingers for frontier justice.

Marco was a regular. Marco was also a close friend of the owner, so he never paid for his meals or drinks. There were lots of them, too; Marco was like one of those parasitic smaller fish that feeds off the larger fish. He was all 'look after me, look after me', but despite the freebies he never tipped. Nothing riles a hospitality worker more than a demanding dick-wad riding the freebie train who doesn't tip—that's the trifecta, right there. One night when Marco had finished his free rib-eye, polished off his bottle of free shiraz and ordered his free espresso, the bar manager Dave finally had enough. He didn't say anything. There was no sniggering conspiracy of 'Hey, guys, guess what I'm going to do?'. Dave nobly and quietly took matters into his own hands when he disappeared, with an espresso cup, around the back to where the staff kept their bags. Dave served Marco an espresso laced with piss. The beauty of it was that Marco was Sicilian. In Sicily, sipping is for sissies, so he drank it in one gulp. He never suspected a thing. And if you're wondering why Dave pissed in the cup *before* adding the coffee, it was because he didn't want to ruin the crema. A true professional.

As the previous example demonstrates, knowing your customers' foibles will help tailor the perfect comeback. Call it bespoke revenge, if you will. Colin had made a fortune in weed removal. He had the straggly ponytail, the blonde mistress he boasted to his mates cost him two grand a week to 'keep', and the manners of a psychotic baboon. He and his lady friend would sit there for hours drinking Champagne and arguing. When the bottle was empty he'd stand on a chair and wave it over his head. That was his version of 'Please may I have another'. Classy. Anyway, Colin also liked to drink Coopers Red, a beer that naturally comes with sediment in the bottom. You're meant to leave the cap on and tip the stubby upside-down for a few seconds to disperse it. Colin liked to do this himself. All part of the ritual, you see. Which made it very easy to ease the cap off, replace it so it looked like it was still intact, and present it to Colin. He upended it and promptly covered his pants in a golden shower of beer. It was beautiful.

Costa was the waiter equivalent of a ninja warrior. A master of the dark financial arts. If anyone had pissed him off—and he was always being pissed off—you'd see him writing down their credit card number on a slip of paper and putting it in his back pocket. I don't know exactly what he did with these numbers, but knowing Costa's tastes, it was something very expensive.

Attacking people in their financial goolies is always a good move when the Dead Eyes, forgotten order and chair kicking hasn't made an impact. A business jerk showing off to a bunch of other business jerks is best targeted directly via the hip-pocket nerve. After a night of being treated like a lowly serving wench, Anja only pretended to run the Alpha Jerk's credit card through the machine. 'Your card. It's no good,' she told the flustered diner in front of the business contacts he was desperately trying to impress. What made it even better was that Anja was German. Just imagine those impassive Teutonic tones, sternly telling the squirming customer, 'No. You have no money.'

Tony was one of those show-off drinkers. A guy who needs other people to know he's a top-shelf kind of a guy. His drink of choice was Johnnie Walker Black Label whisky. Expensive stuff, but he'd always drink it mixed with Coke, which is kind of like adding raspberry cordial to Grange. The joke at Tony's expense began accidentally. We were out of Johnnie Black and I (yes, this is me) grabbed the bottle off the display shelf. I didn't notice it was actually a stunt bottle full of iced tea—really old iced tea, with all kinds of disgusting floaties in the bottom. When the manager realised I had served Tony a glass of aged iced tea and Coke, and that Tony drank it, smiled and asked for another, it was decreed that he should receive it henceforth. Tony smoked Marlboro Reds, for god's sake. His palate was shot to pieces. Over the course of a few months he drank his way through the whole bottle.

And then there was the fly. The fly in the bottom of the customer's long black. A big, fat blowfly that only revealed itself in the last dark dregs of coffee. Reports differ over whether the fly wound up in the cup by accident or design. It was noted by at least one observer that if it was indeed an accident, it was uncanny that it had been camouflaged in a black coffee.

Social media has changed everything, of course. A waiter's revenge can now be served up as a big steaming pile of ordure on the internet. It's not as elegant, certainly—there's always a price to pay when anything artisan goes into mass production. Social media demands that you can still smell the blood. Bystanders want to see the victim thrashing about in the water, pleading for mercy while the shark circles ahead of the final attack. It's revenge as a spectator sport.

Take, for example, the tale of a New York waitress named Laura Ramadei, who posted on her Facebook page an open letter to the man who put his hand on her bum and asked if he could take her 'to go'. Using the name from his credit card slip, a quick Google search had revealed Brian Lederman's occupation (banker—was anyone really surprised?) and her missive struck enough chords that it went viral. In Lederman's defence, he vehemently denied this particular incident of arse-grabbing when the *New York Post* came calling ('I've grabbed plenty of girls' asses in my life, but I've never grabbed hers,' said Mr Charming), and, look, she *had* provocatively asked his table if they needed anything else. Lederman then responded in the manner of any self-respecting hedge-fund titan: with the promise to make sure she never worked in New York City again.

There is another alternative when it all becomes too much. You could remember the freedom you sold for twelve dollars an hour and all the juice you can drink. The day is churning with possibility. It would be like wagging school on a sunny afternoon. There will be consequences, you're aware of that; you can see them shimmering in the distance. But you suddenly realise your days have become a thing to climb vertically, something forbidding and sheer. And you feel the tingle that scampers along your vertebrae when you stand on a precipice. It's the temptation to . . . just . . . step . . . out. To see what happens. This is the thing you will battle your entire life: the lesson ingrained in all children when they understand their only power over the world is contained in the word 'no'.

A bag describes a parabola as it's swung onto a shoulder. The action is weighted with meaning. The choice is easy.

IT'S A MAN'S MAN'S MAN'S WORLD

Maybe it's a genetic thing. The odds stacked against my table-waiting career, I mean. It's chromosomal. See, I'm XX. That's my deficiency, right there. I don't have a dick. I am *sans* penis.

I'm not saying possession of a Y chromosome will save anyone from the manifold perils of restaurant life. Not a bit. It won't save you from half-decaf-soy-lattes, from miserly tippers, from summertime thigh chafe. But it will save you from the unspoken query that lurks in the undergrowth of so many innocuous tableside negotiations. The query that hums beneath the 'still water or sparkling?', the 'butter or oil?', the 'medium or rare?'. The query that grounds your interactions like a bass line. 'Are *you* on the menu?'

It's just different for men, alright? Men don't cop half the crap women do, not in everyday life and certainly not in waitering life. Yes, waitering. I don't like the term waitress. It's only jobs looked down upon as frivolous that get the gender stick waved at them. Waiter, waitress. Steward, stewardess. Actor, actress. Why don't we distinguish between doctor and doctoress? Because we don't want to distract them from the business of saving lives, that's why. Waiter and waitering will do nicely, thanks very much.

But yes, women. We all cop it, us waiters of the female persuasion, whether fat or thin, big or little, up or down. I've been sexually harassed by proxy, for god's sake. A small boy who can't have been more than three started stroking my legs, moved onto my rump ('Nice bum, nice bum,' chanted the wee tyke) and started to rummage around the best china. His parents, you ask? His drunk dad sat on the sidelines egging him on with paternal pride. At moments like that, it takes all your strength not to howl for the future of humanity.

Any male readers might want to skip ahead at this point to the relative safety of Chapter 7; I promise there'll be no hard feelings. But please stick around, fellas. I'll try to make it worthwhile. If you do decide to go, take this thought with you: a woman working the floor of a restaurant is a bit like that line about Ginger Rogers. She did everything Fred Astaire did, only backwards and in high heels.

There was a framed black and white photograph on the wall at the Sabatini Cafe. Apparently it's quite famous: a street scene of 1950s Italy featuring a Sophia Loren type, a va-va-voom human volcano walking down the street, her hourglass figure vacuum-packed into a white skirt-suit. The woman, shot from behind, remains anonymous but the street is thick with men, every set of eyes locked on her and glistening with intent. They look exactly like a bunch of jackals spying a lame zebra limping across the savannah. A bunch of hungry jackals who haven't eaten in a month. Occasionally a customer would ask me what it was like working at the Sabatini. I'd point wordlessly at that picture.

I meet Eda on my first day. Eda is the apprentice chef. I'm on my break, sitting in the courtyard, flicking through a true crime book abandoned next to the overflowing ashtray.

'See him?' she says, pointing over my shoulder at a photo of a self-evidently dead body, supine on concrete in a dark halo of blood. 'That's my cousin.'

Eda was an anomaly. Albanian. Traditional. Married. Only nineteen. But tough. Boy, she was tough.

You've got to be tough to survive in a commercial kitchen, no matter what your gender is. The unwritten rule is that chicks have to prove they're as tough as the blokes, if not tougher. It's a big ask. When they don the chef's whites men often seem to wind the clock back about 20,000 years. It must be the proximity to naked flame, I've decided. 'Toughness' is also considered in purely masculine terms. I've seen one or two women maintain an unruffled sense of self. They wind up in the pastry section. The way it usually goes is they over-compensate into a parody of the tough chick. You know the tough chick? The tough chick can take it all then give it back, double. The tough chick is a bitch on steroids. The tough chick has a dick. The tough chick is ready to rumble.

Fuck, yes. Yes, fuck. Right fucking away. Fuck fuck fuckity fuck.

Eda was creamily pretty, built to the specifications of a porcelain doll, and when she wasn't saying fuck, given to flirting with Maurizo, the sous chef. Mo responded enthusiastically in kind. He was a pink-cheeked, baby-faced northern Italian who, at the age of thirty, still lived with his parents. They shared a kiss in the coolroom. It was a fairly chaste thing by all accounts, but Eda either had an attack of the guilts or a twisted desire to have a man fight for her honour. Whatever the case, Eda's red-faced husband arrived soon thereafter to belt the bejeezus out of Mo.

During service, too. That shows he was really mad. Everyone knows you leave personal matters until after 3 p.m.

He burst through the front door bellowing 'I'm going to kill him!' which gave Mo a chance to scurry for the storeroom. Humiliatingly, he was dragged out by one leg like an errant puppy. For the next week Mo nursed a black eye and a far more deeply wounded sense of pride. The incident wasn't spoken of again. Not when Eda was the cousin of Akhmed the Switch who'd taken a bullet to the head outside a city nightclub. Who knew how many other crazy relatives she had who were still breathing?

Looking back, the Sabatini was the kind of place destined to have '63 per cent rating on Urbanspoon' carved on its tombstone but for that moment in time, at least to my impressionable eyes, it was dazzlingly Old World. It was the intersection of spaghetti marinara and romance. It was the place to make you maudlin with Europhilic nostalgia even if the closest you'd been to Florence or Rome was the plaza at Preston Market.

I lived close by, only a few hundred metres up the road. A two-bedroom terrace house shared with three other people, none of whom were sleeping together. It was cosy. To escape our lack of living quarters I'd sometimes collect coins off mantelpieces and down the back of the couch and splash out on a coffee at the Sabatini. At university I'd sit next to kids who'd take a bottle of

Grange from their parents' cellar for a casual dinner with friends, and I was pilfering loose change for a cappuccino. *Vive la différence.*

The owner, Gino, was a nuggety pit-bull of a man who had arrived on a boat and spent the next thirty years in grim pursuit of the Australian dream. Think of Vito Corleoni, transplanted to Melbourne instead of New York and in the trade of caffeine and *cotoletta* rather than bootleg liquor and extortion. The Sabatini was Gino going legit. He'd made his money in a few shabby suburban places and this was his big roll of the dice. It worked. In the eyes of this calmly affluent suburb, the Sabatini ticked plenty of boxes: the boxes for gilt-edged mirrors, 'Nessun Dorma' and pumpkin risotto. Even walking through the door gave me such a thrill it bordered on illicit. A tingle down the spine that spoke of what life might be when I no longer lived in a house where someone slept in the kitchen. 'I work at the Sabatini.' The words trickled off my tongue like honey.

Gino had a thing for his floorboards. A fetish thing. The wood was a deep mahogany, polished until it seemed to glow with its own light source. It was like a ripe olive, ready to burst. And Gino himself was dark and polished and perma-tanned. The floorboards were almost an extension of himself. Adding to the psycho-sexual overtones, he demanded that they be meticulously, scrupulously clean. We swept a dozen times a day but it was never enough. He'd kneel down in supplication, inspect them like an entomologist studying a line of exotic ants, stand up shaking his head sadly and demand yet more sweeping.

Roger the English waiter knew the direct route to Gino's heart. He ducked out to the back alleyway and brought back a pile of dust that he presented triumphantly as the fruits of his sweeping labours. 'Yes, Rog-er, very good, Rog-er!' beamed Gino, trying out a rare smile on a mouth more permanently set into a thin line of disapproval. But the floors were a far greater source of angst than pleasure. For a while there was a waiter at the Sabatini named Cesare. Cesare disappeared, presumably to the bottom of the bay wearing concrete boots. His crime was to knock over a stack of chairs. It was a heart-stopping moment when Gino rushed over to midwife the fallen tower off his floor, lifting it gingerly as though a baby was trapped underneath.

The staff all froze, mid-action, a still life of horrified anticipation. And there it was. A dent in the floorboards. Their mirrored perfection sullied by a 3-centimetre gouge. Cesare knew he was fucked. Gino maintained his composure long enough to get out to the courtyard where he let rip, hurling around everything that wasn't nailed down while screaming as if his testicles were in a vice. Picture a 68-year-old man roaring like an outboard motor while he throws chairs around like matchsticks. He was strong, old Gino. And he certainly had a set of lungs on him.

I'm not even Catholic but was tempted to cross myself. There but for the grace of God and all that.

MELISSA

There was a heavily pregnant woman who was a week overdue—we'd been having a little chat about it when I seated her and five of her friends. A while later one of the waiters says to me, 'Where did that table go?' All six of them had gone and the food was untouched. They'd left money on the table but there was a huge puddle of amniotic fluid on the floor, and it had destroyed the floorboards. They could have told us.

The Sabatini was a family affair. If Gino was the Godfather, his oldest child Arna uncannily mirrored the fictional Godfather's daughter Connie. Self-centred, spoiled and bossy, Arna was talked of in hushed tones by her Italian family because—*sotto voce*—she'd almost been an old maid. Over thirty and single: a fate worse than death, or even lesbianism. But then she found someone who agreed to marry her and all was right with the world once more. Ari was six years her junior, an easy-going schlub of a man who had worked with her when they were public servants in some inconsequential government department. Why he married her, I don't know. Maybe they gave him an offer he couldn't refuse. The outcome was inevitable. The minute they were back from the honeymoon he was fastened onto the chain gang to take his place in the family business. From the outside he and Arna were a loveless union, although somehow they had managed to conceive Adriano, the first grandson and therefore the Sun King destined to grow up into a hideous brat.

Ari looked like a grown-up Mediterranean version of Kevin Arnold from *The Wonder Years* and carried himself with the bemused air of a man who had popped out to buy milk and suddenly found himself with a wife, a kid and a bunch of in-laws only slightly removed from The Mob. Ari was Greek, which might have had something to do with his disconnect from the family. The fractious history of Greco-Italian relations meant they treated him like the hired help. He wasn't really One of Them. This was a man sentenced to probation for the rest of his life.

Ari was sweet but he was a pushover. Possibly none too smart with it, either. He thought the verb 'capitulate' meant taking a dump. Each morning when the effects of his first espresso started to make themselves known in his lower intestine, he'd cheerfully announce to whoever was around, 'It's that time of day, I have to capitulate,' and disappear with the newspaper to the men's for twenty minutes. I'm still not sure which was worse: the serial over-sharing or the crimes against vocabulary.

A lot of hospitality jobs mimic the trajectory of a doomed relationship. You go through the initial honeymoon phase where it's all unicorns and rainbows and shared jokes across the bar. When you meet Gino's son Carlo, another family member sentenced to work day and night for the term of his natural life, he says, 'I've heard all about you,' and you know he means good things. It's a warm feeling. A better-than-good feeling. You are officially a professional waiter. You feel so at home you even adopt their idiom, the way they pronounce Italian words with a frightening rise of volume and a determined accent—and here is your *ESPRESSO* and *CANNOLI*; most certainly sir, *PREGO!*— in a way that only italics and capitals can convey.

But then you start to hear an old, familiar tune playing faintly in the distance. What is it? Oh yes, it's the saxophone solo from *Yakety Sax*. And wait, is that Benny Hill skulking in the corner?

∾

In my version of the story the problem begins with Carlo, a young man who has accumulated twenty-seven years' worth of frustration at being the indentured servant of a domineering father. Carlo's life is mapped out for him. He is the Michael Corleone of the Sabatini. A decent man being slowly yet inevitably corrupted by the family business. While he is measuring out his life in coffee spoons, Carlo is looking for entertainment.

'Ari's in the office. He wants a word with you,' Carlo says to me one morning. I trot dutifully to the office only to cop an eyeful of Ari changing into his work uniform. It's possibly more than Arna has seen in quite some time. At least since Adriano was conceived. For the rest of the day, Ari and I avoid looking at each other.

Another time Carlo orders me to follow him out to the kitchen. I follow him out to the kitchen. 'What the hell are you following me for?' he says.

The chefs jump on the gag. 'What are you doing following Carlo around like his little dog? *Ar-oooo!*'

In their version of the story I might be young and naïve and ridiculously gullible. But it wasn't just me with 'victim' written on my forehead. Another waiter named Jacinta copped it as well. Her tailor-made indignity was the managers all piling into the toilet after she'd used it. Ostensibly they were making sure she hadn't been taking an illicit cigarette break. I wasn't a big fan of Jacinta—she was a chronic whiner with a married lover who liked to sit at table eight and watch her; sometimes he'd even bring his unsuspecting wife with him, which appeared to be part of their sport. Still, sniffing the toilet? That seems a bridge too far.

Things got even blokier with the arrival of Malcolm, a self-styled Casanova waiter with Coke-bottle glasses and a wife whose pregnancy he used as an excuse for visiting hookers each Friday night. An occasion he looked forward to with unembarrassed relish. Who's it to be tonight, Cassandra the Asian temptress or Monique the French slut? Choices, choices . . . He was the kind of guy who'd trot out the old 'who's the mother and who's the daughter?' cliché, a line he believed was both timeless and charming.

Malcolm tipped the Sabatini's delicate balance of flora over into outright testosterone overload. To use the modern parlance, we reached Peak Bloke. Eventually we abandoned separate sections and triaged diners based on gender. The arrival of an attractive woman would send the male waiters into a huddle at the bar, where they'd analyse her attributes in the kind of detail otherwise reserved for the football. The male customers were all mine. Or was I all theirs?

The jury has reserved its decision. Exhibit A for the prosecution: Sergio the professional gambler. Sergio arrived every morning at precisely 11 a.m. wearing the trademark shiny green lycra bicycle shorts in which he had power-walked from his house 3 kilometres away. Every morning at 11.05 a.m. Gino would shove me at Sergio's table, hissing 'Smile!' through gritted teeth.

Sergio was independently wealthy—his words—and in the process of having artwork specially commissioned for his house. The artwork was to be based around his burnt orange feature wall. He wanted me to come and advise. Not only that, he promised he could treat me to a—his words—Champagne lifestyle. 'You go to his house,' Gino says. It's half-question, half-command.

Gino is confused. It's a service industry. It's not *the* service industry.

We had a regular for a while who would often sit alone reading *Men Are From Mars, Women Are From Venus*. It was a best-seller at the time, but in that febrile environment he deserved a bravery award. Years later, after Harry and I had become friends, he told me that he and his mate debated for a long time whether to ask me out but they never had the guts. 'You always looked so unhappy.'

You bet I did. The dream of a better working life was crumbling into dust.

I turn up for my 11 a.m. shift and because it's quiet Gino commands, 'You. You start at twelve,' which is totally flouting workplace laws, but so is the Sabatini's cash economy. And it was always *You*. I never heard him use my name. Not once.

Anyway, it's a blazing hot day back before global warming became a news story, when Melbourne still greeted each heatwave like an unexpected houseguest. The Sabatini does not have air-conditioning. It's brutal. Customers are tetchy. No one's tipping. Six hours of working in a sauna and I've paused to grab a cloth to stop the sweat dripping onto my notebook.

'Daydreaming again, huh?' Gino hisses in my ear. He snatches my pen and hurls it across the bar. It clatters under the espresso machine. I have to get down on all fours to retrieve it from among the historical coffee gunge and dustballs. He stands there looking at me, his eyes glinting with something close to contempt.

Gino's older brother Raphael starts working at the Sabatini. Raphael is sixty-nine years old and illiterate. Everyone tells me on the first shift I share with him. 'Raphael—he's illiterate,' they whisper when Raphael is out of earshot, as though he must remain unaware of his inability to read and write lest the shock be too much. Much like a blind person supposedly has super-sharp hearing, his memory has jumped into the breach to compensate, I'm told. You can give Raphael an order for twelve different drinks and he'll get it right every time. Unfortunately this is a complete fiction. But he is the owner's brother, and so you must never mention it while patiently reciting the order to him for the third, fourth and fifth time.

Raphael has a face that reminds you every time you look at it that the nose and ears are the only parts of the human body that keep growing. He wears a permanent half-grin underneath a friar's bald pate with a desperate fringing of white and blows his nose with a startling honk.

'When you think, do you think in Italian or English?' I ask him one day during a lull behind the bar, a question intended to display that I have no problem with the fact he is an illiterate peasant from

Puglia and that I'm as hip as any Gen-X to oral history, the wisdom of the elders passed down from one generation to the next.

Raphael's chuffed. 'Why . . . why . . . thanks for asking me what I think. Yes, I think. I think quite a bit.'

Later he hands me a card. It has his name written in childish, spidery letters and an address. 'Because we both have next Tuesday off. So you can visit me.' He looks at me meaningfully. He winks.

It dawns on me that Raphael is stupider than a bag full of compost. And he has misinterpreted my being-nice-to-the-aged routine as romantic interest.

'Raphael?' I begin cautiously over a mountain of wet cutlery after the last customers have gone home. 'You know I'm not interested, don't you? I mean, it's the age gap and everything . . .'

'I don't mind that you're young.' Raphael is missing the point somewhat. I decide to leave it. I need to work more on my honesty.

∼

He has a parrot. Allegedly. The alleged parrot can talk. Raphael likes to imitate the parrot. He walks around the bar squawking, 'Raphael has a big dick.' Apparently Raphael's parrot has done the necessary background checks and discovered its owner has a penis larger than the average human male. 'Raphael has a big dick.' It goes on for days.

A few months later Raphael returns from holiday in the Philippines with a batik shirt, a carton of duty-free Marlboro Reds and a 21-year-old bride. He proudly shows off her photograph. The men congratulate him like he's just had a child. In a way, he has.

He tells me about their first intimate encounter in forensic detail. To paraphrase Michael Bolton, maybe Raphael thinks if we can't be lovers we can be friends. Or maybe he's trying to show me what is now so cruelly denied. It sounds like something culled from *Penthouse Forum*, minus the bit that begins, 'I don't normally write letters like this but . . .'

I will spare you the bulk of the story. Suffice to say, it is prolonged and displays Raphael's eye for intricate detail. It culminates in this: 'She took my vest off for me. Then I popped her. She was definitely a virgin. Only twenty-one. But *she* wasn't too young.'

The wife does a runner. A 21-year-old Filipina who speaks no English has turned out not to be in love with Raphael after all. 'She's crazy!' he says, twirling one finger around an ear in the globally recognised signal for insanity. 'She gambles.'

When I am sixty-nine years old and a much younger co-worker says 'hello' and 'goodbye' and maybe even 'a caffe latte for table twelve please', I will not assume he wants to get into my pants.

This I promise.

One night we go to the casino.

We go after work. There has been talk. Everyone is going. James the kitchenhand is going. He is a wriggle-thin sinew of a boy with a quick-draw wit. I have a crush on James. So I am also going.

Sergio tags along. Thankfully he is not wearing his green lycra bicycle shorts. He has changed into pants and a shirt but is no less annoying.

It turns out James is not going. He was only joking.

Dammit.

We wind up at a nightclub of which I remember little, save for two women dirty dancing with each other while most of my workmates ogle from the balcony. I end up back at the Sabatini

NICK

A table of six had been going really hard on the
alcohol. A bottle of white was sitting in an ice
bucket on a stand but then I noticed someone had
put the ice bucket on the table. One of the guys
gestured at it and said, 'You should know my wife
has been sick.' I went to remove it but he grabbed
my arm and said, 'No, no, we don't want to make a
fuss, my wife will be embarrassed. Just bring me
another ice bucket.' They spent the rest of the meal
with a bucket of vomit on their table.

with Carlo. For a nightcap. Talk turns to Gino and his floorboard
obsession. 'He's a hard man,' Carlo says emotionlessly, sunk into
his whisky. 'You have no idea.'

I am twenty-two years old and have not even reached the base
camp of understanding other people.

Carlo grabs his car keys. 'Ride?' I go with him, not even
thinking about eight hours' worth of alcohol sloshing wildly
through his bloodstream. He stops outside my house and turns the
engine off. Sits looking at me silently. Those dark, inscrutable eyes.
Just like his father's.

Was anything meant to happen? I'm still not sure.

You don't have to be a brain surgeon to figure out that one of
the reasons the restaurant biz is so full of flux, drama and terror

is due to the relative youth of its workforce. But maybe it helps. Dispatches from the frontiers of neural science indicate the human grey matter doesn't reach maturity at eighteen, when you get to legally drink and drive (albeit not together) in Australia, or even twenty-one, when you get to have a massive party involving the presentation of a giant novelty key.

Turns out it's the rental car companies that are right on the money. They'll stick expensive restrictions on any driver under the age of twenty-five. That's when a person can be considered a fully-fledged adult. The beautifully named 'executive suite'—the brain's prefrontal cortex that calibrates things like risk and reward, thinking ahead and regulation of emotion—isn't fully baked until a quarter of a century after life springs forth. Crazy stuff.

So therein lies my theory of why the hospitality industry is so fractious. You've got an essentially itinerant workforce of young people with under-developed brains, fuelled by alcohol and other substances, smashing about like atoms. It's a recipe for disaster.

I'm no brain surgeon but I do have a law degree being eaten by silverfish in a drawer somewhere. The legal concept of contributory negligence is a handy tool when analysing the chaos of the average twenty-something waiter's life. In layman's terms it goes something like this: if I can't even figure myself out, how the hell am I going to understand my co-workers or the customers?

Through my jaundiced prism, for example, I firmly believed that the well-dressed middle-aged couple who turned up each Saturday in their shiny European convertible were absolute, utter and complete wankers. Why anyone would drink Champagne before noon was beyond me. They did look terribly self-satisfied, which was a permanent mark against them, but now I'm prepared to admit they were ahead of the curve. Brunch is the new national pastime. Australians are brilliant brunchers. Brunching should have been our exhibition sport at the Sydney Olympics. Smug couple, I'm sorry I treated you with disdain.

And the women I decided were ex-nuns, forced out of the convent by a harsh, patriarchal culture. Two plainly dressed, sensibly shod middle-aged women who came in once a week to order a single entrée risotto between them. I was studying feminist history at the time but clearly didn't have as vivid a sexual imagination as I might have. Ari hated them. Less because they were probably lesbians, more because he was an absolute tight-arse. If he caught me giving them bread and butter with their one-entrée-risotto-two-plates he'd give me the look he reserved for the local wino who'd stop by to cordially inquire about any half-empty bottles that might be lying around. But I liked sprinkling a little sunshine on their day, even though Ari eventually screamed at me about my 'stupid fucking bleeding heart'.

I cried. Of course I cried, despite deploying all my mental tricks—thinking of puppies, feet and violent movies—to prevent it. Crying at work is inevitable if you're a woman, although the way it's frowned upon makes you feel like you've failed a really important PowerPoint presentation. There's something brutally embarrassing about crying at work, simply because it's so baldly human and you're not meant to be human at work. But it's not a sign of weakness. It's not. Women just produce more water in their eyes when they're sad or angry or even happy. We're more . . . tidal.

There are more things to cry about when Roger and Anna, the English waiters and the combined voice of reason, leave to return home. Then Jacinta gets the chop. Somehow I find myself the only female left standing on a speedway of out-of-control masculinity.

They start sniffing the toilet after I use it.

I become quiet. And quieter. Then quieter still.

It does occur to me that there are other places I could feel insecure when walking in the door carrying an apron rolled in its own strings. It occurs to me so violently that I regularly exclaim to my housemates: 'I'm out of there! Watch this space, I am so gone!'

Marina, who is an apprentice chef at an Italian place across town, merely nods her head and keeps combing conditioner through her thick blonde hair. Marina has been the ongoing butt of a thousand 'jokes' at the hands of a sadistic chef-employer. What I am going through is nothing. And so the inertia that marks the whimpering end of so many relationships betrays me.

The Sabatini gets to be the dumper. I am the dumpee. Ari calls one afternoon. He sounds awkward. Says it's not his decision, it's come from the others. A bold hospo twist on the old dating furphy 'It's not you, it's me'. After I have hung up the phone I cry, and then I am furious.

I let them win. Dammit. *Dammit!*

I have revenge fantasies about Gino. Why Gino rather than Raphael, or Ari, or Carlo? They say a fish rots from the head down. Gino was the head of the fish. Ergo . . .

Actually I have revenge fantasies about a few people I crossed paths with as a waiter. I try to keep them thematic. Gino's buys into the whole Italian thing. It's a *Godfather*-lite confection, so I've got a Luca Brasi-styled sidekick, a hulking yes-man to do my bidding. He's gaffer-taped Gino to a chair and gives him the occasional slap across the cheek while I go to work with a blowtorch and a set of pliers. Say my name, bitch. Say my name, you dip-shit of a man.

I start with the pliers, delicately pulling out his nails one by one. They resist at first, then come out with a satisfying little— pop! By now Gino's shrieking something unintelligible in Italian. It sounds like an imprecation to the Almighty to strike me dead but I continue, regardless. I throw the nails in the corner, then jump up and down so the loosened floorboards undulate like a xylophone in an earthquake. Then I go to work with the blowtorch, close and meticulous, until all that is left of their glossy tyranny is a blackened, smoking ruin.

It keeps me warm at night. But I guess the best revenge on Gino was simply that he had to be Gino. Even I have to admit that was punishment enough.

— 7 —
HOW TO MAKE NOTHING OUT OF SOMETHING

You know a sure-fire way to make money from restaurants? Start a support group for everyone who's lost theirs chasing the ownership dream. Set a modest annual membership fee, charge a dollar for a styrofoam cup of instant coffee (extra for milk and sweetener) and you won't look back. There'll be tears (you can charge for tissues) and there'll be anger (there's nothing more comforting than carbohydrates—charge for sweet biscuits). The upshot is that there'll be more money to be bled from that sad circle of plastic chairs in a disused scout hall than any of these guys found tapping into the Great Australian Dream of restaurant ownership.

Stick around the hospitality industry long enough and you'll see people doing their dough in kaleidoscopic ways. Some, realising the end is nigh, choose to go out in a spectacular display of fireworks and embezzlement fury ('If that's how it's going to be—cop this, universe!') that invariably ends in furious creditors, a locksmith, and the disembodied voice of the recorded phone message advising, 'The number you have dialled has been disconnected. Please check the number and dial again.' You may never see this person again, although South-East Asia is probably a good place to start looking. South-East Asia is the industry version of going into witness protection.

Much like confronting death itself, staring down the barrel of fiscal annihilation is a very personal matter. Some go under with a quiet whimper, some are bitter, some sociopathic, some merely pathetic. Whatever the case, the view from the cheap seats is never pretty. Sure, there's always another place willing to hire a waiter with a chequered work history and her own wardrobe of black and white separates. Waitering is a movable feast, after all. But watching people who have poured their life savings into a business coming to terms with its terminal diagnosis is like watching the human condition in time-lapse.

You know the Kübler-Ross model of the five stages of grief? It's like that, only—hopefully—without the human body at the end of it. It kicks off with denial and anger. Little explanation needed here. This is the bit where the boss starts acting more volatile than usual. Of course, he might simply have renewed his coke habit or be spending too much time with the form guide, sinking his dough on the fifth race at Randwick. Time will reveal all, but if a hitherto well-balanced person snarls 'What the fuck's your problem?' when you walk in for your shift, chances are things are on the slide.

Then it's onto the bargaining stage. This is the bit where a previously clean line of credit receives a sudden downgrading. It's like Moody's or Standard & Poor's demoting a nation from a gold-plated, triple-A credit rating to BBB junk status. Sweden one day; Uruguay the next. As if there's been a secret memo go out among the suppliers—and quite possibly there has, because these guys swap intelligence like ASIO operatives—goods are being delivered on a strictly COD basis (that's cash on delivery—no way is the supplier going to get stiffed on two cases of pinot gris when the dining room is apocalyptically empty).

There will be meetings. The meetings might be formal: an overly cheerful bank rep fronting up to talk about that little outstanding debt. The meetings might be informal: loan sharks arriving with their glittering dead eyes and flinty air of menace. There will be other 'meetings' conducted in the kitchen. Loiter casually nearby and you'll hear the head chef being implored to stay. The chef usually knows what's going down. The chef deals with the suppliers, and probably has the closest relationship to the boss. The chef is the bellwether of the business. If the head chef position is a revolving door of sudden, unexplained departures—be afraid. Be very afraid.

Next up, depression. Look out for the chain-smoking, the quiet weeping in the office, the bottles stashed in the bottom of the boss's bag making soft little clanks, the muffled chimes of doom, foretelling another night of self-medication on the couch.

And then, finally, acceptance. Or arson, an eventuality the Kübler-Ross model failed to consider. It could go either way.

Whatever your personal feelings, it's not good for the soul to watch a person go down like the *Titanic*. No one enjoys working through that awful twilight zone when the writing's not only on the wall, it's in 10-foot-high neon letters, an emergency flare seared into the night sky. It's professional masochism.

Anyway, the clued-in staff will have abandoned ship at the first sight of the iceberg. No shame in that. It's the only smart move, because by this stage there aren't enough lifeboats to go around. Don't go feeling any misplaced sense of duty. If you're on the books the owner has probably stopped paying superannuation to save a few hundred measly dollars a week. If you have holidays owing, you'd better grab them while you can, because you're about to go on the holiday with no end.

Few things depress the hell out of me more than walking past an empty restaurant at 7.30 p.m., the time when it should be pumping, the kitchen cranking, the waiters bustling, the place full of bonhomie and cheer. Whatever the joint might be—upmarket, mid-market or the kind of place with 'cheap-arse Tuesday' daubed in fluoro lettering on the window—the net effect is always the same. There's the empty stage-set of folorn tables and chairs. The hopeful cluster of waiters at the counter. Doing what waiters do when times are bad—waiting. Waiting and waiting and waiting. Odds-on one of them is an owner, rostered on to cut staff costs. It's easy enough to identify this person because even through plate glass they reek of the eau de cologne known as D'Spair. This person will eyeball you as you walk past, hoping to make like a tractor beam and pull you in against your will.

Fat chance. You think I'm going into a place with no one else in there? No effing way. I'm like everyone else. I see an empty joint, I assume it's no good. Even if by some chance it is good, it's no fun to eat in an empty dining room— and anyway, they're probably forced to push dodgy produce that's been in the fridge just a little too long.

See? Failure is a self-fulfilling prophecy.

Of course, there are stories about brilliant comebacks from the abyss. They're traded like talismans across an industry where hope is just about the only thing in short supply. David Chang made a multinational mega-success of Momofuku only after going all gonzo on his traditional Korean stuff that had been greeted by New York with an unimpressed 'meh'. The story is carved on a stone tablet high on a mountaintop somewhere, alongside a copy of the *Time* magazine with his grinning mug on the cover. But if you're going to base your business plan on a Chang-like resurrection, you might as well start writing letters to the Tooth Fairy. Best treat it as nothing more than a beguiling tale told to restaurateurs after their Stilnox has kicked in and they're being tucked whimpering into bed at night.

So I went to work for Salvatore.

Salvatore had been the Sabatini's head chef. Yes, yes, I know. But I'd been out of work for six months, surviving on handouts from the Bank of Mum and Dad (interest rate: guilt) and it was time to get back on it. And Salvatore had been the least-worst person there.

ERIC

It was an outrageously expensive hotel with a sushi restaurant where the chef's specialty was lobster sashimi. He wouldn't kill the creature first; he'd simply lift the shell off, scoop the tail flesh out, put it back in and serve the whole lobster, which presumably had died by this time, on ice at the table. One night I put the lobster down to the usual ooh and ahhs and turned away only to hear a massive crash and people screaming. The lobster had crawled off the platter and onto the floor. The whole table went berserk.

There was an element of kindness to his broad-framed Italianness. He could dick-joke with the best of them but his flirtations were chaste, he occasionally gave me a lift home in his classic Mercedes, and he didn't mind it when I nicked sun-dried tomatoes from the plastic container on the prep bench. So when he called and happily explained he'd ditched the well-paying, steady job he'd held for more than ten years to throw his hat in the ring as what is stiffly known as a chef-patron—well, 'yes' seemed a reasonable answer.

'Fuck that Gino,' Salvatore exclaimed with passion, the dark circles under his eyes more pronounced than the last time I saw him, but with the unmistakable air of someone quivering on the cusp of their own destiny. 'Fuck him. I've been dreaming about this for a long time. Finally I'm doing my own thing.' He drew it out for emphasis, nurturing the consonants into a sing-song lilt. 'Fi-na-lly.'

Let's call it Niente. Nothing. Because Niente might as well never have existed. It lasted less than a year. Horrific stuff. It was like a car crash, only without the screech of tyres, the quasi-satisfying shattering of glass and crumpling of steel. Niente went so quietly into that good night the casual observer would never have realised it took the life savings and the very spirit of two decent men.

It was a business on dialysis from day one. The decisions made by Sal and his brother Ronny, who'd taken early retirement from the police force to throw his money into the venture, contravened all accepted wisdom. They also prove, as if further proof were needed, that a decent-enough chef does not necessarily make a decent-enough restaurateur.

First mistake: they leased a blank space that merely boasted four walls and a roof and built a restaurant from the ground up. This meant they needed specific opening-a-restaurant permits. They needed to satisfy specific opening-a-restaurant health regulations.

They needed to jump through so much red tape that they became gymnasts of filling out forms in triplicate.

It's fairly obvious why someone would want to throw open the doors—tah-dah!—on a box-fresh, shiny, never-before-seen space. The thrill of the new is ingrained in us all. Buying a restaurant that someone else has sweated over, nurtured and cajoled into being, is like buying a second-hand car. Where's that beguiling new-car smell? It smells like someone else. It's not really *yours*. Not for a long time, anyway, until you've asserted your own chips-and-gravy preferences and can eventually kick the tyres, thump the bonnet and say 'yeah, baby' with satisfaction.

It could be a lemon. Maybe the books were cooked beyond recognition. Maybe the genial cafe owner implored all his friends and family to eat there the week you spent observing it in action before signing on the dotted line. On which note, where the hell are all those customers now? Maybe the owner let you in on his little tax-avoidance secret: he's been skimming 100K off the business each year. Or so he says, hoping to explain the discrepancy between the official takings and his asking price. It's not so far-fetched. Plenty of operators do it. But do you believe him?

There are the sites haunted by the ghosts of restaurants past. Some become so perfumed with the stench of failure even the I-Chang couldn't make a go of it. A conga line of hopefuls take it in turns to do their dough. The place will go from Greek to Japanese to Jamaican soul food to a Polish grill, seemingly each week a new cuisine, a new continent. All the while Joe Public becomes more and more suspicious and eventually crosses the street to avoid the bad juju. Any place that's changed hands three, four times in as many years? Take my advice. Just say no, because it will never fly.

But opening something new takes time, and patience, and, above all, money. Money was the one thing in short supply for Sal and Ron. All the while they were satisfying a particularly assiduous arsehole from the council who delighted in rejecting permits on fanciful grounds (he didn't like the choice of tiles; the wheelchair ramp to the toilets was 4 degrees too sharp), the rent was backing up like sewage in a pipe.

Niente had actually been a strip club. Rumour had it Salvatore had been a frequent visitor. Nothing unusual there—it's not uncommon to freshen up midway through a double shift with a buttfloss-clad arse waggled in the face. It was clear that between lap dances he'd taken the time to look around and decide it had potential for his dream project. His dream was to open a restaurant just like the Sabatini. When I say 'just like the Sabatini' I mean 'exactly like the Sabatini'.

This was part of Sal's problem. The Sabatini was all he knew. After a decade working for the little dictator Gino, he was totally institutionalised. You see guys like this, they get used to the little flap in the door opening three times a day, the prison-issue tray sliding through. The paycheck turning up once a week. Someone else to make the hard decisions. To take care of the bills. In terms of running his own restaurant, Sal couldn't even wipe his own bum. That's the overlooked beauty of being a wage-slave. Most problems are someone else's problem. A good restaurateur is a regular Mr Fix-It. You don't want to be bringing in the fridge repairer unless the fridge is in need of the last rites. Same goes for the ice-machine guy, or the dishwasher whisperer. You're pissing your profit away if you don't know at least a few rudimentary band-aid solutions for all the gear keeping the restaurant's engine-room humming.

That was the second mistake. Not only had they gone to the huge expense of installing a commercial kitchen, being a typical chef Salvatore had needed the best of everything. Nothing second-hand for this little black duck. It's easy to see his way of thinking. I mean, this was *it*. His workplace for the next fifteen years, until he retired to Noosa or the Gold Coast with his golf clubs and a whole wardrobe of checked shorts and white slip-ons. Why not enjoy a little comfort, a huge coolroom, a reliable ten-burner oven with no hot or cold spots, a super-duper ventilation system that could suck the dentures out of a mouth, an ice machine that could have reversed the thinning of the Arctic shelf.

They did take one punt that deserves respect. They'd chosen a stretch of shops best described as up-and-coming rather than fully arrived. Call it the eternal appeal to the gods of real estate. A busy restaurant paying too much rent is not a profitable restaurant. Only the landlord is the winner. Anyone who leases on a strip described as 'hotter-than-hot' in the food glossies is a fool unless they get some unbelievable sub-market deal. Ha. Like that's going to happen. Sal and Ron rolled the dice on lifting the fortunes of a tired shopping strip not too far from the Sabatini.

Yet it was somehow just plain wrong. Wrong by way of Wrongtown. Imagine a well-known work of art. The *Mona Lisa*, for example. Then ask your average five-year-old to replicate that painting. That was Niente. I don't believe in the Chinese art of feng shui, the practice of harmonising the environment through negative and positive energy flows. But I do believe in crimes against interior design, and here they were manifest in every strange nook and cranny constructed with cheap fibreboard ('To texturise the space,' Sal explained) and in every bilious daubing on the wall. Basically they'd senselessly tried to replicate the feel of a rather bijou, old world cafe in a huge 200-seat former warehouse-slash-strip-club.

And Ron. Oh god, Ron. Ron was out of his depth from day one. A huge former cop complete with authentic drug squad moustache, now crashing around behind a bar trying to come to terms with not-so-newfangled drinks like the Cocksucking Cowboy. What's that they say about old dogs and new tricks? His hearing was totally up the spout, too. It was a liability in the force—it's good to be able to hear someone yelling they're going to shoot—and it was a liability here. 'Ron? Ron? RON!' Sign language wasn't able to convey the kind of detail needed in 'a chardonnay, two espresso martinis, and a bourbon and Coke, no ice'. We tried to communicate in writing but he didn't have the best eyesight, either, and was always losing his glasses. Sal bought him one of those cords so he could hang his bifocals around his neck but he didn't want to wear it. Said it made him look too old. The sweet bird of youth had flown a couple of decades earlier, but who was I to tell him?

There weren't so many customers to worry about Ron's glacial drinks preparation, anyway. Sal took to skulking nervously around the bar. A chef outside of his lair is a dangerous thing. Unnatural. Seeing a guy in chef's jacket and clogs cooling his heels in the dining room is like going to the zoo and seeing the door to the tiger cage hanging open. It unnerved the few customers they did have.

Conversations with Sal became increasingly awkward.

'So Sal . . . how's it been going?' I'd venture at the start of each shift, trying to keep the cheer in my voice even though the quiet pall of doom hanging over the joint indicated he was facing his own personal Hiroshima.

'We did twelve covers on Thursday night and sixteen on Friday,' he'd say, groping for the bright side of the moon. 'Last Friday we only did eight. That's gotta be a good sign, right?'

'Totally. That's an excellent sign.'

'Yep. Yep.' He was there but he wasn't really there. Behind his bushy monobrow and the wreaths of cigarette smoke, there was a brain torturously computing the money it cost him to open each day, every hour, every minute.

ANDREW

I used to work at a really fashionable restaurant in a super-trendy but pretty gritty area. It was opposite a methadone clinic and all the staff were expected to eat their meals in the alley behind the restaurant surrounded by a sea of human faeces and needles.

Eventually I couldn't take it anymore. I rang one Saturday afternoon. Criminally, I was rostered on that night. 'Sal . . . It's just getting too much. With uni work and everything. I'm going to have to quit.'

There was silence on the other end. Four seconds, five seconds. Deathly silence. I coughed nervously. I wondered if he'd hung up in disgust. Then Sal came back. 'Yeah . . . sure.' It was the last bit that killed me: 'I understand.'

Other chefs would have been angry being left in the lurch at such rudely, obscenely late notice. They would have given a huge, expletive-laden smackdown. They would have used my cowardice as the perfect excuse to release the pressure valve on the stress bubbling inside. But Sal said it so gently. There was a world of understanding in that 'I understand'. He was a good man, Sal. He didn't deserve his fate.

It was at Niente that I came up with a brilliant idea to help fledgling restaurants when they're at their just-open most vulnerable. There was plenty of time to observe the world through the plate-glass window and watch people walking along the street. When they got to Niente they'd pause. Everyone pauses at a new business. People always get excited about new ways to spend their money. It's one of the reasons capitalism won the Cold War. They'd look at the menu taped to the window. It read okay. Italian bistro 101, a boring but sound collection of arancini, beef carpaccio and chicken involtini. It worked just fine at the Sabatini, so why didn't it work here?

Here's the thing. Restaurants generally get one shot. I don't mean one shot at critics. Critics aren't the real concern. Maybe a critic will come in. Maybe not. It's not so important. It's the locals whose hearts and minds you want. The everyday people who make or break restaurants are generally willing to take a punt. They'll visit once in the spirit of neighbourhood loyalty. If they like it they'll return and, more importantly, they'll tell their local friends, who will tell their local friends, and so on. It's like throwing a rock in a local pool and watching the concentric circles go further and further out. But Niente actively repelled people. Most passers-by who peered in the window would recoil in horror, partly at the décor but mostly at the empty room. I could read it on their faces. A big, fat NO.

Of course some would walk straight in before realising their mistake. It's embarrassing to turn on your heel and walk out, so the overly polite would suck it up, sit down and take the menu being shoved in their faces. That was my job. To get people to stay. To put myself bodily between them and the door. To cut off their escape route while grinning like an idiot and reciting the evening's specials. I was a combination of bouncer, pimp and Andrew O'Keefe on *Deal or No Deal*.

I felt bad for the people who did stay—like the elderly gent who sighed and said, 'If it matters so much to you, dear,' then surrendered himself to house arrest. Diners cajoled, begged and forced into seats would sit there miserably, in emotional consort with owners who were obviously bleeding from every orifice in some mutation of restaurant ebola. The bolder ones who walked into our web of despair would then slink around pretending to inspect the new joint, but with all their energy focused on edging for the door. The restaurant equivalent of 'I'm just browsing, thanks'.

Which made me think: what about monetising the rent-a-crowd?

To some extent this already happens. It's known as the opening-night party, where the liberal application of Free Stuff lubricates the pleasure receptors of bloggers and journalists, who then go home and hopefully write glowing things before the booze wears off. But take it a step further. How about paying people—secretly, of course—to sit around eating, drinking and making like they're having a whale of a time? Do it each night for as long as it takes the general public to catch the good-time virus. It would be like a flash mob for the restaurant scene, only without the dancing. It would be like the laugh track for a sitcom, only not annoying. Everyone passing by would look in and think, 'Gotta get me some of that.' Humans are pack animals, after all—or at least we were, until the internet came along and turned us all into introspective halfwits tapping away on tiny screens while ignoring the world around us. But we'll get to that later.

And what of Sal and Ron, you ask? By the end they were as defenceless as baby sea turtles, flapping uselessly for their lives along a scorching stretch of sand as the gulls swooped and pecked. I drove past sometimes and the augurs of doom were painted on the window for all the world to see. From 'brand new menu' to 'kids eat free' to 'free glass of wine with every main course', from being open lunch and dinner seven days a week to just dinner, to just Wednesday to Sunday, all the while inching inexorably towards the grave.

Salvatore was forced to go back to working in someone else's kitchen. Talk about the world's biggest comedown. When you're still on the pans each night at the age of fifty, it means something has gone horribly wrong. Every year spent in a commercial kitchen exacts a terrible toll on the body. Oh, the back. Oh, the legs. What do you do when you're sixty, older? It had been his one shot, and it had blown, badly. I saw him a few years later, in the supermarket late one night. It was Sad O'Clock, the hour favoured by drunk uni students, druggies and insomniacs. His basket was filled with microwave meals for one. I'll blame it on survivor guilt that I tried to slip away unnoticed into aisle six, but he waved me down. Genial to the end. I asked about Ron. Turned out Sal had survivor guilt of his own. He shook his head. Cursed himself for leading his brother along the merry road to hell. 'It turns out no one wants to hire an overweight 56-year-old with hearing problems,' he sighed bitterly. 'Who woulda thought?'

Time and fashions move on. That stretch of neglected shops has become a buzzing restaurant hotspot, the sort that people get in their cars and drive across town to visit. Wannabe restaurant and cafe owners are paying above-market rent to secure their stake in the gold rush. As for the former Niente, it was snapped up by an Indian family who make a good living buying failed restaurants for a song and turning them around. Buy low, sell high. That's the creed. It's now a Teflon-coated success story with a queue out the door. The bit that really bites? It's Italian.

— 8 —
BABY GOT BANDWIDTH

By this time I'm working in an internet bar, although I have no idea what Linux is. Actually, scratch that—Linux is the kid from the Peanuts cartoons, right?—but my cyber-gag doesn't go down well with Altus the militant hippy. Altus gazes at me pityingly through his web of dirty blond dreadlocks before bowing his head back over a computer screen embedded in the bar. Altus is so busy saving the world from itself he has no time for frivolous things. A sense of humour, for starters. Money, for seconds.

He's been one of the Base Station's repeat customers from the day it opened, but he is also the living symbol of why it is doomed to fail. Anyone over the age of eighteen is welcome to use the computers, which are free albeit reliably dodgy thanks to the mysteries of the Linux operating system. All they have to do is buy something. Anything at all. The Base Station is deliberately non-prescriptive. The owners, a couple in the twilight of their youth breaking free from the invisible shackles of soul-sucking corporate jobs (now where have I heard that one before?), had imagined an energised community of like-minded people jawing over beers and sharing the latest information about—oh, I don't know, hacking, and the evils of Microsoft, and *code* or something—but the reality is only slightly less engaging than the drooling demented wearing adult nappies in a nursing home. No matter how gloriously the interweb glows in three-dimensional technicolour with freaks and geeks, flame-throwers and perverts, everyone confronts the online universe alone.

In the future, the internet cafe ought to be studied as an anthropological blip that flared and sputtered out due to technology's relentless forward march. They sprang into being—the first was in Seoul, the second in San Francisco—thanks to humanity discovering it urgently needed to communicate all sorts of vital things RIGHT NOW, such as celebrities with cellulite and cats that look like Hitler. And then they were rudely superseded by the very technology they celebrated. They're the Beta video of the hospitality world.

The internet cafe wasn't the only weird hospo-hybrid of the 1990s. Businesses that tried to combine everyday tasks with socialising became a bit of a thing. It was as if a general expectation arose that the boredom could be drummed out of workaday life with the liberal application of downlights and swizzle sticks. This is the era when the bar laundrette also made a fleeting appearance. History now relates that 'edgy' and 'fabric softener' are not terms that mesh naturally together, but that didn't prevent a few hardy souls proclaiming the future was all about fun, and if that fun was to be had while doing the weekly wash, then hooray. They missed the memo that a laundrette is purely functional. You cannot pimp a laundrette. People don't want to drink cocktails and flirt while their smalls are on spin cycle.

Technology quickly caught up with the internet cafe then zoomed right on past, but for a brief halcyon period it was a window into an imagined future. Base Station owners Marlon and Danae made the strategic error of imagining it as a bar, and a cafe, and an art gallery, and a performance space. Nuh-uh. Do not pass Go. Do not collect $200.

Internet cafes still exist, of course, but they've beaten a strategic retreat to boring old practicality. They've given a deep sigh and resigned themselves to the orange laminate and the brown carpet, the bad coffee and the fluoro strip lighting. They're a no-frills transit lounge into cyberspace for tourists wise enough not to pay global roaming data fees on their wireless hand-held devices. You can't pimp that.

A quick note: these days it's common for cafes to provide free wi-fi. This, in my opinion, is madness. Those cafes might as well stuff a wheelie bin full of cash, pour petrol over the top, and strike a match. Their free wi-fi says to the tight-wads of the world, 'Welcome. Please take a seat for four hours and sip on a single coffee until we indicate we are closing by putting chairs on tables around you.' It's a great deal, beyond question, but only for one of the parties involved.

The Base Station deserves a respectful eulogy. It was a noble social, technological and artistic experiment. Its computer system was based on open-source software, about which I know precisely nothing, save for the fact that at the time it was hideously unreliable. (Maybe it still is. I couldn't say, because I don't really know what open-source software is. When my computer needs fixing, I have a guy who comes and fixes it. It's a very satisfactory arrangement.) It was meshed together by Marlon, who in fairness really did seem to know what he was doing. But however much he pored over it while muttering unintelligibly about Java, it remained a web that tore and rent in places unexpected; that at times seemed a cruel psychological experiment on humans and their capacity for optimism. It crashed with unerring regularity—maybe a half-dozen times on a bad night—yet every time an anguished wail would go up from the chubby Brazilian guy who liked to sit in the beanbag and flirt with persons unknown on the other side of the world.

Part of my job was to help people with the computers. Irony alert. Just as Bill Clinton wasn't the person to be left in charge of interns, I wasn't the person to be trusted with computer problems. The Base Station's worked on some Unix system. I still don't know what that means, exactly. I have a lot of sympathy for Thomas Watson, the former chairman of IBM who will be derided at trivia nights forevermore for declaring there was a world market 'for maybe five computers'. That was 1946, mind you. I think the man had a fair excuse for underestimating the computer market by a couple of billion units. As for me, in 1994 I heard about this newfangled thing called *email* from my university friend Elise. I was just back from Europe, where I'd gaily ducked into post offices from London to Moscow for their post restante service. The concept still makes my head spin: anyone can send me a letter—*anywhere in the world*—and the post office will hold it for me. What need I for this electronic messaging business? How could it possibly replace the great romance of ink and paper? Ha. Hahaha. (In my defence, it does seem to run in the blood. My great-great-great grandfather was an English convict transported to Australia during the Industrial Revolution for machine breaking. Which means he was a Luddite in the true sense. I am merely carrying on the family tradition.)

Marlon was so busy being at the cutting edge that he was in acute denial over the technology on which his business relied. It was as fractious, unpredictable and disruptive as a newborn baby, yet each time it crashed he responded with what appeared to be genuine surprise. In those halcyon early days he and Danae were encased in a soft golden bubble in which nothing could go wrong. They were living the dream: sleeping above their very own niche business, the kind that spawned newspaper articles about trends, written by journalists who never failed to assume an avuncular 'oh gosh' kind of tone about what the young people were up to these days.

I guess Marlon and Danae, and a good number of their customers besides, would be called hipsters if they were gallivanting around now. The signs were clear: he liked to wear a beret and cultivate his facial hair. She was overly fond of black. But this pre-dated full-blown hipsterism by at least a decade. Back then these people, young men and women both, were simply slightly odd, artistically inclined individuals. Before they unionised into the fiercest social clique the world has ever known—yet shadowier even than the Masons, denying they exist at all—they were the keepers of the geek flame.

Hipsterism's over. It's OVER. It was tagged and bagged when the Sunday papers started to include them in their 'know your tribe' features. It's an era now locked safely away inside the parameters of time; a bygone historical moment to squirm over. But, oh how innocent the Base Station days when a customer's first transgressive piece of ink was displayed shyly on an upper arm. So many sweet little things with their edgy barcode tatts, all intent on proving they weren't part of the herd and that individuality was a principle worth dying for.

The Base Station's system crashed, and it crashed often. Each time I'd put on an Oscar-nominated performance of knowing what I was doing that basically consisted of switching things off and on again. My go-to move. A pagan appeal to the gods of electricity, in part, but mostly something to appease the baleful eyes of customers abruptly torn from their online chats and random cat searches. The place ran on the smell of an oily rag so there was only ever one bartender rostered on at a time. This was both blessing—it's indisputably fun to rule the bar as a benevolent dictator—and curse, because there was no one else to blame if things went wrong.

The script ran like this. I'd switch things off and on, mutter a bit, say something about 'Java', concede defeat, then trudge up the stairs to knock nervously on the apartment door. Marlon and Danae had made it very clear: they didn't like being disturbed. I never saw inside their living quarters. It was all very mysterious. After a five-minute delay (what the hell were they doing up there?) Marlon would appear, descend the stairs and rummage around doing whatever it was he needed to do, and the screens would give a hopeful glow that made everyone's hearts leap with joy, like when ET came back to life. Smiles all round. Marlon would give a satisfied nod and retreat upstairs to his lair. Five minutes later—crash. Fade to black. Loud wail from Brazilian guy who was about to get to second base with some anonymous male cybertext lover in Norway or Peru or possibly even at a rival internet cafe a suburb away.

Pad pad pad pad pad. Back up the stairs. Knock knock. 'WHAT IS IT?' Marlon would yell, more exasperated this time. (He and Danae had no TV, so I ask again—what the hell were they doing up there?) The charade would go on until the few souls remaining in the bar would realise there was no more cybernetic fun to be had and slink off into the night.

Once the honeymoon gloss wore off, Marlon and Danae realised they had fallen into a trap common to new parents. They'd dealt with the anxiety of a new business by adopting a strict routine. A routine known as 'becoming paranoid agoraphobics who never go out'. These early-prototype hipsters looked in the mirror one day and didn't like what they saw. If they were going to reclaim their edge, they would have to break out of their monastic existence to engage with the world once more. 'We're going out for a few hours,' they announced unexpectedly one afternoon as I turned on the coffee machine before opening the doors. Now that I've had kids I recognise the way their voices were just a little too loud, the cheerfulness just a little too cheery as they willed themselves not to think about the multicoloured disasters that might occur in their absence.

'Sure! Yes! Go!' I responded in a similar fashion, trying to inject my voice with every bit of positivity I could muster while inwardly thinking 'Oh shit, oh shit' because I was about to be thrown to the nerd wolves.

They lasted only an hour that first time. I saw them sitting in a cafe across the street, keeping an eye on their beloved internet bar in case it caught fire or stopped breathing or something. It was kind of sad, yet also strangely comforting.

They must have taken heart that no major disaster ensued, because after that they made a real effort to get out. Baby steps, but each occasion helped stretch the apron strings a little more. The next time they ventured further—maybe 100 metres down the street to the dodgy Chinese restaurant—then the next time as far as the pub on the corner. It was unprecedented when they went all the way across town to a party thrown by some people they used to know before they opened an internet bar.

That time wasn't such a success. They arrived home to a bank of computers without a pulse and the bar empty save for a massive guy with ginger plaits mounting a spirited case about getting a refund on his coffee because we hadn't held up our part of the deal. 'You. Did. Not. Provide. Me. With. A. Computer. That. Works.' His voice was shaking with outrage but I held my ground. No way was I going to concede defeat to a six-foot-six hippy with braids to his bum. Whatever happened to peace, love and understanding?

Okay, so I missed the peace train by about forty years.

The hippies who populated the Base Station—first courted by Marlon and Danae as the kind of countercultural icons who'd be good for business, then merely tolerated once it was clear they would only ever cough up for a single soy chai latte—were an opportunistic bunch who'd try to steal whatever wasn't nailed down. I guess they were living the creed that all property is theft. It's a defensible political position, but there were only so many times I could tolerate smacking their filthy hands away from the jar of mixed nuts before wanting to sell them out to The Man and call the cops.

Plenty of them were Hallmark hippies. Kids, really, trying on a fashion, artfully arranging their rags as intricately as if they were Comme des Garçons. They were the sort of people who wrote on the toilet door, 'If you love something set it free. If it comes back to you it's yours, if it doesn't it never was.' Not everyone at Base Station was sympathetic to such curdled sentiment. Underneath it someone had added: 'Then track it down and kill it.'

Altus, however, was a breed apart. He was the quasi-despotic leader of a hippy splinter group, a hardcore bunch of ferals who would disappear for months at a time to the Tasmanian blockades then pop up again looking even wilder and hungrier than before. Altus wasn't his real name, if you hadn't already guessed. I'd love to know what was on his birth certificate but he wasn't the kind of guy you could ask such profoundly personal information. You didn't chew the fat with Altus. 'Yo Altus, wassup?' No. Definitely not. His nom de guerre was taken from the Latin, meaning 'noble or profound', he told me without so much as a blush on his tight, pinched face half-hidden in the shadow of a dreadlock mass that relayed his character as succinctly as his charge sheet. He rarely wore shoes, bathed infrequently, and had no aspirations towards worldly goods—in fact, he took great satisfaction in being able to lug everything of value in his life in a filthy army disposal backpack.

Altus was grimly committed to his cause of Generalised World-Saving like the purest of ascetics. Some people feel they were born in the wrong body; Altus was born in the wrong era. He would have been brilliant tooling around with half of Dickens' mob in the laneway grime of Victorian England. I could imagine him in a hairshirt, whipping himself into the exalted frenzy of a bloody pulp. If he'd lived in biblical times he was the kind of guy who would have sat on a plinth in the desert for years and then been sainted after a hideous death involving wasps.

'Don't give them your real details,' he scolded when I conceded defeat in my moral battle against email. I was setting up my first Hotmail account while he stretched his soy latte out to a third hour. 'If you use your own information they can use it against you.'

'They?' I asked.

'*They*.' He scanned the room as though they were already there, listening to every word.

It pains me to concede his paranoia about government spying might have been warranted. But then I'm the sort of person who'll gladly cough up all sorts of personal information for the chance to win a $5 supermarket voucher. Altus and I were at cross-purposes. When he called me 'a willing victim of capitalism', he was right on the money.

I don't know what became of him when the Base Station closed down. He's probably still down at the blockades, older and grimmer and grimier than before. There's a good possibility he's been chained to a tree for the past ten years. If he's wearing a suit and holding down a nine-to-five job I'll be deeply disappointed. I doubt he is, though. He was too far gone for that, although in one respect he was unimpeachable. No dope. 'It makes you weak,' he'd spit to his hippy mates as they went on the nod. It was the same old story. Generation after generation, heroin kills the collective dream. They'd come in, order a single drink between two or three, head to the toilets and fix up. The saggy old green couch was very popular for a lazy-hazy afternoon. The music we played must have helped the heroin dreams, too. Arty electronica: all beeps and whirrs and fuzz that uncannily mirrored the sound of early internet dial-up static. It must have been nice to Major Tom the interior universe like it was one giant mainframe.

I was living at the time with a hippy-junkie. It's really not a great combination for a housemate, particularly one still wanting to claim the moral high ground. Caz didn't believe in tea bags— the staple attaching the string to the bag might leach toxins into the tea, she argued—yet she was perfectly comfortable with the idea of sticking a needle in her arm. I don't think it was the actual metal that was her major problem, mind you. It was the toxic shit coursing through her bloodstream.

She did have one decent party trick, which was to get a sheet of aluminium foil and cut a negative image into it using a Stanley knife. Stick it over the TV, put the screen on fuzz and it makes a nice psychedelic display, perfect for looking at for hours when you're ripped. Credit where credit's due. But that one bit of pos didn't make up for a whole heap of neg. She was on the gear then off the gear then back on the gear while swearing she was off the gear but all the while the rent was suspiciously backing up. Take a rummage around her room and there they are, a whole bunch of fits and foils—oh, and that's where the teaspoon collection has been hiding.

Like most hippies Caz didn't believe in property unless it was hers. When it was her turn to buy toilet paper, inevitably she'd leave a stack of torn newspaper on the bathroom floor for bum-wiping duties. 'It's fine for me,' she'd whine when ordered to fork out on some two-ply. She was also a waitress. It was our only common ground, aside from being female and breathing oxygen. She rarely did laundry, so when it was time to go to work she'd pinch my black tops off the washing line. Often I'd have to throw them out afterwards because they'd be so impregnated with her body odour even industrial-grade disinfectant couldn't shift it. Of course she didn't believe in deodorant, either. One time she even took my undies.

Moral of the story: never share a house with a hippy. They'll make you cry.

The Base Station was a novel introduction to the world of the bar chick. Bar work is vastly superior to waiting tables, namely because it provides protection against the Visigoths, aka the customers. That half-metre or so of solid, immovable structure between You and Them represents a blissful breathing space. A sort of demilitarised zone, minus the UN.

HAMISH

A bunch of office girls were drinking heavily on a Friday night. They ordered the eight-course degustation but by the third course one of them wobbled off to the toilets. We found her lying on the bathroom floor. She refused to move so for the next two-and-a-half hours other diners had to step over her. Her friends ate her dinner and drank her wine and they didn't check on her once.

And it was really quite necessary at the Base Station, where the customers were odder than most. It was an unofficial lonely hearts' club. This was before Facebook, Instagram and Twitter, and long before Grindr and Tinder. Being able to order sex like pizza was only a flicker in a young programmer's eye. But there were rudimentary ways to hook up. Closed chat rooms, mainly, where people got together for a bit of analog naughtiness. We didn't ban porn but asked that it be used—you know—discreetly. Not that you'd want to masturbate in a public access bar (well, hopefully not) but all the staff knew to strategically cough before approaching the terminal in a dark corner. That was where the Brazilian guy lurked. A discreet bit of throat-clearing would give him time to switch from whatever hardcore gay sex act he was looking at to pictures of cats in cowboy outfits.

It never ceased to amaze me how many customers didn't bother logging out of their email accounts before they left. Did I read them? Are you crazy? Given half a chance, wouldn't you go rifling through the electronic files of a goth girl with the login name of Madame Bones? It kept me sane, in between performing the other unofficial duties of my job, such as talking the arthouse cinema manager who looked like *Seinfeld*'s Newman through a torturous break-up, and being friendly to the bank economist who made a small fortune each year but was so socially inept he'd ask every single woman who crossed his path for a date. These days he'd be pegged kindly as someone on the autism spectrum. Back then he scared people.

The weirdest incident involved a Canadian skateboarder I'd met in Italy years earlier. One of those over-familiar, talkative, all-round annoying people who latched onto my group at a youth hostel and stuck to us despite rigorous discouragement. We wound up shaking him by sneaking out the back of a bar. Cruel, but necessary. So fast-forward five years and one night at the Base Station a group of backpackers comes in. They do a bit of emailing and piss off again. Enter Canadian guy. Same buzzcut, same three-quarter shorts with pretentiously long key chain, same annoying personality. 'Have you seen my buddies?' I point him in their direction before he can remember me. Later that night they come back in. I tell them their Canadian mate was searching for them. They respond in horror: 'No, man, we've been trying to get rid of that little dweeb for three days now.' I almost felt sorry for him. He's probably still out there travelling the globe, wondering where everyone went.

Marlon and Danae tried hard to make their business fly. They tackled it head-on with 16mm film nights, with poetry slams and DJs who played more of that electronica that was like catnip to junkies. All ignored the central business truth that when your clientele is penniless your business will not flourish.

That was why employees had to pay for their coffee. A cup of coffee cost the business about 20 cents but Marlon and Danae made us cough up market rates. Tight? Tighter than a camel's arse in a sandstorm.

They were going down the gurgler but I think the penny-pinching came naturally. A corporate lawyer barrelled in one afternoon, desperate to send some faxes ahead of a settlement deadline. Marlon, spotting an opportunity for shameless profiteering, introduced the bespoke faxing fee of $20. This was peanuts to the corporate guy but once he left and Marlon tried to pocket the cash, complex negotiations ensued.

'But I get the tips.'

'But I own the place.'

'Yeah, but I'm the bar bitch. The tips are mine.'

'But I'm the one who can work the fax machine.'

'You realise you're breaking the bartenders' covenant?'

'Okay, well, how about we split it?'

It's never a good sign when you're bartering with your boss over twenty bucks, but there was non-monetary compensation. If it was quiet—which it usually was—Marlon and Danae didn't mind if I had a smoke at the end of the bar. That was quite forward-thinking of them, and noticeably boosted the profits of the Peter Stuyvesant Corporation. They turned a blind eye to drug dealing in the kitchen. (Maybe some explanation is needed here: it was New Year's Eve, and Marlon walked in just as a friend and I were exchanging cash for pills. To his eternal credit he rolled his eyes, walked out and later asked me not to do it again.) Nor did they care if I swore in the line of duty. In hindsight, working at the Base Station was a complex system of swings and roundabouts.

There was one moment when hope shone through the fog. The annual street festival, in the halcyon days before the evils of public liability insurance put an end to communal fun. Traffic was diverted and the whole road became a big, boozy thoroughfare with a slow-moving crowd jazzed up to the max on beer and pills and I don't know what else. Somehow—I know not how—the Base Station became the place to be.

And it was fucking brilliant. The place was thick with people dancing on the bar, on the tables, everywhere. I pulled the afternoon shift and was practically whimpering with exhaustion by the end with the amount of booze we'd shifted. I occasionally caught a glimpse of Marlon and Danae through the crowd, grinning from ear to ear as though their faces would split open. It was easy enough to read their exaltation. This was it. The turning point. Their reversal of fortune.

The next night—dead. And the next night after that. The tide had not turned. It was just a blip. We went back to flatlining. They went back to their mysterious half-life upstairs.

Just like their business, Marlon and Danae were on the rocks. People confront their demons in different ways. He took to drinking. She took to eating. She comfort-loaded a good 20 kilos. Marlon started flirting with the female customers, which drove Danae insane and forced her into the illicit arms of more of her favourite cheese-flavoured corn chips. It was a vicious cycle.

They were looking for a way out. One time they lit on the brilliant idea that they could make a bunch of money by franchising the business. Because what the nation desperately needed was a whole chain of failing internet-bar-cafe-gallery-performance spaces. A lawyer put a bullet in that one in their first meeting, telling them it was impossible to franchise a failed idea. Ouch.

I could forgive them for wanting to Ponzi scheme the Base Station. They were desperate. Those corporate soul-sucking jobs weren't looking so bad anymore. But then they proved they didn't have my back, and I couldn't forgive them for that.

We had a regular customer named Carmichael. Regular? He was so regular you could set your watch on him walking in the door on the dot of 6 p.m. each night and staying until stumps. He didn't do much. Just sat there, alone, and drank beer. A lot of beer. He spent more money than a dozen hippies on Welfare Thursday put together, so Marlon and Danae loved him. He was practically keeping the place afloat. But he was creepy, in the blandly non-specific way of all major creeps—like Ted Bundy. Or Jeffrey Dahmer. One night he silently handed me a letter proclaiming love, lust and a bunch of obsessive stuff that made me fairly confident there was gaffer tape and a meat cleaver in his bag.

RICHARD

A customer died. It was a country restaurant and
Neil the pig farmer—in his early nineties, almost
deaf—would pull up every day in his brand-new
Range Rover. He'd always order a cheese sandwich
with the crusts cut off, which he'd then gum
for hours because he only had one tooth. One
afternoon Neil was asleep in his cheese sandwich
for quite some time before we realised he was stone
cold dead. After they took the body away, we saw his
tooth sticking out of his sandwich.

I kept the letter to be used as Exhibit A if my dismembered
body was found in a dumpster, but Marlon and Danae tried to
play it down. Thing is, he was by far their best customer, which
meant there was absolutely no way they were going to give him
his marching orders. Not even if it meant sacrificing a loyal staff
member. Eventually we reached a compromise where Carmichael
promised to stop staring at me unblinking for hours at a time and
I'd try to get on with smoking cigarettes at the end of the bar. It
worked for a while, albeit with a fair degree of discomfort. Then
he stopped coming in. We heard that he'd been admitted to a
psychiatric hospital after he started acting erratically. Even more
erratically than usual, I mean. Vacuuming the front lawn at three
in the morning, things like that.

Quite coincidentally, but perhaps (in hindsight) ominously, I
was dating another guy named Carmichael at the same time. The
chances of two Carmichaels intersecting in a particular time and
place are not great. In fact, statistics show you're more likely to

be hit by lightning while being attacked by a shark. Maybe the universe was trying to tell me something. The one I was dating styled himself as a biker bohemian, but in reality he was just a knuckle-dragging Neanderthal with a bad ponytail. Clearly, Carmichaels and I don't mix. We're the human equivalent of oil and water. Given the superstition about bad luck running in threes, if I ever meet another one I'll go screaming in the opposite direction.

Boyfriend Carmichael was just as much of a bad news story as Base Station Carmichael. Less in a sinister-psychotic kind of way, more in a garden-variety alcoholic, poor personal hygiene and anger management issues kind of way. In a small miracle I decided to divest myself of him. It seemed a straightforward split until the night I got home late after dealing with the usual Base Station weirdness and there he was, sitting in the darkness after breaking in through the bathroom window. He waited until he had my undivided attention before cutting his throat from ear to ear with a razor blade. Something you never really expect to see, especially at 2 a.m. on a Saturday in July. I remember thinking through the shock: how ironic that I would have been better off backing the other Carmichael.

It was kind of a relief when the Base Station went on the computer crash that never ends several months later. After the throat-cutting incident I didn't enjoy coming home late after work. Turning the key, wondering what waited on the other side. Ex-boyfriend Carmichael survived, in case you're wondering. I hear he ended up a suburban solicitor. And maybe I did learn something from the *Hippy Life Manual* after all, because that's karma, baby, right there.

— 9 —

THE THINGS WE DO FOR LOVE

I didn't fall in love with hospitality. That much should be fairly clear by now. But I did fall in love with someone who had fallen in love with hospitality. And that, as they say, has made all the difference.

And no, he wasn't a chef. Hell, no. It's a constant source of wonder to me how chefs have become sex symbols. The only explanation I can come up with is that it's a primal thing (remember: primal is related to *primate*). You know: a man, a knife, a naked flame. If you find something compelling in that triumvirate, a crotch-focused frisson, you might be suffering from the pagan practice of chef-worship. Beware. That way there be dragons—or at least the people hilariously called celebrity chefs.

Just for the record, I've dated one chef. A celebrity-free chef. I don't know if he was up with the latest sous-vide techniques or if he could deconstruct a pavlova, but he was nice. End of story.

But plenty of women have a *thing* for chefs. I've seen an otherwise sane woman acting all hot and bothered over some kitchen idiot who had failed Year 10 and said 'somefink' as if he were the Beatles. All four of them. I've seen a young married hottie put the moves on a TV chef like a professional assassin. I didn't know whether to applaud or take grainy, illicit photos to sell to *New Idea*. And I've seen chefs who enlist their wives and children into their all-round good-guy media personas then act like alley cats when the cameras stop rolling. 'The way I see it, you get chocolate cake at home,' one such person grandly said, swaying slightly at a bar one night while his wife and kids were safely ensconsed at home. 'But sometimes you want *cheesecake*.' He seemed pleased with his food analogy.

Can we be honest with each other? If I'm going to admit to any dating peccadilloes here, I prefer a front-of-house guy. Ah, the irony. I definitely prefer waitering as a spectator sport. But there is an addendum. Only the professional need apply. I could never lust after a bad waiter. If I met the male equivalent of me, I would recoil in horror if the he-me asked me out. There's something about a man in an apron that just does it for me. There's a world of psychoanalysis in there. (Is my subconscious mind making the highly assumptive equation that chefs are too aggressively male, while apron-clad waiters are in touch with their feminine side? Do I need to give my subconscious mind a stern talking-to about stereotypical gender roles?) And don't get me started on waiters who make me laugh. Therein lies an important precept for life: anyone who can deal with the horrors of the job and come up smiling is a person worth getting to know.

So. Ben. Ben was working at the Duke Hotel, which was a place I'd taken to meeting some friends for a boozy Sunday lunch. This guy behind the bar caught my eye. Like all garden-variety crushes, it was precipitated by a whole lot of superficial box-ticking, but after ample observation, reflection and note-taking, it became more than that. He had an energy that could power the city grid. He laughed a lot. Most tellingly, nothing ever got to him. There was plenty of time to witness this guy in action, and he could backhand a troublesome customer as gracefully as Roger Federer. More importantly, he could leave the customer smiling as well. It was a classy performance. As someone who stung with every slight, real or imagined, of every diner who thought me inferior because I was the one on my feet, it was revelatory. It was like being an Amazonian explorer stumbling through thick jungle into a clearing and discovering a whole new tribe with previously unimaginable customs.

At the wind-up of those Duke lunches—exhausting affairs where I would laugh continually for three hours and generally carry on in a manner designed to telegraph I was an altogether fabulous individual who would make a top-notch girlfriend—I'd strategically bypass the waiter and take our bill to the bar to interact on a more personal level with Cute Barman. I was probably smiling like a juvenile delinquent allowed out on day leave, so I forgive him for never giving me more than the tenets of professionalism. He was polite and all that. But as for anything else—*nada*.

Very disappointing. Especially when he should have been flirting for tips. But I have never been one to take no for an answer. In fact, I take it as a personal challenge. So I did what any self-respecting young woman would do.

Reader, I stalked him.

Not psychotically. Not dangerously. Not in a way to make him invoke the legal system for his protection. But the Duke did quite well financially that year out of my desire for its barman. Not that he noticed.

And then one night he came into Base Station. With his girlfriend.

Of all the internet bars in all the towns in all the world, they walk into mine.

She was pretty. Blonde. Big tits. Your basic nightmare. But something wasn't quite right. He had a beer. She had a lemonade. They didn't talk. They sat slightly apart, faces turned ever-so-slightly away from each other. Their body language screamed Splitsville.

I have been on one proper date in my life. It was torture. My date and I pulled out our cigarettes only to have the waitress point to the No Smoking sign. We asked for a drink only to be told the restaurant was unlicensed. It was a failure of due diligence on both our parts, and we thoroughly deserved to spend two heinous hours making small talk and drinking mocktails while silently despairing 'Oh Lord, will it ever end?'. The modus operandi of my generation is a simple three-step process. Go out, smash a face-full of booze, and pick up.

The night after Ben and his cusp-of-ex-girlfriend appeared at the Base Station—the very next night—I had arranged to meet my friend Naomi at the Night Cat. The Night Cat was a legendary pick-up joint. It had been opened by smooth man-about-town Henry Maas as a sophisticated, cosmopolitan club for discerning people. It didn't live up to his expectations. I read an interview once where he lamented bitterly that it was the kind of place people took backpacks.

As fate had transpired I was running typically late and Naomi, being a very practical sort of a girl, had taken an ecstasy pill to fill in the time. I checked my backpack in the cloakroom and walked in and there she was, gabbing furiously to Ben. Come in, spinner. It was early summer, I was in my favourite dress, and the gods were smiling. It took a few minutes to get rid of Naomi and another two hours of solid work, and several bourbon and Cokes, before Ben got the look that means 'you're *nice*' instead of just 'you're nice'. He told me later he'd gone out with his housemate that night to talk about how they weren't going to bother with girls for a long, long time.

Bully to that. Thus ensued the typical semi-alcoholic, frolicsome time that marks the honeymoon phase of a twenty-something relationship. We developed our repertoire of Things We Like To Do. There was 'our' cafe, 'our' beer garden, 'our' Thai restaurant (cigarette between the spring rolls and *por plaa*), each of which obliquely cemented an 'us' onto the world where previously there was an almost unimaginable state called 'no us'.

I tell you this simply because life has a funny way of seeming like there was a grand plan when you look at it retrospectively, when there really wasn't. As far as I can tell, life is simply a series of coincidences the brain arranges into meaning to obscure the fact we're all staring into the abyss.

But Ben's love of hospitality has impacted my life like an asteroid slamming into a planet that was innocently going about its business. I am not exaggerating. At its worst, it's like being shackled to a prisoner who makes a run for it through a field of trip wires with a hungry German Shepherd in pursuit. At its best, it's like peaking in a field while a waistcoat-wearing rabbit offers a tray of Mint Juleps. And all of it, whether good or bad, was entirely unexpected.

Because not only did I not love the hospitality industry, I did not love food. Truth be told, I did not even particularly like food.

I was brought up in a family where meat was brown, chicken was white, and fish and chips meant Sunday night. My older sister and I were true children of 1970s suburbia. We hated each other—there were several attempts on my life in the years 1975–78—yet in one thing we were united: food was, at most, a necessary evil. One of our earliest shared memories is of our mother begging us to eat. 'Please try something,' she implored one afternoon, real tears in her eyes as she gazed upon the spindly, twig-like limbs of her offspring, no doubt fearing the neighbours' talk and the dread word 'neglect'. Our skin was translucently white and mottled, the outline of the veins beneath glowing blue in a horrible road-map of our circulatory systems. 'Please eat. I'll make anything you want. Anything.' To which Sis and I, two healthy girls who just happened to be catastrophically thin, chirped 'no thanks' and dashed off to do another thousand laps of the backyard pool.

Saturdays were particularly dread-worthy, because Saturday night meant one thing: my grandmother's lamb roast. Yes, I know, I'm a foul ingrate. And may Nanna's soul rest in peace. But truly, her leg of lamb could have been an exhibit from a crime scene. A particularly horrid one. Maybe where the victim was immolated in a car and investigators had trouble telling where the person ended and the vinyl car seat began. The smouldering lamb would be dragged triumphantly from the oven and once my father got to work with the electric carving knife, the interior would reveal its colour—no sweet baby pink but a genre-busting puce, with outbreaks of mission brown. For twenty-eight years that was how I thought a lamb roast should be while simultaneously shaking my head at the gustatory weirdness of the world. Compounding the travesty was the fact that my grandfather, Nanna's husband, had been a butcher.

Escaping Nanna's lamb roast wasn't at the forefront of my mind when I did the typical teenage girl, aged thirteen-and-three-quarters thing and announced I was giving up meat. Nor did it hinder it. Her roast potatoes were marvellous and the dietary switcheroo meant my ration of those golden-crisp babies was increased. Win.

No real lover of food goes vegetarian. You can go vegetarian and then discover a love of food from within the confines of your straitened circumstances. Yum, yum, nut roast! Far more difficult—impossible, even—to be in thrall to richly comforting veal ragout, the salty toffee'd shatter of pork crackle, the quotidian delights of a roast chicken, and then one day say 'From henceforth you are a stranger to me'.

So there I was, a vegetarian non-lover of food—someone surviving on a diet principally composed of instant noodles (Oriental flavour preferable), spaghetti with tinned sauce and that crumbly faux-parmesan scattered on top, and Vegemite toast—who had just hooked up with a food-obsessed boy so in love with hospitality that he hung about the chefs at work, pestering them for cooking tips.

Ben should have run for the hills at that point. To his credit he stuck around and made me a toasted cheese sandwich instead.

I don't believe in any sort of afterlife, but if there is a heaven all the angels will be eating Ben's toasted cheese sandwich. He won't mind. He loves cooking for big crowds. And his toasted cheese, while hardly the finest thing in his repertoire, is truly worth dying for. You get white bread—delicious, high-GI, ultra-refined white bread—and slather it in butter. Then you get a non-stick frypan and melt more butter. You fry the bread in the pan, then when it's golden and buttery-crisp on both sides you introduce it to slices of cheese, which should be a combination of parmesan and good old tasty cheese. The principle is not unlike French toast, where the egg soaks into the bread so it becomes a hybrid, only here you are dealing with half bread, half cheese. The bold move is to put the cheese in direct contact with the pan so it goes all nicely caramelised and corrupted and slumps irrevocably into the bread like a 3 a.m. drunk. It's crucial to add sea salt as it cooks. Scatter, scatter, scatter, so it melts into the sandwich. Add the final layer of cheese and melt it between the two pieces of bread, a touch more butter, and finish with more salt crystals on top. You might as well slap it straight on your thighs, but it's totally worth the weight gain.

But let's fast-forward a couple of years, during which time Ben has eaten more mushroom risotto than anyone should reasonably be expected to, and patiently put up with the full gamut of vego quirks. The obsessing about gelatin, the ongoing philosophical crisis about wearing vintage leather and the plaintive question 'Is it fried in animal fat?' (NB: waiters will always say vegetable oil but seven out of ten times they're lying.)

We are on a boat. We are on a boat with his family. His family are farmers. Sheep and cattle, mostly. It's brutally cold. A wicked

CHRIS

A guy celebrating his fiftieth birthday with his wife and kids went to the toilet and came back ashen white. It turned out he'd never eaten asparagus before so he had no clue what that unique asparagus urine smell was—he was convinced he was rotting inside and about to die. Maybe his mortality had been weighing on his mind.

southerly, which blew away the money from the Monopoly set while we were boarding, howls across the lake. The shoreline is covered in $15,140 of useless Parker Brothers denominations. And inside the small cabin, a bubbling tray of lasagne with a rich bolognese sauce has just been taken from the oven. The smell is intoxicating. It's like in the Looney Tunes cartoons when Sylvester the Cat turns into a zombie following the scent of the Tweety Bird pie. The smell says, 'Eat this, and you shall be made whole.'

Don't ask me why it was that lasagne and not another that lured me back to the dark side carrying a letter of apology for my canine teeth. I'd encountered other meaty things that smelled good during those wilderness years. I'd been freezing cold plenty of times. None had tempted me to renounce the thing in my life closest to religion.

Maybe it was osmosis. These were people completely at ease with the cycle of life and death. Let me tell you a story. When they were children, Ben's little sister Kate had adopted a one-eyed calf. She named him Blinky, and each day she fed him warmed milk from a bottle. One night when the family was sitting down to dinner—roast beef with potatoes and gravy—their dad turned casually to Kate mid-meal and asked, 'How does Blinky taste?' And indeed it was the little one-eyed calf on the table that night. I didn't say it was a good story.

To their credit, the family didn't make a big deal of the lasagne incident. They were no doubt looking on surreptitiously as I made the first tentative incursions into the cheesy, delicious mass, my nervousness giving way to sheer gluttonous delight. I half-expected jeering to break out around the table, but instead they kept quiet. Probably they sensed that at this stage my eating habits were like a flighty wild bird and if they made any sudden movements I would flit off back to vegetarian land and they'd have to provide an alternative dinner for me forevermore.

Oh, it was all innocent flirtation to begin with. A sneaky spaghetti bolognese. A cheeseburger. More spag bol. But it's a slippery slope from mince to harder drugs. One day you're eating a sausage in bread at the election day fundraiser, the next you're eating a bacon sarnie and by the end of the week you're gnawing on a chop bone. I reached rock bottom a long time ago: the carnivore's answer to living underneath a bridge in a cardboard box. I can now eat lamb's brains despite the little veins running through them that make them look horribly like—I don't know . . . *brains*—and say, 'Mmm, creamy.'

The most difficult part was telling my own family, whom I'd lectured, harangued and generally annoyed the crap out of for fourteen years. As the joke goes: How do you know if someone's a vegetarian? Because they'll tell you in the first five minutes. Reparations were in order. In particular I anticipated a big, shit-eating 'I told you so' from my sister. So I over-compensated. In journalistic terms, I buried the lead.

Now, as it transpires, if you announce to your family 'I have something to announce', it elevates expectations somewhere north of sky-high. If you do it while the family is gathered together instead of picking them off one by one, it also creates the feeling of An Occasion. So after I announced that I had something to announce and blathered on in a generic way—there was a fair bit of material about choices, and growing older, if memory serves me right—by the time I actually got to the point, they all thought I was about to say either: I'm pregnant, I'm engaged, or I'm dying. All of which made the real news a bit of a comedown. Everyone simply shrugged and went back to talking about the football.

A worthy lesson to learn. Best to break unpalatable news by making family members anticipate worse news. Next time there's something bad to tell them, I'm planning to sprinkle pamphlets from an oncology unit around the house just to soften them up.

～

Ben could have used a similar tactic when he dropped his own bombshell. This particular bombshell was atomic. He was giving up university to plunge into the restaurant world full-time. In the eyes of his parents this was like the Pope handing back his cassock to go clubbing on Ibiza.

He'd been studying geology. Rocks are about as far as you can get from a human-friendly profession, and Ben was wildly unsuited to a lifetime in the outback or down a mine, but his parents wanted more for him than a lowly (in their eyes) server's job. This was not what they had in mind for their cherished first-born. His mother wept when he broke the news he was going full-time at the Duke.

But Ben was a step ahead of them and, indeed, of me. He had happened along at exactly the right time, starting as a lowly busboy at the Duke when it was turned from old man's boozer into shiny gastropub. It was one of those places that captured the zeitgeist— I mean, the mere fact that it attracts a wanker's word like zeitgeist should tell you all you need to know. He had sniffed the wind and foretold the potential for a food-loving, people-loving kid from the country.

The tale of the Duke was shared by many inner-city pubs during this era of renewal. It had been a respectable bloodhouse back in its day. The home of the finite possibilities of the working-class man. A drinking hole and an unofficial betting shop, a couple of cheeky pots before going home to dinner on the table. It's there on the local historical society's photo board, a pub just like every other that punctuated Melbourne's grey inner suburbs with alcohol's golden promise. That was back when the word pub meant something static, blissfully unchanging. Now only a pokies joint can hope to prompt the feeling that you know exactly what to expect when you step in the door—more of a portal, really—guiding you to another reality with its own unflappable internal logic.

The modern pub has fractured into a kaleidoscope of sub-groups. There's the sports pub. The stripper pub. The uni pub. The gastropub. The family pub. The really fucking scary pub. It's complicated. The pub used to be just the pub. The constant around which life ebbed and flowed. Even religion, its rival in the grand illusion stakes, ran a poor second. My Catholic forebears tell me this was rarely a problem for the priests, who understood their place in the wider scheme of things. Their relegation didn't offend. Plenty of those priests drank themselves woolly most evenings. And they got served first, of course. God would have approved. It cemented the symbiosis: a captive audience of guilt and redemption.

There were remnants of the old suburb when I started drinking at the Duke. This was a pre-renovation Duke. A pre-Ben Duke. For the old guard clinging to its dingy front bar, it was a refuge from a rapidly changing world that meant their footpaths now teemed with people confusingly called yuppies and their roads rumbled with gleaming European four-wheel-drives. They gathered around the beer-soaked barmats each evening like figures out of an Edward Hopper painting. Leader of the grizzled pack went by the name of Charlie No-Name. 'That's right. No-Name. With a hyphen. Mr No-Name. But you can call me Charlie.' He had the soul of a sozzled poet and the face of Chet Baker, although sadly for the ladies it was the post-heroin Chet Baker, not the baby-faced jazz ingénue. Charlie had a Scottish brogue, an ancient ponytail tufting optimistically at his nape and a great range of waistcoats. As barflies go, he was dapper. His best mate was a Greek guy called George who spoke in increasingly incoherent drivel before finishing each evening slumped over the bar or occasionally face-down in the metal trough while his buddies thoughtfully ashed their cigarettes around him.

It was a meeting of two cultures. One a dispirited old crew huddling against the winds of change. The other a bunch of youngsters—my mob—on a hand-wringing search for identity. It was no accident that we stumbled into this downtrodden corner pub with its faded green vinyl floors, stale beer smell and one-dollar billiard table. Our university peers were playing drinking games at college pubs but we were engaged in different coursework: the pub as political statement.

We were gormless twats, of course, but much too young to realise. And Charlie and co kindly made room for us at their bar, even though they could have run us out without raising a sweat. Angus Macgregor, a former private schoolboy from Eltham desperate to renounce the privilege of Riverside Road despite still living there with his parents and two golden Labradors, became determined to win Charlie's respect. His Scottish approach was rebuffed—there were none so Scottish as Charlie and Robert Burns, and that was the end of the matter—so he changed tack and went in politically. Charlie had been a stalwart of the Builders Labourers Federation before he hung up his overalls to concentrate on beer and roll-your-own durries. Angus was an arts undergrad and he gave it everything he had. I heard terms like solidarity, workers' rights and direct action. It was stirring oratory from someone whose mum would be picking him up in an hour's time.

Charlie listened thoughtfully as he stared into his half-empty glass, paused, and winked. 'How about a blow job?'

~

So much for the *ancien régime*.

Only a few years later that corner pub had become a sandblasted metaphor for the relentless march of an upwardly mobile world. New owners charged in like storm troopers and tweaked it with the fervour of a plastic surgeon going to work on a mid-life crisis. It was lifted, spak-filled and reconceptualised. People armed with colour swatches dashed about saying important things like, 'We need to embrace the northerly aspect.' It was transformed from duckling into swan, if a swan could have bi-folds, polished timber so shiny you could use it to check for parsley in your teeth, and an 'al fresco area' protected by a row of concrete planters too heavy for any drunken miscreant to tip over.

The Duke was a classic case of right place, right time. Not for Charlie and his crew, who were pushed out to search for another sticky vinyl home to call their own. Even the upstairs ghost occasionally sighted by the alcoholic barman disappeared, never to be seen again. But it rode a new wave of newly moneyed people newly interested in food and wine. Once they'd eradicated the 100-year stench of cigarettes and tap beer and thrown it open to the zombie hordes of Diners Club members, it was the sort of place that prompts everyone to go 'Why didn't I think of that? Why didn't I get the lease on that tired old pub and turn it into a goldmine?' Why didn't you think of it? Because you didn't. Now shut up and stop whining.

The news of hospitality's rehabilitation took its time getting to Ben's family. His mother, a proud farming-family matriarch, was very big on respectability. Waiting on other people was not her definition thereof, even when his job came with the title of 'manager'. But it wasn't the first time she had underestimated her son. When he moved out of home she gave him a Country Women's Association cookbook. It was a book designed for young people with—how

SCOTT

They'd met online and this was their first meeting.
It seemed to be going pretty well but when I was
clearing their mains he made a joke to me about
how girls never look as good as they do in their
profile pictures. She silently got up and walked out.

to put this kindly—perhaps not the full range of experience in the
kitchen. A sample recipe is worth repeating in full.

MIXED GRILL
Ingredients: Two sausages, two chops, one packet of
crisps.
Method: Grill sausages and chops until cooked.
Open the packet of crisps and serve on the side.

Ben's tale is just an isolated example of the prejudice waiters
experience in a country with no proud tradition of the craft. And
in later years his parents would be madly proud of their son, the
hospitality professional. We'll be getting to that.

But that's enough about him for the moment. Back to me.

After the Base Station I had drifted into the nefarious world of
catering. Catering is essentially freelance waitering. You're in
charge of your own destiny. You can pick and choose the jobs you
want. And you get to perve on all the big events. Births. Deaths.

Marriages. It's like being in 'shuffle' mode professionally. Catering means never having to say you're sorry. One minute you're accidentally serving the gluten-free chicken pie to the vegan, and the next you're outta there, packing away the heavy dishwasher-safe crockery into the back of the truck before dashing to the next job. Catering is number 668—the neighbour of the Beast.

Working in catering blew the lid on this whole wedding caper. The 'best day of your life' is nothing less than a massive scam designed to bleed as much money as possible out of young couples who would be ten times better off using it as a house deposit. Mark my words: marriages fail, but real estate is forever. If it's a wedding, everything goes up by at least 50 per cent. The food, the booze, the venue hire, even the bloody balloons. If you want to be smart about a wedding, try booking it as a cocktail party. Don't go anywhere near the 'w' word. Sure, they'll be pissed off when a woman turns up looking suspiciously bridal in a puffy white meringue gown, but just think of the savings you'll make.

Catering weddings is the most stressful. Funerals—whatever. Everyone's too busy grieving to notice if the food is rubbish, and if anyone does happen to notice they can't say anything because it'll look like they're not sufficiently sad. Christenings are kind of the same, if only because people seem to have lower expectations when it comes to kids. The liberal application of sparkles certainly goes a long way for the under-ten set. But weddings? Weddings are meant to be the best day of not one but two people's lives. They're also unofficially meant to be the *second-best* day in the life of the parents who've helped stump up the cash, and maybe the *third-best* day for the bridesmaids, and so on. Tot it all up and you've got quite a mountain of expectation. Try catering for that.

I worked for a caterer who got into the business because friends kept telling her she was a great cook. It's a sadly common story. Throw a few dinner parties, get a few compliments, and hey presto—a caterer is born. It's better than being flattered into opening a bricks-and-mortar restaurant—god help those pathetic souls—but it's still not the money-making lark it seems from the outside. By the time she'd crawled through all the red tape, however, there was nothing for it but to keep on crawling to try to recoup the set-up expenses.

She could make a decent salmon and cream cheese blini, and her mini-quiches were excellent, but she was no businesswoman. Nor was she so good a cook that she could be trusted with the $250-a-head extravaganzas with lobster and wagyu and all the marquee ingredients people these days want to wow their guests with. She was a classic case of bad ideas happening to good ingredients. Everything essentially got minced and turned into a mini-pie. Easy to see her way of thinking—everyone likes a pie, especially a mini one—but a function cannot live on mini-pies alone. And who else takes a booking for a wedding in a scout hall and doesn't bother to check the site before the big day? Having running water in the kitchen and more than one lonely power socket for her battery of pie warmers would have been a big help. It was off to the hardware store for a whole bunch of power cords that overloaded the system and led to a complete blackout while the dance floor was heaving to 'Love Shack'. At least the mobile DJ had his own generator.

She took a booking for a medieval-themed wedding in the country. The couple had been university sweethearts. They'd met at a club for people devoted to medieval battle re-enactments, and he had broken down her ramparts. They were comforting proof that there is someone for everyone, and if a blushing bride sees fit to spend The Happiest Day Of Her Life™ wearing a long conical structure like an historical wind turbine on her head, that's her

business. But when the staff arrived at the wedding function, in
a field, in the middle of nowhere—just the kind of place those
damnable Normans might conceivably be attacking come night-
fall—we were directed to a tent with the ominous words, 'Go get
into your costume.' A maroon and gold velvet puffy-sleeved gown
might have a certain arresting quality but it is not designed for
the serving of pies, whether of the four-and-twenty blackbirds
variety or not. The crumbs stick to the velvet like metal filings on
a magnet, for one, and the heavy skirt is easily trodden on by any
knight of the realm making a grab for the last wagyu mini-pie.

It was a terrible wedding. I think everyone who had the
misfortune to attend would agree. It was an unseasonably hot night
and everyone was getting about in costumes that weighed ten kilos.
The local mosquitoes, some of them the size of elephants, had been
busy telegraphing the message that there was a whole field of fresh
meat ready to be sucked. There were men in chainmail sinking very
un-gallantly into chairs with rivulets of sweat pouring off them—it
was my first wedding where rust was a very real concern—and
women in tight corsets were gasping fags and saying 'fuck' a lot,
which wasn't particularly in keeping with the theme.

The bride was blushing. Beetroot red. The poor girl was
dying inside her twenty layers of velveteen drapery, and just to
compound matters she was under siege from a rogue band of
mosquitoes attracted to her like a tiny, buzzing death squad. As
I handed around a tray of fish mini-pies I noticed one of them
setting up shop on her head.

I did, in my defence, preface my rescue operation with a 'hold
still', but maybe I should have elaborated further to say, 'Hold still,
there's a freakishly large mosquito sucking blood from your
forehead.' My aim was true—the mosquito died where it squatted
on the bride's face, and in dying left a sticky stripe of blood across

her brow. It was not a good look; doubly so to the people across the tent who saw the bride being assaulted by a waitress.

After that incident my saviour, my very own knight in shining armour, whisked me away on his white steed. 'Prithee, fair maiden,' said he, 'dost thou wish to bide awhile at my place of toil?' Actually, his words were something more like this: 'Do you want to do a few shifts at the Duke?' And thus it was back to the fray.

— 10 —

WORKPLACE POLITICS: A SURVIVAL GUIDE

I highly recommend sleeping with the boss. The fringe benefits include decent shifts, free sample bottles of wine, and the occasional lift to work. The negatives include everyone else in the workplace hating you, losing your job if the relationship doesn't work out, and co-workers snarking about the easy ride you're on while your boss-slash-squeeze is trying to show you're not getting an easy ride by being hard on you. Let's just call it even, then.

So you think it's a good idea to date inside the workplace? Do you think it will be cosy, convenient, cute, or a dozen other words starting with C? Better rethink, sugarplum. Whether you subscribe to the gospel according to *Cosmo* or not, it's Rule Number One: Don't shit where you eat. It's unprofessional. Yet romance in the hospitality industry is as inevitable as it is fraught. We have already established that waiting tables is a young person's game, like enjoying the music of Katy Perry, saying 'like' as a form of punctuation, and midriff tops. Young people, as everyone knows, are so chock full of hormones they could be classified as clinically insane. They're working cheek by jowl in an environment not unlike the siege of Stalingrad. It's squeezy. A statistically significant number of hospo relationships begin because someone grabs someone else lightly around the waist to get past them behind the bar.

But wait, there's more. It's a transient population. There is alcohol. There are drugs. It's a powder keg of sexed-up pheromones waiting to explode.

Plenty of romantic scripts play from beginning to end in the time it takes to bump the dining room out from lunch shift to dinner. The concept of discretion can be hilariously loose, especially when the air crackles with the tension of two people impatiently looking for an excuse to smash each other's faces off in the coolroom. Any new couples prepared to go public, do be aware that while your co-workers might seem supportive, they're actually gagging behind your back. There's nothing so nauseating as two people being all cute during work hours, giggling as they help each other fold the napkins, touching hands over the cutlery, calling each other 'babe'.

It can get ugly, fast. 'Babe' can turn into 'bastard' before Tuesday's slightly dodgy oysters turn into baked oysters au gratin on the specials board. If it doesn't work out, someone has to quit. Few mortal souls are so emotionally sturdy they can go from shagging someone to seeing them flirt with other people while they work. There is no quick-fix rehab for the heart. You can't simply disappear into the anonymity of a big corporation by requesting a transfer to accounts. Unless one party to the split decides to walk the plank, who stays and who goes will be a matter for the manager's adjudication.

I would like to take this opportunity to reaffirm that I didn't start sleeping with the boss. I started sleeping with a person who then became my boss. An important distinction. Ben took a big professional risk in putting his girlfriend on the roster. He must have really liked me. Or been sick of my empty bank account. I must remember to ask him.

Workplace politics. Where to start? The average restaurant will be riddled with factions whose deep roots stretch way, way back into the mists of time. Your run-of-the-mill gastropub like the Duke can be eerily similar to the former Yugoslavia, where seething ethnic tensions began about a week after the Big Bang. No one remembers the details of the actual events, but everyone claims to carry the festering wounds like a personal scar. Ask someone to explain and you'll get something like, 'Well, there was this bar manager, and he was late for work one day and . . . Hang on, I'll get Gav to explain it.'

It is vital for the newcomer to ferret out, as quickly as possible, these factions and sub-groups and shadowy cabals. It's going to take you months to get your head around it all. The stakes are high. There are undercover agents as ruthless as the Stasi. They'll rat you out if you so much as smile at the hapless individual marked for execution. There's always someone marked for execution. The restaurant answer to the dead man walking. Accidentally befriend this person, and if you manage to keep your job you could be the last-tapped for staff meals for the rest of your life.

This is why smoking is so important. Not meaning to sound like an envoy from Big Tobacco or anything—tobacco will kill you, children—but being a smoker has a twofold benefit for any hospitality worker. Most obviously, it's the only way you're going to get a break mid-shift. There is a tacit understanding that smoking is an addiction and that a nicotine-dependent worker must have a regular hit in order to be a productive worker. I once worked at a place where a non-smoker—an annoying, sanctimonious, bead-wearing, bike-riding non-smoker—floated the idea that she deserved a five-minute fresh air break. Guess who was suddenly rostered on the 7 a.m. starts each day?

Smoking is much more than the lifestyle opportunity to sit on a milk crate in an alleyway for five minutes. Smoking is your inroad into the densely compacted intrigue of the workplace. You will often be joined on your cigarette break by other staff. Use the time wisely. Make some friends. Figure out who's currently doing whom, who used to do whom, and who's about to do whom. This is crucial information. Crucial enough that the tax office really ought to give waiters a deduction on nicotine-related expenses.

However, in the interests of saving a new generation from emphysema and the unsightly pant indentations caused by milk crates, here are a few guiding principles to help you on your way.

KNOW YOUR ENEMIES

The waitress who's been there forever, and I mean forever

She has been there for so long she remembers when the colour scheme was chosen. She calls the regulars 'love', has attained the status of neutrality—in the eyes of the kitchen she is Switzerland—and she knows where the bodies are buried. Mostly because she carried the spade. This is one mean bitch you do not want as your enemy. She can crush you, and she won't even break a fingernail while she's doing it. The strong women of history—Joan of Arc, Catherine de Medici, Heather Mills—were merely the test run for this broad. She protects her turf like a Rottweiler in a car yard. She has been there the longest, which means she has unofficial voting rights. Voting on what? On you, dear one. On you. She'll be friendly at the start. She'll be very friendly. It's a cat-and-mouse game in which she's trying to gauge if you'll play nicely and not attempt to usurp her power. There's only one thing for it. Show respect. Defer to age and experience. She wants to know you're on her side. Play it right and you'll be friends for life.

The friendly slacker waiter

Everyone likes this guy. Even the chef likes this guy. Hell, *you* like this guy. No career waiter, he's either an installation artist or in a band. He's not taking this waiter gig too seriously. He ambles in five minutes late, but always in such good humour, complete with a crazy story about something that happened the night before. Gosh, he's chilled. He makes everyone laugh. He's good for morale. But stop. Take a good, hard look at what's going on here. Why does he always get his dinner first? Why does he get an extra cigarette break? ('Mate, you don't mind if I just pop out back again? Gagging for a smoke. You know how it is . . .') Why does he get to knock off first and sit around drinking beer while you finish scrubbing the bar? Go out drinking with this guy, by all means. He's a helluva lot of fun. But don't let him take you for granted, you pussy.

The second-in-charge

Sometimes known as the deputy manager or the duty manager, the second-in-charge is a loose cannon. This is a person inching up the slippery pole towards official management status who has gotten stuck between floors. The 2IC is a professional halfway house: neither one of the drone workers nor one of the true bosses. From within their half-life twilight zone the 2IC is always on the make. They'll enjoy throwing their weight around when the real manager isn't there. Favourites will be rewarded and enemies punished, but remember this: their power extends no further than the shift. Suck it up and pay no heed. It's important to note that the manager has hired the 2IC to be compliant and bossable. This person is sent in to clean up any shit-storms that blow up. They are management's gimp. It's a thankless job. The manager doesn't respect the 2IC. Neither should you.

The waiter who started just before you

Hey, let's be besties! We can learn the ropes together! High five!

Think again.

Think about what's going on in the mind of the waiter who used to be the most junior member of staff but now, thanks to your arrival, is just a little more legit. Finally this person has someone on whom they can pull rank. Not only that, you're in direct competition for shifts. Repeat the maxim: *Keep your friends close and your enemies closer.*

The hospo brat

A new and frightening sub-species emerging from the sewers like a two-headed reptile, the hospo brat is created when *Restaurantis parentis* quite reasonably decide it's time for their progeny to learn the value of hard work. In the way of all dynasties, the long game is on this pimple-faced, chronic masturbator PlayStation addict eventually assuming control of the empire his forebears worked eighteen-hour days, seven days a week, to create. There is a one-in-two chance he will end up pissing their years of sacrifice up against the wall by deciding to open a Champagne bar with gold-plated toilets and plasma screens showing Victoria's Secret runway shows. Put yourself in the shoes of the average sixteen-year-old who knows he doesn't have to sweat the small stuff. You know: education, maturity, figuring out what he wants to do with his life. No. It's all going to be handed to him on a platter. No wonder this kid is swaggering about with the arrogance of the Mafioso made man—no dealing with garbage or blocked drains in the ladies' loos for this fine upstanding young fellow—and the managers can only push him so far before he runs off to Mummy or Daddy with a fictitious story about bullying or embezzlement.

The chef

Ah, yes. Chefs. Finally we come to the waiter's arch-nemesis.

The cobra to its mongoose.

Trapped in a sick symbiosis of misunderstanding and hatred.

Plunging together in a twisting ball of pummelling rage over Reichenbach Falls.

It's an eternal mystery why chefs and waiters have not yet realised they're actually on the same side. The real fight ought to be against the common enemy. That, of course, is the customer. The customer is the Hun, the Mob and the Mongols combined. Yet the evils of the diner are completely overshadowed by the dog-and-cat antipathy between kitchen and floor staff. Somehow the diner has become the fly that buzzes in the room while the heavy artillery blams away across the kitchen pass.

What a waste. If the kitchen and floor teamed up, they could be formidable. Remember: World War Two would have had a very different outcome if half the German forces didn't suddenly have to be diverted to the Russian front. What we need is a non-aggression treaty negotiated by someone up to speed on all the latest techniques in diplomacy. What's Kofi Annan doing these days?

The kitchen-versus-floor apartheid reaches its weird apotheosis each year at the work Christmas party. At the Duke that meant a few baskets of fries, a few rounds of beer at the restaurant itself after service one night, which put the occasion on a cheer-par with any of the other 364 nights of the year. At my very first Christmas party at the Duke, I didn't recognise the entire kitchen crew for the first half-hour. I assumed they were some random gang of slouchy guys who'd wandered in—maybe they'd gotten lost after robbing a 7-Eleven, maybe they were a bunch of delivery drivers invited along to share a bowl of potato wedges. After service, chefs always duck out before the floor staff; it's one of the many reasons they feel superior. I'd never seen them in their civilian clothes before, hair wetted down after a quick post-work spruce-up in the upstairs bathroom and enough deodorant to send the chemical-sensitive into anaphylactic shock.

A couple of hardy souls attempted to make small talk across the great divide, but it was absurdist theatre without the wit, the waiting without the Godot. Each conversation sputtered out after a few exchanges. It was a bit like the story of soldiers putting down their weapons on Christmas Eve and embracing each other in No Man's Land, but there was none of the joyfulness that makes it such a heart-warming tale, just a fervent desire to get this goodwill business out of the way so we could get back to shooting each other.

The Christmas party was a band-aid on a malignancy. There were various secondary cancers riddled throughout the place but the primary cancer went by the name of Jonathan. He was the head chef. One of half a dozen who graced the role during my tenure at the Duke, which at times seemed more a revolving door of graceless opportunity than a proper restaurant, and certainly the most memorable, albeit for all the wrong reasons. He wasn't that old but he was old-school, clinging stubbornly to the habits of a less enlightened age.

Times are changing. Kitchens can now be pleasant places to work. Honest. Plenty of chefs have a handle on social expectations and prefer to lead by example. It's the triumph of the carrot over the stick. Change is slowly coming, although it's taking its damned time about it.

I'm not saying that playing tricks on workmates doesn't have some comedic merit. If the kitchen decides to leave a dessert of chocolate and caramel-striped deliciousness on the prep bench to be discovered after they've all knocked off for the night and it turns out to be layers of duck fat and pig fat with whipped cream on top—well, that's funny. Empirically funny. Harmless funny. No one got hurt in the making of that joke, although the memory of the palate-coating rancidness will haunt for years to come. And if retaliation takes the form of a pint of apple cider vinegar gulped down by the chef who likes to start each day with apple juice—well, whose fault is it if he hasn't told anyone about his stomach ulcer and winds up doubled over in the emergency department?

Jonathan, however, had come through the ranks in the days when apprentices were bastardised as relentlessly, thoroughly and mercilessly as army recruits, and he was not going to be denied the karmic retribution owed to him. It wasn't just the endless dick-grabbing and poetic speculation about what objects had been inserted into his colleagues' anuses. Nothing unusual there. So long as kitchens are mostly male they'll continue to be as dick-obsessed as the toilet queue at Poof Doof. There was a special layer of bully-boy viciousness in Jonathan that went above and beyond the call of duty. He liked to demean. He liked to humiliate.

It's not like he had anything obvious to be angry about. The Duke had a nice kitchen and staff who were relatively well paid. There was nothing to explain why he was such an arsehole, except for the fact that he was born an arsehole and will one day die an arsehole. Possibly it was because he was a New Zealand boy working in a world of Italians and his greatest contribution to the canon was the tandoori chicken pizza. Or because the Duke's reputation was built on two previous head chefs who had been women. Italian women. They were the bomb. They worked hard, partied hard, made some brilliant food, won a bag of awards, and were well liked and respected. They've gone on to bigger and better things.

Jonathan was a pedestrian chef whose pedestrian food was never going to raise a critic's eyebrow. He was vain—when his first child was a few weeks old he bought a Harley Davidson motorbike and started visiting a solarium 'to set a good example for my son'—and maybe his vanity whispered in a little voice that he was not well liked and respected even less. He has not gone on to bigger and better things. He eventually disappeared into dowdy little suburban joints. Years later I accidentally stumbled into an anonymous restaurant in middle-suburbia one night and there he was. Knock me over with a feather if he wasn't running the exact same menu. It could have been carbon-dated to 1996.

One thing about Jonathan, he knew how to game the system. He surrounded himself with a doltish bunch of followers. Boys, mostly, straight out of culinary school and too stupid to resist the whole 'yes chef, no chef, how high chef' thing. Italian mama's boys, on the whole, like Mario, who was twenty-one and had just spent $40,000 on his car stereo and approximately one-hundredth of that on his fiancée's engagement ring. Or Artie, the bodybuilding hulk of a chef de partie, all muscles and steamed chicken and hunger, who displayed flashes of decency but would revert to a grinning man-brute whenever Jonathan appeared.

Not only did his crew diligently prop up Jonathan's unstable ego, they allowed him to effectively control a power bloc. They were his bargaining chip for better pay, better conditions, whatever took his fancy, because he could threaten to walk and take the entire kitchen crew with him, and the owners knew they'd go trotting after him like well-trained dogs.

There was a swing door separating the kitchen from the dining room at the Duke. It was a magical door, like the door to Narnia, because walking through it transported the waiters to a different land where none of the usual rules applied. There were no friendly talking mice and pretty water nymphs in this land, alas. It was more like a less-welcoming version of an Egyptian prison.

The era wasn't kind to waiters. The following decade saw the discovery of smears and foams, which act like high-grade adhesive and keep everything in place, but the 90s fashion was all about stacks of food reaching for the sky. The Duke boasted a signature vegetable stack—roasted eggplant, red capsicum and pumpkin smooshed together with goats' cheese (new ingredient alert!) so precarious that it teetered like a giraffe in stilettos, constantly on the brink of collapsing on its side into an oily, goat-cheesy mess. If it fell before the hapless waiter got it out of the kitchen, Jonathan's pupils would retract into tiny pinpricks of fury in his psychotic ice-blue eyes as he bagged out the useless . . . fucking . . . idiot . . . responsible. If it fell once it was through the magical swing door— Too bad, customer. Stack it up yourself. I'm not going back in there.

Jonathan did have his light-hearted moments. For several weeks he happily led a chorus of Warrant's 'Cherry Pie' every time I walked into the kitchen. I know it doesn't sound like much but when it happens fifty times a shift, five shifts a week, it really messes with your head. It's water-boarding with words. It's meant to be a gratuitously fun slice of spandex rock but I still can't listen to it without wanting to go somewhere very quiet and weep a little. But what was I to do? Seriously, what was I conceivably to do? Go running to my boyfriend and get him to sort it out? Go on strike? Demand the entire kitchen crew stand up and apologise to their parents, classmates and the school? Not bloody likely. The only thing for it was to put on my waterproof big girl pants, hold my head up and get on with it. And I guess in some ways I was lucky.

Being the manager's squeeze meant I was quarantined from some of their more creative endeavours. Jonathan and Artie cornered another waitress when she went into the coolroom to get lemons for the bar. They shut the door, turned off the light and casually talked about how easy it would be to rape her. 'Just weirdly conversational . . . as if they were talking about the weather,' Nella told me later. She came back out to the bar, white and shaking. Being real grown-up men, they resorted to the time-honoured defence of 'It's just a joke!' when they were challenged, and naturally enough nothing ever came of it—except Nella never again went to the coolroom alone.

Now for the $64,000 question: what do chefs think they're achieving, exactly, by bullying staff to the point everyone pretends they can't hear the bell? Okay, so maybe they have a dog-eared copy of Marco Pierre White's *White Heat* at home, the book that single-handedly invented the rockstar-chef and in 126 pages transformed its subject into the Keith Richards of the kitchen. All sorts of shitful kitchen behaviour owes its origins to *White Heat*. It really ought to be banned; it's the *Lady Chatterley's Lover* of the kitchen set. Take a close look at all the ink snaking down that young chef's arms. 'What would MPW do?' is probably lurking somewhere near his wrist. Little do they know that even Marco Pierre White (who the hell goes by three names anyway?) is trapped in the prison of his own legend. Little do they know that most guys who shoot for Marco Pierre White wind up at Gordon James Ramsay, minus the fame and the wealth, the product endorsements, TV shows and international string of restaurants. Plus these guys are simply too busy being rockstars to acknowledge some central truths. That making staff afraid to go into the kitchen to the point they 'forget' to put in dockets is going to make everyone look bad. That it's not the height of comedy to shove a scorching hot plate in some hapless waiter's hands so an impression of their fingerprints is permanently soldered to it.

Okay, okay, the Reconciliation Commission is demanding both sides make concessions. So I'll concede that spending every shift in a commercial kitchen might send even a well-adjusted person a little troppo. A commercial kitchen is often no bigger than your average bathroom. There's no concept of personal space for chefs who work long hours in an inherently stressful job in the company of artificial lighting and relentlessly harsh industrial surfaces. Tile. Stainless steel. Concrete.

This is not a plea for soft furnishings. It's a plea for under-standing.

All the re-education programs in the world won't be enough to deter a chef determined to cling onto his reign of terror like some moth-eaten Middle Eastern dictator. I've got my hopes riding on the open kitchen to be the thing that puts a bullet in the old-fashioned, zucchini-up-the-bum kind of bullying. A restaurant

159

WORKPLACE POLITICS: A SURVIVAL GUIDE

isn't complete without an open kitchen these days. The mantra of the modern food age: Not only must cooking be done, it must be seen to be done. It's all about providing eye frottage for the diners. Food porn foreplay. Accepted wisdom now holds that food tastes

---

MICHAEL

It was an inexplicably popular cafe where one of the most popular items on the menu was the tuna melt, a mayo-heavy tuna salad with a bit of onion, celery and grated carrot splodged onto stale bread, then covered with a luridly orange cheese and grilled. The chefs, if you can call them that, would make the tuna salad mix in huge white plastic buckets, throwing in the ingredients and then mixing it with their bare hands (literally up to—and beyond— their elbows). One morning the chefs were in the kitchen gathered around one of the big white plastic buckets. There was a large dead rat curled up in the centre of the tuna salad. The bucket was fairly full and the owners hated waste, so there was a debate about what to do. A few thought the whole lot should be chucked. Others thought just the rat should be ditched. In the end the chef who had been there the longest made the decision and picked the rat up by its tail and chucked it in the bin. He then scooped out a thin layer of tuna salad around where the rat had been lying and threw that in the bin, too. Then he put a lid on the bucket and slid it back into the coolroom, ready for the breakfast rush.

---

better after seeing people sweating to make it. The happy by-product for waiters is a far diminished risk of receiving a stinging flick over the ear with a rolled-up tea towel from the chef.

Sunlight is the best disinfectant, as they say. Institutionalised kitchen bastardry might have received its marching orders. If I ever start getting all misty-eyed about the old days, just shoot me.

TROUBLESHOOTING 101: THE RETURNED PLATE

So you've raised a reasonable complaint about the food and for some unfathomable reason your waiter resists taking the plate back to the kitchen for a spot of rectification? Chances are there's a snaggle-toothed psychopath in there just dying for a chance to take out his frustrations on the poor apron-clad schmuck who bursts through the swing doors saying table three is complaining the steak is too rare.

It's been a tough week for our chef hero. His new iPhone isn't synching with his iPad, his wife is giving him grief for rolling home at 3 a.m. after knock-offs, and Geelong was drubbed by Carlton in the Friday night game. He doesn't care that the customer is always right. In fact, he's dead sure the customer is always wrong, and the waiter bearing bad tidings is simply acting as the misguided representative of a classless dickhead who wouldn't know good cooking if he stuck it up his arse, etc, etc.

Take the Sabatini, for example. Mo couldn't poach an egg if his life depended on it. This was somewhat of a handicap for a breakfast chef, although in his defence poached eggs were only just getting a foothold in the cafe landscape back in the early 90s. Scrambled was all the rage. Poached takes a bit more skill than what is essentially egg mash with a truckload of cream; no one can stuff up that one, unless they commit the rookie mistake of using too high a heat and wind up with a mound of yellow insulation material.

There was at least one cafe on Brunswick Street, ground zero of the then-revolutionary 'breakfast all day' menu, where they'd poach dozens of eggs the night before the craziness of weekend brunch service. They'd leave them in a vat of iced water, bobbing around like so many silicon breast implants. Chef's job was to 'refresh' them to order. Nice. Add a slice of toast and some limp spinach and that'll be $15, sir.

Anyway, Mo's poached eggs were little more than a rock-hard yolk with the memory of the whites fluffed grimly around it. It was an act of awe-inspiring chutzpah simply to put the plate in front of someone. They'd usually look up in dismay. Unsurprisingly they'd often ask to send it back. They weren't to realise, although I was painfully aware, that Mo was in the kitchen sweating out the toxins after a big night at the casino and/or the strip club, and swearing his head off every time another order came in. Mo knew he couldn't poach eggs. That was why they weren't on the menu, and didn't I fucking know not to let anyone order them even if they were a regular fucking customer? Okay, so I was a bit of a softie in that department. My bad.

So here's my advice to any waiter in this situation: nod in a polite but non-committal fashion, turn, walk off, and act *really, really* busy. Sure, the customer will summon you back if they're of a determined frame of mind, but work on the assumption that most people don't like to make a fuss. Steel your resolve with the knowledge that a psychology study proved Australian diners are practically allergic to anything approaching confrontation. A couple of actors pretending to be waiters staged an escalating

series of rows to judge the response from customers. By the end
the actor-waiters were yelling and throwing things at each other,
and still the diners kept their eyes politely averted from the action.

Why? Because most people have been raised to think it's uncool
to raise a fuss. This plays right into the hands of the typical waiter,
for whom 'whatever' is the default position.

It backs up my experience that nine out of ten diners will accept
defeat, complain bitterly among themselves, pay the bill and never
return. You won't get a tip, of course, but foregoing a few bucks
is good value, in my book, if it means escaping a major bollocking
from Vlad the Kitchen Impaler.

~

I have described the inner workings of restaurants in the harshest
of terms. I have described them as places of siege, where the soul
goes to shrivel and die. Yet love blooms in the unlikeliest of places.
When I think of the good that can come of the industry, I think
of Kelli and Will. A couple that should never have been. A couple
that defied the odds and won.

She: the 41-year-old waitress who had been at the Duke the
longest. Not to be messed with. Trapped in a loveless marriage
with a husband whose idea of a good time was to lie in a darkened
room listening to Pink Floyd's *Dark Side of the Moon*.

He: the hospo brat. The 22-year-old son of one of the Duke's
owners. Overly fond of motorbikes, but on the whole a sweet
young man working his way through university.

They should have been oblivious to each other. A negative
charge repelled by a positive. At most they should have politely
nodded across the nineteen-year age gap.

But it was the closeness of the working arrangements that started it. You squeeze past someone in the line of duty enough, you're going to start wondering what they look like with their clothes off. Plus it was reported to Will by his workplace spies that the sexy older waitress had declared, 'I'll have a crack at that boy.' It was a drunken fit of pique about having to listen to all that Pink Floyd, but it helped light the spark. He'd only just lost his virginity, to a different waitress at the Duke. He liked to keep things in-house.

Things were moving in an arse-grabbing-behind-the-bar direction when Will called her one day to say his mum had gone out. Strange words for a 41-year-old married woman to hear, but it wasn't exactly an everyday sort of situation. So Kelli headed over to Will's mum's house, taking with her two of those small bottles of Champagne with straws in them because someone told her you get drunker if you drink it through a straw, and she needed to be drunk. They had sex for the first time in his single bed.

After that—game on. 'We had sex at work everywhere. On the staff meal table, upstairs in the function room, out the back. The only thing out of bounds was the boss's chair. That would just have been weird.'

The world isn't kind to a couple who defy expectations. Grappling with anxiety, Kelli saw a therapist, who yelled at her for being unfaithful to her husband. Perhaps not the world's greatest therapist. She and the hospo brat kept their relationship under wraps for more than a year until enough people started guessing and eventually another of the owners warned darkly that if the rumours turned out to be true, Kelli would be looking for a job. No older waitress messed with a Duke scion without getting her come-uppance.

The truth has a funny way of wriggling out and in this case it was Ben who accidentally dropped the news to Will's dad. I know people often say they 'accidentally' dropped some incendiary piece of top-secret information when they're actually inveterate gossips, but in this case it was true. Lucio had only recently suffered a severe stroke that left him talking slower than a one-fingered typist. He'd had a minor stroke a decade earlier, at the tender age of thirty-two, but didn't pay it any heed. Kept smoking and drinking and generally carrying on as if he was an indestructible teenager who'd snuck into the Playboy mansion while Hugh Hefner was off getting a prostate examination.

It was instinctive to try to prod the conversation along a little to help him out, but one day Ben prodded it along a little too much. Bear in mind that Lucio was a proud Italian man who prior to his stroke had enjoyed an energetic love life. Every week he'd be in the bistro with a different woman. They were always glamorous. Always young. Sometimes two of them. 'Parmigiana for dessert tonight, boys,' he'd crow. That's top-secret Italian man-code for 'Look who's about to get a threesome: jealous much?' But by this stage, although he could think straight enough, he couldn't get the words out. All he could do was look helplessly at Ben—shocked, outraged—visibly struggling to form the words clawing for release from his skull.

'. . . Kelli . . .?'

'. . . Duke . . .?'

'. . . *Old* . . .?'

Nine years later he's still not reconciled to his only son being with a woman almost two decades his senior. But Ben's been vindicated for his loose lips. All that *Dark Side of the Moon* is only a bad memory. Kelli and Will are now living together and happily waiting on the arrival of their new broadband connection: 'High-speed porn, babe, high-speed porn!'

~

And for Ben and me? Our ending was less sunset-over-water, although my rival in the love stakes turned out to be not another woman but a pub. In fairness to him, he had tried his best but we had reached an impasse. There are only so many times you can fight with your beloved at work then make up in the coolroom before it gets really depressing.

So Ben did what men (and women) have done for time immemorial when they want to deliver bad news. He took me to an expensive restaurant.

I've seen plenty of people break up in restaurants. Couples break up in restaurants all the time. From the dumper's point of view, they're a relatively safe place where the throwing of plates and yelling of insults is far less likely to occur than if the news was delivered in the privacy of one's own home. For the dumpee, the only consolation is this rule of thumb: the more expensive the restaurant, the more significant the relationship. If you can count your wedding anniversaries on two hands and get the flick at Sizzler, consult your lawyer.

It was a nice restaurant. Nicer than any restaurant I'd been in up until that point. And Ben was sweating bullets. I actually thought with a little 'squee!' of excitement that he might be about to propose. But instead he dropped a bombshell. 'It's not working out.'

Perhaps he could have phrased it better. It was a relief to find out after intensive questioning that he meant the job. Not us. We were still on. It was the Duke that was getting rid of me. He was merely its emissary, delivering painful news while still hoping I would accompany him home that evening. What a hoot. It will be something we laugh about in the future. Maybe sometime around 2045. Anyway, years later, when he did actually propose, in a carpark next to a dumpster on the eve of Bin Day, it was an endearing flipside to the romantic scene in which he dumped me professionally.

So Ben gave me a reference and sent me out to make my own way in the world. Did I resent him for choosing his career over his girlfriend? Well, maybe, just a little, although it was tempered by the self-awareness that I was patently rubbish. And I suspect, although he denies it to this day, considering what later transpired there, that he got me my next job at another shiny gastropub known as the Rising Star. He also quite possibly intervened on several occasions to stop them firing me. But that's just a hunch. He ain't talking.

These days hospitality and I have reached a truce in our battle over Ben and settled for a slightly resentful ménage à trois. We share him, although which of us has the better part of the deal I really can't say.

— 11 —
THE DARK ARTS OF PERSONAL ADVANCEMENT

The casual observer would have noted the two police cars parked haphazardly out front as a dead giveaway that something was wrong. Maybe the shatter of glass from the pub's door, a glittering arc splayed on the footpath in a tableau of arrested energy. But to the initiate there was one herald of disaster even more glaring— it was early morning, and George was there. This was an event unusual bordering on unthinkable, because George was never early. George was never even on time. George was always late, although in the unfailingly positive self-appraisal of the Rising Star's owner, he could never be late because whatever time he showed up was the perfect time. George was like that.

I said 'owner' but really he was forced to share the title with two other guys. Co-owner: that pesky little prefix was the handbrake on an ego that would happily have gone careening down a hill like a runaway truck and come to a fender-crunching halt in a glorious pile of money. Oh yes, the Rising Star—more commonly known among its ratbag staff as the Rising Damp—was a flourishing business. It must have pained George to share custody, but the consolation was that he held the royal flush because he was the only one with industry experience. The other two were old buddies from the 'hood. Wog boys done good. In construction and real estate. Money to burn.

George was the hands-on owner. The evil overlord, although his business card actually said general manager. The other two left him to it, more or less. They were your Type-B pub owners. Guys who got into it for the boasting rights, to make a bit of extra cash and to pick up chicks. Not necessarily in that order.

Dan was an electrician by trade who'd stitched up a sweet deal with one of those construction giants that bash up thirty-storey apartment towers in a few months that start falling apart a few weeks after the owners move in. Dan, Dan, ladies' man. He thought he looked like Liam Neeson although he wasn't so bold to come right out and say it. 'Some people think I look like Liam Neeson,' was his far subtler tactic for introducing the idea that he was movie-star handsome. Tables of women would sit looking at him slightly befuddled—he looked like Liam Neeson only if you squinted really hard and tilted your head to the right while drinking a second espresso martini—but when they found out he was an owner of the joint, they'd often switch on that invisible sign above their heads that said 'open for business'.

The other owner was Tommaso, the head of the construction company that contracted Dan, destined to be his wingman forevermore. Not much to say except that he was a decent guy with an interesting taste in friends.

George liked being called Boss. The arse-licker head chef Damien complied, but everyone else called him Bubbles. Behind his back, of course, but it was uncannily fitting. Bubbles was the name for a small, inconsequential lapdog. Truth be told, if George was a dog he would have been more of a basset hound—all jowly, with dark baggy pouches under his eyes to match his rumpled, baggy body. His toenails were downright frightening. Gnarled claws the colour of a dying person's urine, stepped with thick, horned ridges. It was deeply disturbing when he wore sandals in summer. They were a moving violation. A walking occupational health and safety issue. Any customer catching sight of those gruesome digits would immediately cancel their order for the fried calamari, but it didn't matter in the long run because the Rising Star was bulletproof. They'd hit the jackpot. George had been in the industry for three decades and at various times he'd owned some big-name nightclubs and pubs, but he'd never had anything like this.

George was one of those figures well known within the industry and not without. Neither a bottom feeder nor a whale, he was a practical fish that sticks to the temperate mid-depths where the middle class likes to swim. That was the Star. Immediately beloved by the people who had priced the suburb out of the reach of its old guard of immigrants, factory workers, bohemians and uni students, it overlooked a park the council had decreed, via Local Ordinance 2.9, be referred to as 'leafy Barton Square' in all subsequent mentions in the local newspaper. Up the road there was a chemist riding a two-speed economy, slinging blood pressure medication to stressed professionals and methadone to the junkie underclass stacked into the nearby council towers. The more entrepreneurial ones would

IZZY

I was working in a fancy restaurant that had a really strict staff drinks policy. Zero tolerance, which was seen by most of the staff as a personal challenge. We drank a ridiculous amount of great wine so it wouldn't look like too much of any one thing was missing. It was back in the day when there wasn't a computer stock system, just a book and a pencil. So we'd constantly adjust the stock levels and usually drink there until dawn at the end of each working week.

duck into the cobblestone alleyway to spit their daily ration of green gunk into a cup to on-sell for profit. It was what passed for spectator sport while setting up at the Rising Damp, lugging tables and umbrellas outside for another day's bruschetta madness. Inside it was the usual story. A glossy curved bar hugged by the bustling bistro. Timber, gloss, glossy timber, mwah, mwah, mwah. The far end of the bar was the invisible start of the restaurant proper, where linen was laid on the tables, garnishes were more extravagant and prices were 20 per cent higher.

And they got it for a song. An absolute song. It pains me to think of it. May everyone in the restaurant trade pause to whisper a prayer for similar good fortune.

∽

And now, as the Tuesday after a long weekend dawns over leafy Barton Square, we find Bubbles' black Holden Statesman parked in the disabled spot across the road while its owner paces the street and sucks another Dunhill down to the butt.

Upstairs his office is in its usual state. Translation: it looks as though a gang of union heavies has done a run-through with a baseball bat. The ashtray hasn't been changed in a week. For a committed chain-smoker it means the paperwork strewn across every available surface is covered in a fallout of soft grey ash. The cleaner was never allowed into the office. Trust wasn't Bubbles' strong point.

His cleanliness-is-next-to-slovenliness mantra is not what has attracted the local constabulary, however. On this particular morning there is a large safe-sized hole where the safe used to be. Overnight it has been jackhammered out of the fireplace into which it had been cemented, dragged to the stairs, and surrendered to the laws of gravity. It must have weighed 250 kilos, easy. It bounced off the walls, punching a couple of safe-sized holes into the plasterwork as a memento as it passed through en route to the ground floor. Next to the smashed-in front door, the alarm system has been disabled. Don't go imagining some crack team of career criminals going all heist-movie on it, abseiling through the roof while sinuously avoiding the laser movement sensors. All they had to do was switch it off at the power point, which was conveniently located next to the unit on the wall. Security at the Rising Damp left a little to be desired.

George was inexplicably nervous, like an old woman at a bus stop. Pacing, sweating, clutching his ciggies for comfort. One can only speculate. He was going through a messy divorce. That safe, to which he alone possessed the combination, would have been the ideal place to hide tens of thousands of dollars in cash from the prying eyes of his soon-to-be ex-wife's lawyers. Money that he wouldn't be able to declare to the insurer because it was money that didn't officially exist. Maybe there was other phantom money residing in that safe. Maybe there was money skimmed off the Star's profits that his business partners remained blissfully unaware of. Yes, that could have explained his nervous cigarette smoking. Nothing stings quite so sharp as being robbed of the proceeds of crime.

So how did this brazen band of criminals manage to spirit away a massively heavy hunk of metal? It's a mystery. There was no CCTV footage. They must have jacked it into a truck and taken it off for a loving date with a blowtorch. The cops never discovered if it was an inside job. Someone obviously knew the safe was full after a festive three days' holiday trade. Not that hard to figure out, really, but did I mention they'd had another business partner, at the very beginning? A guy who only lasted a few months before a mysterious falling out. He owned another restaurant up the road. Occupying a less prominent place on his CV was the fact he'd also done time for armed robbery. Anyway, someone knew what was sitting there after a hectic long weekend. A whole lot of lovely money. I wonder if the culprit took a leaf out of Scrooge McDuck's book and rolled around in it joyfully, like a dog in cow shit. I would have, if it was me, but unfortunately the Great Safe Heist of '96 remains unsolved.

There is no such thing as the perfect crime, but there are the perfect conditions for crime, and the Rising Damp made it easy for a small but perfectly formed kingdom of vice to flourish. Let me put it delicately: those a certain way inclined were able to entertain their upwardly mobile aspirations without sober application to self-betterment.

Less delicately: it bred lowlifes like a petrie dish breeds bacteria. It was just a matter of time before the badness got the upper hand and overran the place, chasing out anything good that might keep it in check. A fiefdom of squalor was born.

And through it all we kept smiling and serving pots of beer to the upwardly mobile clientele, most of whom didn't have to resort to larceny to fatten their offset cheque accounts.

I might have casually mentioned, just in passing, without a trace of bitterness, that George and his buddies bought the joint for a song. An absolute fucking song. It was the Lotto win every hospo worker dreams about, but there was more to it than dumb luck. It was an educated guess. See, Bubbles and his cohorts didn't renovate the place. That happened under the watch of their predecessors, two successful and therefore very wealthy merchant bankers who'd decided to take the lease on a smelly old pub on a promising corner. *They* took the risk. *They* pulled a rabbit out of a hat. *They* conjured a success story out of green vinyl and neglect. *They* were rewarded with a place that heaved with customers, seven days a week. So why did they sell it for next to nothing to Bubbles and Co?

George had owned plenty of businesses before. Bars. Restaurants. Cafes. Pubs. He was a man keenly aware of how the system worked, and his sixth sense was calibrated finely enough to realise there was something shifty going on.

And indeed he was correct. The something shifty went by the name of the Jamaica fund. The Jamaica fund was the invention of the small group of managers put in charge of the Star by the merchant bankers. It made sense. That's what you do in corporate-land. Delegate, delegate, delegate. If you lack the time or expertise yourself, you pay someone lower down the food chain to do the work for you. Unfortunately it doesn't exactly work like that in restaurant-land. Not unless your manager is a devout Episcopalian who fully expects eternal hellfire as punishment for stealing. Actually, not even then.

The Jamaica fund was the byword for a massive operation that stuck a fat syringe into the Star's femoral artery and methodically bled the place dry. It was an absurdly simple scam. Don't ring up that table's bill for $300. Don't ring up those six glasses of fizz. Put it towards the Jamaica fund. It was a conspiracy between three or four guys—none of whom ever made it to Jamaica, as far as I'm aware—but even those without their fingers in the till felt the glow of its largesse. The Jamaica fund's philanthropic program kindly sponsored all sorts of free eating and drinking for off-duty staff.

So why didn't the merchant banker owners twig? Because they were utterly clueless. Lambs to the slaughter. And let's face it: they *deserved* to be fleeced if trust was their primary management tactic. The sooner they were chewed up and spat out the better, although in their defence, a busy business doesn't necessarily mean a profitable business. If wage costs are too high and food costs have blown, you can be the busiest joint in the country and still not be making enough money to buy a six-pack and a couple of pizzas. That was the misapprehension they were labouring under. 'It's a tough business,' they must have muttered to each other every time they were appraised of the week's financials.

But that didn't explain what was going on here. And George sensed it. And he and his buddies swooped and took the place off the hands of two disillusioned merchant bankers who, by that time, were simply grateful for release and rushed off to the safety of securitised debt structures.

Even so, George made some inexplicable decisions. He kept the chef, which demonstrates the persuasive power of Damien calling him Boss. Fox, meet Henhouse. We hope you're comfortable here. And please show the chickens some respect.

Even in the genre of fleeting, transitory occupations—BASE-jumping instructor; nuclear disaster first-responder—waitering is a stand-out performer. In this profession, sticking in the same job for a year is considered seriously long-term. Veteran status. The transience of the workforce means it's ridiculously easy to fabricate a history. Not just a work history. A personal history. In the old days you had to disappear to Alice Springs or Darwin to escape the ignominy of an affair gone wrong, suspicions of embezzlement, a bizarre incident involving a dog and a piece of garden hose. Now you just have to move to a different restaurant in a different suburb and start spinning anew your outlandish tales of personal glory.

Reinvention. Stick that at the top of your list of the good things about being a waiter. For a profession with almost pathological amounts of socialising, it's uncannily often that you look up and think, 'Who are these people, really?'

One of the Star's barmen was called Sam. Because that was his name. Or was it? Sam was the prototype for the international man of mystery. Which was exactly how he liked it. I have a theory that at a particularly impressionable teen phase someone close to him floated the concept that the obtuse man gets more chicks. Something as relatively straightforward as 'How are you, Sam?' would get a response like 'Well, my darling, the sky is blue.' Sam was a bull of a man, his heft held together by high-elastane black cotton and hair gel. If I were in a gang fight, I would want Sam by my side. If I wanted my car to disappear and be discovered burnt out in an industrial wasteland for the insurance money, Sam was my man. Sam was the kind of guy you wanted with you, not against you. One night he threw lighter fluid on one of the more eccentric waiters who wore a pince-nez perched on his nose and his dead grandmother's teeth around his neck. Sam set him on fire simply because he was bored. But then this big, burly, semi-frightening individual was found in the men's weeping like a child. It was cancer, he said. Inoperable. He was dying. And he promptly left work to die. Only he was seen many times thereafter looking fit and well at another restaurant across town. There was all sorts of shit going on with Sam, but cancer was not one of them.

Even George. Who the hell was he? He certainly wasn't the kind of guy you could conveniently pigeonhole. The restaurant industry is about people. George actively disliked people. He was the Anti-Owner. A real professional will be a glad-handler, a bon vivant who likes to press the flesh, say all the appropriately flattering things to the regulars: 'You look great! Have you lost weight?'; 'How about those Doggies?'; 'So you're looking to buy a new car? I know a guy who knows a guy who can get a great deal for you.' George was often seen ducking out the back when regulars walked in, so he didn't have to greet them. He wasn't exactly a great role model of the service industry.

You could get the make of the man from the people he employed. Take his right-hand guys. Jimmy and Johnny. Johnny and Jimmy. As desperate a couple of no-hope, drug-fucked career hoods as you'll ever find. The crime doesn't pay poster boys. Jimmy boasted one of the longest rap sheets in the state. Not the big-ticket items, though. None of your really ugly stuff like murder and rape. He'd lived a full and well-rounded life of petty crime, vandalism, minor assault (overlooking that nasty incident with the finger and the band saw) and thievery, with quite a few drugs charges seasoning the mix. Possession, not dealing. One look at Jimmy and his big galumphing frame—the human answer to Tigger—and you knew he wasn't exactly drug kingpin material. The smartest thing about him was that he knew it, too. If he'd tried to get into the big league, he would have consumed all his own product and eventually been shot in the head by a guy named Pablo. He was better off scabbing along on welfare payments and his Star cash, supplemented with the pawned proceeds of his break-and-enters. He was a well-known figure at the Magistrates Court. Every time he fronted up for a date with justice, the beak, whichever one was hearing his case, would say witheringly, 'And so we meet again, Mr Johnson,' and send him down for another three months or six months or a year. It didn't seem to worry Jimmy too much. It was the only life he knew, and he was living it with joie de vivre. One time I was driving along terrified that I was about to make news headlines as the victim of a vicious road rage attack but it turned out to be only Jimmy, pinballing lane changes and sideswiping traffic so he could wave hello from his beaten-up old ute.

Poor old Jimmy. He was the producer, director and star of his own one-man comedy show. 'My teacher said I couldn't stick at anything, but I bloody well showed her!' he'd say with his big sloppy grin. 'My life's a credit to perseverance!'

Jim had a flat in one of the council towers. He had a long-running feud with the Aboriginal family who lived in the flat below. When he hit the meth pipe hard, he became paranoid that they were getting him back for his latest effort—smearing shit on their front door, or stealing their kids' bikes—by slowly jacking up the floor. Jimmy spent whole nights shooting up speed, plagued by visions of the linoleum moving where his neighbours were pushing it up with broomsticks. In retaliation he'd hammer the floor and scream to keep them awake. 'They've done it again,' he'd bellow, arriving two hours late for work after pulling a few cones to calm down off the speed, his face flushed as red as his hair. 'They've been doing it all night, all fucking night! They're pushing my fucking floor up! I can hear them down there'—pause to look side to side as if a family of four adults and six children had followed him to work and were now huddled unseen behind the fire extinguisher— 'they're whispering about me.'

In the increasingly rare times Jimmy was out of the big house, he was the Star's handyman. It was a loose arrangement. He turned up when he wasn't drunk or drug-ified or sleeping off either of the above, always clutching the classic junkie's accessory of a plastic shopping bag with a 2-litre bottle of Coke and a dozen chocolate bars. By George's inestimable logic, Jimmy was cheap. It didn't matter that he was also crap. George's big fault: he loved a bargain, and if that bargain came in human form, all the better. He also put Jim to use renovating his own house, on the Star's money. The project remains ongoing.

If Jimmy was slapstick, Johnny was horror. Grizzled feline horror. I don't know what crimes he committed so that most of his adult life was spent in jail. I don't want to know. Johnny was the mythical apparition lurking down a dark alleyway. The stuff of nightmares.

He and Jim were professional acquaintances who often teamed up for burgs. They'd hit ten houses a night, a strike team relieving the inner suburbs of its computers, cameras and spare cash. Quandary: when Jimmy and Johnny are planning another round of—their words—'late-night shopping' and ask your address so your own place doesn't get hit, do you: a) tell them; b) lie; or c) change the subject, then cancel all your night-time shifts for the foreseeable future?

Johnny wasn't often out of the clink, but when he was there was always a place for him at the Star's sink. First time I met him was when I sat down for staff meals next to the dish pig station. 'Taste good?' he asked with his gravelly hnar hnar snigger. 'How about I taste you?' He was sexually adaptable, too, thanks in part to his lengthy time in the pen. More than one male waiter came screaming out of the kitchen with Johnny in hot pursuit, dick in hand, bellowing, 'Get on the end of this!'

He was certainly entrepreneurial, old Johnny. He got a loan that was meant to help ex-prisoners get back on their feet and spent his few grand on a high-tech pipe cutter. Cool Hand Luke minus the cool, he generated a healthy cash flow by making off with parking meters. He managed to upgrade his shitty old Ford Falcon, too. One day he turned up in the latest model, a shiny blue number with mag wheels. He'd simply switched the plates over. Some poor sucker went outside one morning to drive his new car to work and found Johnny's beaten-up rust-bucket with their own shiny plates attached. The cheeky bastard.

Somehow Johnny got his hands on a Tazer. This was when they'd just been introduced to Australia and all the shock jocks were riding a wave of concern about them falling into the wrong hands. And there's Johnny, in the alleyway, gleefully zapping away at neighbourhood cats and rubbish bins. Hnar hnar. A week later, there's a report about a woman who had been unpacking her shopping from her car. She was Tazered and robbed. It made the nightly news. All her shopping, her handbag, her mobile phone. Not half a kilometre from the Star. What a coincidence.

Employing human specimens like Jimmy and Johnny showed that George didn't expect to completely staunch the outgoing flow of cash and goods he inherited along with the business. That was never his aim. It would have been too much like hard work, for starters, but there was also a philosophical basis to his apathy. He

JACOB

An old guy passed out in the middle of dinner. One of his sons knelt beside him while we waited for the ambos, but his wife and other kids carried on as if nothing was wrong. It was a really expensive restaurant, and they weren't going to miss out.

was no people-person but he was a practical man, and thirty years in the trade had taught him a crude relativism. He never came right out and said it, of course, but you could make an educated guess he'd lit upon roughly 5 or 10 per cent as the magical figure the business could afford to lose. The micro-manager breed of owner goes on a rampage if their business is out twenty bucks over a whole night's trade. (And that would probably be to their detriment. So much angst. They'd get a stomach ulcer. Have a coronary. Let it go.) George, on the other hand, practised the Tao of staff pilfering.

Occasionally it was brought to his attention that someone was stealing. Usually he'd simply shrug as if to say, 'And why are you telling me this? Why are you wasting my time? Do I look like I can be bothered to sit down with the accused and get to the bottom of the matter, then go looking for a replacement staff member who will no doubt rob me as well? If you need me, I'll be in the office looking at Asian porn.' It set the baseline. Too much theft is wrong but a little theft is okay. That was how it worked in his head, so that was how it should work in others' heads. But did it? Let's see.

HOW TO RIP OFF THE BOSS: A BASIC FIELD GUIDE

Let's start with some ground rules. The three golden tenets of restaurant thieving:

1. Where possible, balance the till.
2. If not possible, confuse the issue.
3. Don't go often, but when you do go, go hard.[1]

Stashing money under the till

The classic move. As old school as the Rat Pack at a Frank Sinatra concert in Vegas. Unsophisticated, risky, and the preferred method of seven in ten waiters. It's quite simple. All you do is fail to ring up drinks while keeping a mental tally of how much cash can be taken. Don't be an idiot and stash it as you go. Twenty bucks here, forty bucks there. Each time you put that cash somewhere it's not supposed to be, you're exposing yourself, so keep it to one swift hit. However. The till will be over if you get stopped in the moment. Just say someone comes in with a request for three margaritas. Off you go, mix mix mix, shake shake shake. Now where were you? Was it $80 you were up to or $100? Only do what you can keep track of mentally. Of course, if someone honest finds your stash of cash under the till, it's bye-bye. In most places, anyway. At the Star, George simply shrugged and poured himself another glass of red wine when told that one of his long-term barmen was found with an unexplained $400 under the till tray. With an attitude like that, he deserved everything he got.

---

1 It probably needs to be stated here that I never had anything to do with the illegal procurement of financial advancement from my places of employment. I am an honest person who pays her taxes, stands up for old people on public transport, and diligently separates rubbish from recycling. Working in hospitality is like being in juvie. You see stuff. You hear stuff. Doesn't mean you do stuff. Thank you.

Voids

The void is a step up from the till-stash. A table or a bunch of drinks has gone through the system as normal, but after you take payment, void the docket and pocket the cash. The problem, as ever, is explaining the void chit to a zealous manager or owner. Always have an explanation. The table ordered but then they walked out because they're allergic to Mariah Carey. They got a call to say the babysitter was on fire. You're a smarty-pants, you'll figure something out.

Credit card fraud

File under 'hardcore'. Void a docket and refund the money onto your own credit card. Worth doing once for a special occasion (Is it your dad's birthday? Buy him something nice!), but do it for long enough and the bank will eventually realise what's going on and you'll be saying hello to the boys in blue. The soft version of this method is to put your own charges on customers' credit cards—small charges they might not notice. Who checks their bank statements anyway? Maybe you ought to.

Stealing stock

Everyone steals stock. Damien never bought steak, but that didn't mean his family was iron-deficient. One Christmas break he was sprung with his car parked in the alleyway while he stuffed it with all sorts of goodies. He'd even put a roof rack on especially for the occasion. His sous chef buddy was up on the top floor, handing boxes of reserve wine down through the window. And Bill the floor manager. He'd leave each night carrying a box. Just leftovers from staff meals, he'd claim, but it would be so heavy with bottles of wine, cheese, even toothpicks and toilet paper that he'd be staggering under the weight.

Undercounting the till

There is a thing called the float. The float is a prescribed amount of money of prescribed denominations left in the till overnight for the next day's shift to pick up and start using. The big question is, will they count it again or take it on trust that what you say is there is actually there? It's a game of chicken. Bear in mind that most people are in a bad mood at the start of a shift and usually willing to take shortcuts.

The phantom bottle

A bartenders' favourite. Bring in your own bottle of spirits, serve it to customers all night, take the money. A great little earner. I've heard of a guy selling his own mineral water. In some busy bars the phantom till has even been known to make an appearance. Respect.

Stealing the till roll

I've seen this happen only once. Even before the days of digital technology (which really has taken a lot of the elegance from the game), nicking this paper roll was an occurrence of great rarity, like an albino whale, or a comet that blazes through the sky once every ninety-nine years. You can only steal the till roll once because it's a one-way proposition. A waiter named Jason had decided he was jack of the Star and he was going out in a blaze of glory that would

have his co-workers talking in wonderment for years to come.
The signs are obvious when someone's going rogue. They'll start
turning up to work five, ten, fifteen minutes late. They'll disappear
during staff meals to 'get cigarettes', which means placing a bet or
grabbing a quick pint at the pub. If this person was your partner
you'd be checking their mobile phone records, looking for lipstick
stains on their collars. Anyway, Jason swiped the entire till roll
from a hectic night's service, so there was no way of accounting
for the money. Where's the till roll, Jason? Beats me, says he with
a shrug and a grin. Clearly the till roll wasn't the only thing he
swiped. This is the moment in the film where Tom Cruise pulls
the pin from the grenade and leaps from an explosion big enough
to take out most of the San Francisco Bay area. Will you survive
similarly unscathed? Depends on the size of your cajones.

Work the suppliers

Do deals. Buy stuff at inflated prices. Plenty of chefs are familiar
with the kickback, where they get commission or gifts for
accepting lower quality produce than they (that's the owner) paid
for. There was a rumour Damien decked out his whole house with
whitegoods from the companies he was running deals with. It's a
common trick among the wine guys, too. The sommelier's job is to
get the price of wine down and pass the savings onto the business.
However, if a somm goes off the grid and makes a sweetheart deal
with a wine rep, she might officially buy the wine at $20 a bottle
when it's really $15. Let's say she decides to make it her favourite
drop, extolled to all the customers in fluent wine-speak, all grassy
minerality and excellent mid-palate weight. When it's purchased in
ten dozen lots, it starts becoming significant. What's the grateful
wine company going to do? Send an extra case to her house? Fly

her to New Zealand for a week? Or simply hand over an envelope stuffed with money? What a pleasant quandary . . .

~

And that's just the tip of the iceberg. There are as many ways to rip off the boss as there are bosses. It's important to note that while cold hard cash is nice, it's also dangerous. Maybe your sensibilities don't thrill to the possibility that your shift is going to finish under unflattering lighting at the local cop shop. It's far safer to go underground. The way owners really get screwed, little by little, every day, is the cashless economy. In other words: free stuff.

Scratch the industry's underbelly and you'll uncover a whole lovely bunch of free stuff. Everyone loves free stuff. Free stuff makes the world go round. It's not really free, of course. Not in the classic definition. Someone is paying for this stuff, and that someone is the owner. Better to see it as the spoils of war. An unofficial tax on all the shit you have to put up with, day in, day out.

There have been incidents where a restaurant's stock of vintage Champagne is found to be no more than water when a particularly thirsty sommelier departs. And how about those delivery drivers? Not only are they a specially cultivated virus that transmits the gossip of the restaurant world, they're the guys who *make* the stuff fall off the back of a truck. A free coffee and a smile go a long way when signing the invoice for the beer kegs.

What about the customers? You know some of these folk quite well. You've workshopped their divorces, their kids, their plans for real estate world domination. Say they have a beach house down the Peninsula they don't use very much these days, what with work being so busy and all. A few odd drinks, the odd free meal, isn't going to go astray. At the very least they might tip better.

Staff from other restaurants have come in? Throw them a bone! Comp their drinks, comp the whole meal if you can get away with it. It'll be paid back in kind when you make a return visit to their fine establishment. And if they don't honour their side of the deal, you can blacken their name all over town, the dirty hounds.

In the clandestine world of free stuff, all roads lead to the bar. Make no mistake: the bartender is the power behind the throne. The kingpin. He takes the money and distributes the drinks. Enough said. Due to his elevated position, the bartender sees himself as a breed apart from the garden-variety losers of the floor staff. He is indeed the very centre of a complex neurological system. He is the nerve that runs from the floor to the kitchen.

He wants to be fed. There is every chance he and the chef will have negotiated a free trade agreement. The unhindered movement of goods between kitchen and bar. This is the worst nightmare of an owner, whose interests are best served by keeping a constant, low-level warfare between the two arms of the workforce.

At the very least, the chef and the barman are looking after each other on the company dime. It's unfailingly civilised. While the waiters are sitting down to overcooked pasta and wilted salad for lunch, the barperson is being treated to a smorgasbord of delight. Here, try these oysters, fresh in today. Would you prefer them with a little red wine vinaigrette or *au naturel*? How about a rib-eye steak—I'm assuming medium-rare?—and would you like some extra pepper sauce? Why thank you, my good man.

If the chef and bartender team up and go to the dark side, they can bleed the place dry. Say the owner questions a bill for $300 that was voided. The bartender claims the table walked out. All the glossy timber was making them sneeze. The owner charges off to the kitchen to check the story for leaks. The chef dutifully denies having cooked the food. Ring-a-ding-ding.

As for the kitchen—is this not self-evident? A kitchen without a compliant barman is like a car without tyres. I've never met a kitchen that wasn't thirsty, and there are only so many times a chef can send to the bar for cooking brandy before it starts looking a little suspicious. The industrious bartender, in return for all that lovely free food, will do well to keep a constant drip-drip-drip of sneaky beverages heading in the chef's direction. It can be good to be chosen as the barman's envoy, anointed from the motley floor crew to be the glad purveyor of fine wines and top-shelf spirits. The grown-up version of the milk monitor, and the only time you're going to walk through those swing doors and be greeted with something other than hostility. It's only reflected glory, of course, but in these matters reflected glory is better than no glory at all.

— 12 —

SECOND STAR TO THE RIGHT, AND STRAIGHT ON 'TIL MORNING

There is a rather famous restaurant in Sydney that could have been tailor-made for the beautiful people. You know the beautiful people? Yes, them. Horrible phrase, really, but it does have a certain agency for describing the intersection of glossy good looks and a smug air of satisfaction. Basically it's a restaurant where people very pleased with themselves go to feel pleased in company. It does accept bookings from the non-beautiful as well—it will even deign to seat them when they turn up wearing last year's shoes—but there's just a certain tone to the place.

Of this rather famous restaurant, a reviewer wrote with impressive perspicacity: 'Everything seems glitzier, sharper and sexier here. Especially you.' Perspicacity? Well, the bartender was dealing cocaine, and it ended quite badly. Actually, I'm not sure if 'badly' is strong enough a word for a police raid in the thick of a lunchtime service. Whatever you call it, it was quite the scandal. Diners sucking down oysters while admiring each other's dental work were startled to see the bartender being led off in handcuffs by officers with a flair for drama. (Like they couldn't have waited until *after* 3 p.m.?) Chances are some customers were left kicking themselves because they hadn't already secured their weekly supply. Reading between the lines, the reviewer was, too.

Anyway, hats off to the bartender, who was carrying on quite the profitable boutique dealership until the drug squad decided to stomp on everyone's fun. It must have required sober application to carry on an underground business enterprise while remaining up to date in all the latest trends in mixology. Thrillingly, it later emerged that he had a special codeword. Those in the know would ask the waiter, who was also in on the scheme, for the 'special seasoning' or some such and a discreet little bag-o'-fun would materialise at the table.

Drugs with a valet service. It's the upwardly mobile version of the urban myth about the takeaway pizza joint that deals drugs on the side. Every adolescent's dream. I'll have the capricciosa with extra onion, a can of 7-Up and a special number 23, thanks. Delivered to your door on the back of a motorcycle. It's the very model of the convenience economy—AND you get pizza.

I suspect not a lot has changed at this rather famous restaurant despite the drug bust. Last time I was there, thoroughly depressed about the state of my hair, my shoes and my bank account, a very fashionable young woman wandered out of a toilet cubicle and stood transfixed by the hand-dryer. I went back in five minutes later, just to see if there had been any developments, and there she still was, staring at the Dyson like it contained the secrets of the universe.

There's satisfaction in knowing the beautiful people at this restaurant availing themselves of the extra service had more money than sense. Cocaine in Australia is of criminally poor quality. It has so little in common with the good stuff it doesn't even deserve the name cocaine. It's faux-caine. Buying cocaine in Australia is like buying tomatoes out of season: incredibly expensive and invariably disappointing. Plus it's usually so cut down with so much baby laxative you can easily spend your entire high sitting on the toilet. And what waiter can afford to flush away their earnings so irresponsibly?

Let's consider our alternatives. Pot? Forget it. Everyone's worked with the pothead waiter, a complete loser everyone hates because she can't hold her section together so others have to pick up the slack. Plus she's mightily stoned most of the time, so she's all like 'Just chill out about it . . . it's cool'. The only thing worse than a pothead waiter is a pothead chef. That spells doom. There was a head chef at the Duke who really liked his weed—liked it so much that he decided he couldn't get through one screamingly busy lunchtime without a whomping fat spliff smoked at the back door. Unfortunately the wind was blowing a mean westerly that day, pushing all the smoke back inside and making the restaurant smell like an Amsterdam coffee house. Diners were giving each other meaningful looks that said, 'Weren't the 60s a blast, darling, but I'm a little worried our food is going to take a very long time.' The waiters hastily cobbled together an explanation. Clearly a ruse, but something had to be done. 'The chef . . . he's grilling rosemary.'

Ecstasy? Very nice and all—not to boast or anything, but I did come of age when there was a particularly potent batch on the market known as the Mitsubishi Magna. Certainly not to be associated in any way with the Japanese car manufacturer. The Mitsubishi vehicle is a sensible, rational and fuel-economic choice. The Mitsubishi-E will blow your head off. But for work—no. It's just not a good look to be stroking a customer's hair saying, 'I love you—I really love you,' when they're just trying to order an extra bowl of fries.

Which brings me to my thesis about speed. Speed, I firmly believe, is the perfect drug for hospitality workers. Yes, I hear you. It's not exactly glamorous. Speed gets a bad rap. It keeps bad company. It's a known associate of bikies. Speed's main image problem, however, is simply that it's a working-class drug. It's for truckies and army grunts and nightshift workers. But that sums it up. It's a hard-working drug, with good value for money, and high accessibility. Any honest, non-judgemental consumer watchdog would have to give it an official tick of approval.

Speed was king at the Rising Damp. Speed kept the place humming. Speed was in the plasterwork and the floors, speed kept the dishwasher door slamming and the steaks sizzling and the shiny, happy people well-fed and watered. Sometimes it felt like you only need cut a little nick into the timber of the glossy curving bar and a fine white powder would trickle out. But maybe that was because we were doing so much of it.

The first time I did speed and experienced the unique sensation that my eyeballs were about to liquefy and leak out through my nose, the reaction was both immediate and straightforward: *Why, hello there! Where have you been all my life?*

Speed appeals to vanity. It slings a friendly arm around your neck, chucks you under the chin and bellows an endless stream of compliments. 'You're fabulous. You're witty and funny and that story about the man with the briefcase and the guide dog never gets old. And did I mention your hair looks FABULOUS in a side ponytail?' It's a good drug for any waiter who lives in a fantasyland of the future—you're waiting tables now but one day you're going to write that novel, oh yes you will . . . It also eliminates the need for food. Any employer would do well to sanction it on a time-management basis alone.

Speed doesn't have that bone-melting dopamine release of MDMA but it does give you boundless energy. It makes the most mundane, onerous task a joy to complete. Done drug-free, pack-down at the Star was a pain in the arse. Just imagine: you've pulled an eight-hour shift and finally booted out the last customers, your feet are so sore it's as if each metatarsal is a separate and distinct source of pain, and the bar still has to be soaped down, the fridges restocked, the chairs stacked and a dozen other skuzzy jobs completed before you can sit at the bar and talk crap with your colleagues.

But what's that? Warren has just had a special delivery.

Let me tell you about Warren. Barman Waz. Wazza to his friends. A head like a Pez dispenser, a nose designed for the snorting of illicit powders, a voice like a drill. Whippet-thin, with a soft spot for the popular culture of the 1980s and—in unrelated yet pertinent information—rotting teeth. A common waiter affliction. All that syrupy-sweet Post Mix is the mortal enemy of dental work.

Wazza's the one who dubbed the congealing pizza we always got for staff meals 'shit on toast'. Wazza's the one with the trademark clap-and-spin dance move. Wazza's the one who nostalgically championed the lesser-known Australian bands of the new-wave movement: Kids in the Kitchen and Pseudo Echo over The Church and Divinyls. A true fan of the underdog.

Wazza was a fashion savant. He could tell you what he wore on any occasion in the previous twenty years. '1992. I'm at Livid festival. I've got on my red and blue flannie, my desert boots and a really cool dragon T-shirt I found at the tram stop.' Or: '1988. House night at Warehouse. I've just gotten my new black Levis and a Champion sweatshirt. It was green. God I loved that sweatshirt.'

Waz wasn't so much the Star's drug dealer as its drug facilitator. It was more of a support and advice role than hardcore pushing. Sure, he could get the gear, pretty reliably, but he didn't have some big enterprise going behind the bar. Waz was the difference between being a large, publicly listed company and a small, mom-and-pop corner shop operation. He was the friendly face of the drug trade. A dealer you could trust. His product was of a decent quality and his mark-ups were fair.

Pretty much anywhere you go in the world, Thursday night is hospitality party night. So is Monday. Monday is the hospo equivalent of a Sunday. But Thursday for some reason is THE night, when everyone piles out after work to other venues where other workers are grinding through a shift until they, too, can join the fray.

Supply could get erratic on other nights but everyone made sure to keep some stash for Thursdays. Waz, too. He enjoyed the glory. He loved being Da Man. He'd give the signal sometime around the last customers dribbling out into the night and we'd take it in turns to sneak out back to the fat caterpillar lines he'd chopped up on the ice machine. Taking a burning snozzful of speed was like being whacked over the head with a magic wand. It's the moment when things shift from the grey bleakness of a Kansas tornado season to a fantasy of Oz technicolour. All of a sudden you've got five self-motivated workers having a whale of a time, blasting Wazza's cherished *Absolutely '80s* collection. Dirty bar? Bring it on! It's like we've gone inside the ad for the amazing new household cleaning product where a happy housewife gets her jollies fighting kitchen bacteria. Blam! Bam! Pow! Take that, germs. My turn for the Windex. No, mine! It's so much fun you're actively looking for things to clean. Even Waz, normally the laziest guy in the world, was once found out the back madly soaping down the door to the coolroom. That was a particularly potent batch, though.

Wazza's girlfriend Cara was getting legally prescribed speed for her weight problem. What better excuse to rail against society's hypocritical attitude towards things that make you feel good? He was so thin he'd disappear if he stood sideways and Cara could have had the initials HMS before her name. If she'd accidentally sat on him he could have been lost in her butt crack for weeks. There was every chance that one day she'd deliberately sit on him, too. They fought a lot. Hated each other, really, but stayed together for the kids. But he loved it when she was back on the diet pills. It didn't make her any less angry but it meant they got to fight in a house that sparkled.

❦

I don't exactly regret the time I spent doing drugs. I'm not exactly proud of it either, but being embarrassed about it would be like being embarrassed about the whole summer I spent fanatically watching re-runs of *The Sullivans*, or that weird sexual fantasy thing about Mr Humphries from *Are You Being Served* when I was in Year 2, or the time I tried to teach the dog to talk. It's just something that happened.

And it's fun. It's fun to the nth degree. It's fun-squared. It's about as much fun as you can have with your clothes on, although the one time I took acid I became convinced I was naked and

POLLY

It wasn't unusual to do four or five straight double shifts at this place. It was really tough, but at least the owner knew he pushed us with the hours. To keep us going he'd rack up brilliant cocaine in the cellar. He'd take us downstairs individually, give us a glass of Champagne, a line and about five minutes to catch our breath. It certainly kept me going.

had to keep looking down every few seconds to check I was still wearing pants. That was weird.

That's why all the lectures about drugs don't work. They ignore the central truth that any kid with a bag of powder and a rolled-up twenty-dollar note will quickly realise. Things like:

Why do people get wasted and decide it's a good idea to measure their necks in units prescribed by a standard Bic lighter and then plot the results on graph paper?

Because it's FUN.

Why do people get wasted and wave a water bottle at a disco ball for six hours straight while listening to music that sequences the same thirty-second electronic coda at 140 beats per minute?

Because it's FUN.

Why do people get wasted and decide it's hilarious to talk in a Jerry Lewis voice for two hours while repeating the phrase 'My good sir'?

Because it's FUN.

What the anti-drug lobby needs to do is film two heavily wasted people talking like Jerry Lewis while thinking they're cresting a new wave in comedy. That would be more effective than a poster of a mournful meth-head with weeping face sores. Or they could use the shoes my friend Martha bought on the way home one morning after a big, club-banging night. Rubber, multicoloured things like flotation devices or offcuts from *The Muppet Show*. Expensive, too. We still look at them and shake our heads in wonder. Was rave culture really that devoid of taste? They ought to be photographed and put on a poster: These Are Your Shoes On Drugs.

But you know what? Young people are ridiculously supple. They're supple of body, they're supple of mind, and they can withstand pushing the boundaries a little. To make myself feel better about having joined the sad class of the middle-aged (young middle-aged, I hasten to add—positively infantile) I've found solace in aphorisms. For example: nobody ever said anything important after midnight. Lately I've revised it to 10 p.m. Maybe 10.30 p.m. if it's a weekend. It's easy to get cranky thinking about all the time I wasted in the stupid belief it was an infinite resource. If I could have it back I'd be fluent in Spanish, have read the whole seven volumes of Marcel Proust's *Remembrance of Things Past*, and be a master in the ancient art of kalaripayattu. But the truth is that any young person who doesn't live a little—I'm simply talking about being open and responsive to the absurdity of the world, in whatever form that might take—is wasting valuable time because one day they're going to wake up and find they've crossed the Rubicon. My moment was when I got prescription sunglasses. That's when it finally hit me as real, concrete certainty rather than abstract notion: I, too, will die one day.

If I got a call tonight to say Mick Jagger was dancing at Honkytonks and to come RIGHT NOW I would probably invent some excuse. Thanks very much, but I was out dancing with him last night. Or, I've just been kidnapped by Uyghur separatists. In the coin-toss between Jagger and sleep, nine times out of ten I'd take sleep.

But back then, there was no mortgage, there were no kids, there were no responsibilities (or not ones that couldn't wait until tomorrow, or the day after, or the day after that), there was no left knee that went slightly dinky whenever a step was higher than recommended by Standards Australia. Jagger—LET ME AT HIM.

It is for the benefit of mankind that Honkytonks no longer exists. A dive-club with turntables in a white baby grand and a relaxed attitude towards its patrons' choice of refreshment, it was a big gaping maw that exploded the known space–time continuum. It swallowed whole weeks, whole years. It was said that some clubbers never went home, just eked out an existence on the mouldy old couches waiting for the next DJ to come on. There was a separate DJ in the women's toilets. The only way to get to the basins was to assume a defensive position through an obstacle course of flailing limbs. Mick Jagger, being at the time a very sexed-up sexagenerian, had hit Honkytonks with his entourage, and hit it hard. By the time we arrived he was surrounded by a female whirlwind all hell-bent on getting their piece of rock'n'roll history. Women were twerking[2] their arses off to get the great man's attention and through the force-field of kinetic energy you could occasionally get a glimpse of a big grinning pair of lips with a skinny scrap of a human being attached. One of those sights a person could never forget—like sunrise over the Serengeti, or the Aurora Borealis.

The way it ended was utterly, pleasingly, textbook rockstar. His bodyguards tapped maybe a dozen of the most attractive women on the shoulder and invited them to a 'private party' back

---

2 Twerking: a US-originated urban dance that symbolically presents the female partner as eager for sexual penetration via a reverse-entry method.

GERALD

There was a small room next to the cellar where two
of the chefs set up bucket bongs to visit through
service. I'm not a smoker of pot but I'd always chat
to them while they were indulging—the portions
were always larger after they had tucked in.

at Jagger's hotel. You might have expected them to sabotage each
other's stilettos with deftly timed kicks and gouge exposed flesh
with painted talons. But no. There was a palpable camaraderie
among this fragrant bunch of chosen ones. They danced off
together up the alleyway, a joyful band of merrymakers, to claim
their brief share of a charmed life.

～

The waiter's conundrum. At work: exhausted. Go home: wide
awake.

There must be some kind of medical explanation for it. Inertia
of the mind. You focus hard on the same activity for eight hours,
it's impossible to take a sharp left once you get home and go
straight to sleep. You can't just turn off the light, reach for blankie
and be miraculously rendered unconscious.

That's why the post-work debrief is an important psychological
process. Skip the knock-off drink and you risk winding up with
acute post-service stress disorder. It's not unlike getting plaque off
your teeth. Scraping off the mental gunge increases the chances
of sleep.

Even if you do manage to drop off easily, there are the dreams. The bloody service dreams. Like the one where the coffee orders are piling up and there are a thousand angry caffeine-deprived people waiting for their soy lattes and you're working that machine like a crazy person but it's not enough to placate the restive mob. After a nightshift Ben and I would lie next to each other in this twitching, tortured fog of half-sleep, saying sweet things like 'BUGGER OFF TO YOUR OWN SIDE OF THE BED. AND STOP KICKING ME. I MEAN IT!' We still sleep with a line of pillows jammed between us—a sad hangover from the days when it was used to block flailing limbs while a zombie army of caffeine addicts marched on us in our sleep.

Professional athletes have all the luck. To get off the adrenalin high of performance, footballers and swimmers have powerful sleeping drugs shoved down their throats by medical professionals. Socially sanctioned drug taking—cruelly reserved, as are so many things, for the warrior caste. It's completely unfair. A busy restaurant service is an endurance sport. It's Olympic racewalking with plates. The body hurts in joints, muscles and crevices. It aches in places it didn't know it had. The soles of the feet feel as though they've been subjected to ten strikes of the rattan cane for some minor littering misdemeanour in Singapore. Stick to it long enough and eventually you will find yourself googling 'varicose veins + operation'. You will say something unintelligible like 'oof' each time you get off the couch because of your sore lower back.

Yet there is no ticker-tape parade, no breathless commentary. ('Just look at the way Dubecki sidestepped that toddler while carrying two fish and chips and one soup of the day—I've got no words other than *magic*!') There is no post-race rub-down (unless you're very lucky) and no accredited doctor waiting with a few magic pills. Waiters are forced into the shifty arms of self-medication. There's always booze, which helps you slow down post-shift but increases the chances of going out. Or the more pathetic dabblings in over-the-counter pharmaceuticals. In any waiter's medicine cabinet you are guaranteed to find several packets of day-and-night cold and flu tablets with only blank spaces where the mildly sedating night ones used to be, each absence a whispered prayer that tonight, somehow, be different.

I still have a dream every month or so where I'm failing university. A classic, unimaginative anxiety dream. Whatever weird sub-plots my brain decides to add to spice things up—sometimes I'm being chased by a tiger in the library's folio section, sometimes there's a ski run in the student union—it's always grounded in the same narrative: it's the end of semester and I suddenly realise with a sick thunk of dread that I haven't attended a single lecture. Waking up is always one of those moments flooded with relief. Thank god, I feel like sobbing. Thank god those days are over.

Living with that feeling as a day-to-day reality rather than a dream directed by Cecil B. DeMille exacts a psychic toll—hence the mental vomit that still bubbles up from time to time. Not enough of a psychic toll to elicit a brisk 'Right! Time to make a few changes around here!' That would be *waaaay* too optimistic. After pulling a double shift, getting to that exciting 10 a.m. lecture about constitutional law seems as far-fetched as sprouting wings overnight and flying to university instead of catching the tram. Even when hitting the snooze button, however, the dull understanding that life has gotten dangerously out of whack inhabits the room like a small flatulent dog.

Here's a typical shift from those days, set to the jaunty yet whimsical theme song from *Cheers* and arranged in a montage from a riotous sit-com about a young woman pretending to be a university student while she sabotages her future for a devil-may-care existence limping from paycheck to paycheck:

Arrive at work a little shaky—nothing serious, just a few heart palpitations—after working the night before. Drink first coffee. You've been saving yourself all day for this baby, hoping to time that first caffeine hit for maximum impact (the only instance in the last couple of days you could call yourself a model of restraint). Unfortunately it doesn't have the desired effect. Gulp a second coffee. Hmm. Might need something a little more. Maybe a couple of Red Bull chasers, just to really get the engine pumping. Ooh, that's the ticket. But what the hell is that banging sound? Oh, only my pulse. Might need to eat something. Head out the back and scavenge some cold chips left over from staff lunch. Hey waddya know—cold chips aren't so bad. Might add some more salt, though. Wash them down with Post Mix lemonade. Hang in there—it's nearly time for the first vodka tonic, disguised as soda water. The trick is to get mildly tipsy, just a warm tingle without getting all sloppy. Still a couple of hours on the feet ahead. No point getting tired.

'Have a Jagey,' I can hear Wazza say in his chipper twang, the Australian answer to Cockney. Jagermeister. Horrible stuff. It took me a long while to learn there's actually no such thing as a digestif. It's just more alcohol. Even now when I'm a few sheets to the wind the instinct is to turn in the direction of a German spirit that tastes like road tar melted down with fifty-six herbs and spices.

I don't know if it will digestif anything but Jagermeister will give you a little buzz. A mini-buzz. Nothing more. Being properly high at work is tempting, but not such a good idea. Even less so if you're a chef. Let's take time out to pause for a salutary tale.

There was a chef at the Star named Brad. Brad liked his speed. Not just a dabbler—Brad was an authentic, A-grade certified speed freak, going for Winter Olympic snowfield gold. He was either all up or all down but a psycho either way. So one day Brad is all juiced up, bug-eyed and chat chat chat and madly chopping a huge pile of onions and—crunch—off goes the top of his finger. A classic chef injury. The top joint of the left-hand middle finger amputated clean through on the diagonal. Any chef who's distracted or going too fast is at risk of joining the club, and old Brad was slicing those onions like a madman. Why? Because he was a madman. So there's blood spewing everywhere, Brad's yelping, they wrap his injured hand in a tea towel and one of his chef buddies bundles him to the doctor down the street. Brad comes back half an hour later, slightly whiter than before, his hand swathed in bandages and uttering the dread words 'Where's my finger?' He's been told to pack the half-digit in ice and take it to the hospital to have it sewn back on. By that time the finger was in the bin. George had heard what happened, came down to the kitchen cursing his head off, and swept the onions, blood and finger into the bin in disgust. Another poor chef had to go sifting through it all for the mangled little stump. The upshot is, Brad gets it stitched back on and three weeks off work to recuperate. George's pissed because it means he has to pay him sick leave. Brad thinks he's the luckiest bastard in the world, pops into the kitchen occasionally to wave his bandaged hand about like a trophy and gloat about how it's all PlayStation and speed, on the company dime. He finally comes back to work, off his head as usual, and within half an hour he does it again. Clean through, in exactly the same spot. There was no point trying to save it this time. The wound was already a needy little blackened stump clinging limply to its reattached blood supply and it was beyond the ken of medical science to make it regenerate twice. He lost his job, too. No way was George going to pay him for another three weeks of amphetamines and PlayStation. 'Fucking idiot, no fucking way I'm paying that fucking cunt.' That was the last we saw of Brad.

Maybe the Brads of this world are a sign. Wrong Way—Go Back. Because one day it doesn't look so enjoyable anymore. The morning's painkiller-guzzling contrition doesn't make up for the night's idiot adventures. You realise with a flicker of shame that Jerry Lewis wasn't really that funny first time around. You realise speed has sipped on your adrenal glands until they're dusty and expired, little puffs ready to blow away in a light breeze. The visitations are getting worse, too. Those monkeys in the peripheral vision whenever you're tired are just plain freaky.

Tonight, you tell yourself in the don't-mess-with-me voice of your primary school teacher Mrs Palmer, tonight it's straight home, a cup of SleepyTime herbal tea and bed. You will wake refreshed after your medically recommended eight hours' sleep and greet the day with a yogic sun salutation before heading off to pilates and the farmers' market.

But then the dealer turns up on his moped. Mopeds are the vehicle of choice for any middle-class purveyor of proscribed drugs. They think it differentiates them from the blue-collar dealers, who are self-evidently scum. He was just swinging past, he says with a sly smile that shows his evenly spaced teeth, thought he'd pop in to say g'day. Wazza disappears with him to conduct business in the alleyway and comes back looking sprightly and refreshed when only five minutes ago he was quiet and despondent after another fight with Cara. There's a glint in his eye as he hops around behind the bar doing his Michael Hutchence impersonation while mouthing the words WANT SOME?

The air crackles with the tension of a young woman deciding between tomorrow's lecture about the Torrens Land System and a well-deserved pick-me-up after a hard shift.

Okay then, just a dabble.

And somehow—inevitably, groans the audience—all of a sudden it's five hours later and she's sitting in a dark club with sticky carpet, nursing a seventh beer while discussing the problems of the world in depth. '1984,' Wazza's saying. 'I'm at Chevron. I'm in my eight-up Doc Martens, my ripped Levi 501s and a black singlet top . . .'

~

Even if you're not lending your nose to the scientific study of harsh acids on mucous membranes, hospitality is an unhealthy industry.

Take Bubbles. This is a man who only imbibed fluids if they were espresso coffee or red wine—he preferred a heavy, teeth-staining cabernet—and only swallowed calories if they were steak. I once saw him bite into an apple. He reeled back in surprise as if an exotic parrot had just materialised in his hand, looked from the apple to me, raised his eyebrows as if to say, 'Interesting . . . so this is what a so-called *fruit* tastes like,' and threw it in the bin. His gallstones played up each year. It was an annual event, like Christmas or the grand final. One year the pain was so bad he wound up in the emergency department, running head-first at the wall trying to knock himself out. Did the experience make him increase his fibre intake? No, it did not.

There were other casualties. Sadder ones. The ghost of Nancy Reagan flits through with a Just Say No poster.

My old boss Ari from the Sabatini used to work in a video store. He told me that a surprising number of times he'd call up the really late returns only to be told the person had died. I think I mentioned Ari wasn't that smart. There was a good chance he was speaking to the allegedly deceased person who was simply trying to get out of paying late fines. But the same thing started to happen at the Sabatini, only for real. First to go was Anthony, a devilishly handsome waiter whose slightly turned-down eyes made him look like a friendly koala. Anthony was late for work one day, Ari called his house, Anthony's mum trotted off to see if he was in his room, then all Ari heard down the line was screaming. Nothing suspicious, the autopsy showed. Apparently it is possible for a 25-year-old to die of natural causes in their sleep. Another good reason to avoid sleep.

Next to go was Mick. Drink-driving accident. This was the point when Ari stopped calling when a waiter was late, and started just hoping they'd eventually turn up.

Then James. My dish pig crush. A delightful wastrel of a boy in love with wordplay, the comedic possibilities of the Germanic umlaut, and drugs. In a kitchen where 'fuck you, motherfucker' passed for an interesting use of language, he would throw in something like, 'Did you know the name for a llama birth is an unpacking?' James showed that going to the 'right' school doesn't always mean a return on investment.

His dad came in to eat one night. I served his table: a grey-haired lawyer with three of his grey-haired lawyer buddies. When it was time for dessert James had decorated a cake with 'I love my Pa' written in swirling chocolate letters. It could have been a cruel piss-take—James's rebellious streak would have caused his parents grief from the moment he learned to throw toys out of his pram—but there was an eye-shining sincerity when he took it out. There was plenty of water under this father–son bridge but his dad was chuffed.

James was a sweet kid who worked like wildfire. If he'd grown up he would have been a thoroughly decent human being, but he didn't get to grow up because a couple of weeks later he was found dead on his share-house brown modular couch. His housemates hadn't noticed he stopped breathing until hours after they'd all fixed up together, when his skin was cold and his mouth blue.

And then the Star. A barman called Gabriel. A good Italian boy, an aspiring photographer who didn't really take photos but like plenty of guys in their twenties wanted to define himself as an artist. He was initially into speed but then upscaled it into a taste for heroin.

Gabriel got the blame for a lot of stuff that wasn't his fault. Bill, the waiter who stole everything that wasn't nailed down, took two bottles of reserve wine and let Gabriel take the rap. He chose his victim well. Gabriel was one of those people who could deny accusations until he was blue in the face but no one ever believed him.

Gabriel didn't steal the wine, but he was nicking from the till to fund his habit. Another case brought to George's attention where he just shrugged his 'So what?' shrug. Gabriel went into rehab once and came out and picked up pretty much where he left off. His parents were beside themselves. They used to drop him off at work and pick him up straight afterwards to stop him heading into the city to score. They took his paycheck, too, but he sidestepped that one easily enough. He'd take off mid-shift saying he was just going to the toilet, then reappear forty minutes later with blitzed pupils. He overdosed once, which gave him enough of a fright to rethink his activities. For a couple of days following the Narcan shot that jerked him back to life, he told me the world had shimmered with beauty. 'Everything looked so amazing. If I could feel that way all the time then I won't need drugs. I have to learn how to hold onto it.'

As it turned out, Gabriel couldn't hold on. His golden glow and the fear of death lurking underneath it saw him through a couple of drug-free weeks before abandoning him with no forwarding address. Back to Russell Street and the arcade where his skinny dealer lurked inside the pinball clang of the games parlours.

George didn't even bother showing up at the funeral, a gut-wrenching Catholic service with wailing Italians and the coffin decked out in Carlton Football Club colours. Even though he'd known what was going on and did nothing to try and stop it. But it wasn't his fault. It wasn't anyone's fault. That was more than fifteen years ago now. Sometimes I can't even recall his name without pausing to think. Gabriel. His name was Gabriel. It takes a few seconds before it comes back. One day I know it's not going to come back at all.

— 13 —

THE GOOD, THE BAD, AND THE REALLY BLOODY UGLY

You could grapple endlessly with the idea of the good waiter, much in the way of Christians and the parable of the Good Samaritan or Scientologists and the notion of an evil galactic emperor named Xenu. I'm content to approach it in a similar fashion as a purely abstract, theological exercise. By any objective measure I was a terrible waiter. Shit-tastic, Ben once put it in a fit of kindness. Save for being exhumed at the occasional dinner party, my 'skills', such as they were, have been blessedly dormant for the past decade. In all probability I remain a terrible waiter. If one day I go stark-raving mad and decide to get into the profession again, an injunction should be sought immediately. An apprehended service order. It won't be too hard to find a judge I once served who'll look kindly on the matter.

What makes a good waiter ought to be straightforward enough. Someone who bathes daily and flosses their teeth. It's very important when reciting the daily specials not to smell like a small rodent died in your mouth. Someone with a basic grasp of social niceties. Start with hello, end with goodbye, and in between throw in a playful bit of banter—something along the lines of 'And what can I get for you today?' ought to do nicely. If you want to get really fancy, a memory capable of remembering the regulars' names, the verbal flair to make dishes sound exciting, and the self-composure to not start crying when saying, 'Certainly I'll ask the chef if he can make everything gluten-, dairy- and fructose-free.'

Someone who makes a great waiter? Now that is a far, far trickier subject. The temptation is to talk about the special intuition the best waiters seem to possess; the Jedi mind-reading skills evidenced when one appears with a glass of vermentino just as the words 'I really feel like a ver—' are leaving your mouth. (And if you were about to say 'I really feel like a verdicchio'—well, what then, hey smarty-pants wait-person?) If all else fails, grasp at the pop-cultural shibboleth known as X-factor. But this is where we cast off from the safe shores of objectivity and head out into choppy waters. To the ongoing detriment of humankind, a great waiter can only be in the eye of the beholder.

On paper at least the Rising Star's head waiter Marcello was among the greats. He had been one of the top waiters at one of the best restaurants in town, an Italian house of indulgence where the masters of the universe congregated to indulge in spaghetti neri and Barolo and left equally corpulent tips on their corporate

HENRY

A regular customer wanted to propose to his
girlfriend. He was incredibly nervous about it so
we started workshopping it four months before the
actual night. He'd call me every few weeks to talk
it through and I ended up being a pseudo-mentor
for him, feeding him lots of positive psychology:
'It's going to be okay.' So on the big night he
gave me the ring before she arrived. I put it in a
Champagne glass, but when I brought it out to the
table she didn't look at the glass, she looked at me,
perplexed as to why a glass of Champagne she
didn't order had just arrived. The guy was totally
useless. He was just sitting there without saying
anything, waiting for her to notice, so I said to her,
'Look inside the glass.' She looks in the glass, sees
the ring, and looks back at me in utter surprise.
He's still sitting there like an idiot so I had to say,
'It's not from me—it's from him!' Luckily it turned
out okay. They still send me a postcard on their
wedding anniversary each year.

credit cards. It was the kind of place where the famous chef and
the famous clientele treated each other with the manly disdain
that underlies a clubbish good humour. For example, there was
a notorious businessman who one day announced he was sick of
spaghetti neri and demanded a burger. Italians don't do burgers,
generally speaking. Or at least they didn't until burgers stormed

the barricades of world gastronomy. So the chef sent a waiter out to buy a Big Mac, which was promptly served on a white plate.

'That looks like a Big Mac to me,' said the notorious businessman.

'Yes sir,' replied the waiter, 'it is almost exactly like a Big Mac, except this one is twenty-five dollars.'

Even among this rarefied company of top-flight professional waiters, Marcello was a stand-out performer. Why? Because he got the sales. He sold more wine, more desserts, more sides than any other person there. That was the secret to Marcello, and the basis of his claim to greatness. He was a salesman first and a waiter second. He was also the only person I have ever wanted to stab in the neck within five minutes of saying 'Hello, nice to meet you'.

When I think of Marcello I immediately think of eyebrows. Wiry, bushy, crazy face-growths that acted as verandahs for his eyes and quivered with satisfaction whenever he was upselling garlic bread. Such eyebrows can define a man. Marcello was a fizzing spark of electricity expressly devoted to the pursuit of making money. Salesman first; salesman second; waiter third.

Marcello was a man who liked to put the 'me' in team. Every conversation was an opportunity to affirm his greatness—both to himself and to the world at large. To the customers it was a constant, coddling song in the key of Marcello.

'Let Marcello sort it out for you!'

'Marcello will take care of it!'

'Lucky for you Marcello is here!'

'You only need to ask-a Marcello!'

Anyone sensitive to overuse of the exclamation mark will be cringing but I assure you it's impossible to covey Marcello's syntax, and by proxy the true essence of the man, in its absence. Marcello was a walking exclamation mark (by extension that probably makes George a walking colon) who habitually talked in the third person. He pronounced his name with a resounding *Mar-cel-lo!*, three syllables rising to a sonorous inflection on the 'o' like the second coming of the Lord being hailed joyfully to the heavens. Slightly louder than his other words, too, so the emphasis was on *blah blah blah MAR-CEL-LO, blah blah*—a tactic since imitated by commercial TV networks when switching from normal programming to advertisements.

Talking in the third person is known to lower anxiety. It's been identified as a good mental trick to employ when going for a job interview. Don't say it out loud—anyone will think you're a complete douche—but inside your head change 'I' to 'Felicity' (if indeed Felicity is your name) and the feelings of self-empowerment will follow. Or so they say.

I don't know if Marcello had ever read about this and decided to banish the 'I' from his life henceforth. Marcello considered reading an effete indulgence one step removed from visiting a sauna. Education was simply time-wasting when he could be making money. 'Marcello is from the school of life!' he proudly proclaimed while puffing out his scrawny bantam rooster chest. If Marcello was anxious it was in the way of a person who dances naked at a party while setting their farts on fire and then claims to be really actually quite shy. Maybe Marcello went home after each shift and shed a quiet tear about the world's cruelty towards a short, hirsute Italian waiter who liked to wear his apron tied almost obscenely high, just under his nipple line. It's far more likely he tucked himself into bed thinking, 'Marcello good. No, Marcello great. Marcello sleep now.'

Marcello's approach to sales was simple. No grand philosophy, no Anthony Robbins seminars, no 20-point cheat sheet. Screw that namby bullshit. Marcello's success could be distilled to this one simple precept: do not take no for an answer.

If a customer says no, hear yes.

If a customer says yes, double it.

If any waiter decides to follow this professional path—and the financial rewards can be high—it's important to cultivate an air of ownership. It doesn't matter that you don't actually own the establishment in which you work. People respond to being looked after by the boss rather than the second spear-carrier on the left. I don't know why, they just do. Maybe it's a mark of their own seniority in the dining room's brutal hierarchy. Giving the impression every transaction occurred through the prism of his own generosity was a tactic Marcello practised often. Hence this scenario every time I started a shift:

Marcello: 'Larissa, Larissa, Larissa. So good to see you. So good. How about Marcello make you a coffee?'

Me: 'No thanks, Marcello.'

Marcello: 'Just a little caffe latte . . .?'

Me: 'No, thanks.'

Marcello: 'Go on, Marcello makes the BEST caffe lattes.'

Me: 'No.'

Marcello (more insistent): 'Nah, nah, a coffee, a coffee, a coffee, let Marcello, let Marcello.'

Me (sharply): 'NO.'

And so on. There is a good chance Marcello will depart this world lying on a restaurant floor with one of his co-workers standing over him in a daze, bloody knife in hand, saying, 'I really don't know what came over me, officer. One minute he was saying Marcello insists on making me a coffee, the next I just snapped.'

Bill was another good, potentially great waiter with fruitful insight into the illusion of ownership. A man-mountain with the friendly manner of a golden retriever and ankles that swelled alarmingly so that by the end of each shift he was shuffling around painfully with his shoelaces undone, Bill shouldn't have been waiting tables. He was too old, he was too fat, but he flogged computers during the day and worked at the restaurant at night to get back on his feet after his own restaurant went under. Sad story redux. It was a well-reviewed restaurant. It was popular with the big-spending business crowd. But it was on a strip that had the misfortune to become the epicentre of Melbourne's latest heroin epidemic. You can insure against fire, you can insure against theft, but you can't insure against tabloid headlines screaming 'Street of Shame'. Bye-bye business.

We all quietly sympathised with Bill at the beginning, imagining that his ego was finding it hard to let go the glow of being *el patron*, but it turned out there were other reasons customers bailed us up to quietly inquire: 'That large waiter . . . is he the owner?' Bill was the only other staff member at the Star who could have rivalled Marcello, but he had gone to the dark side. Probably a problem gambler, possibly a kleptomaniac, Bill was well and truly on the make. He called from Queensland with a story about having his wallet stolen and all his holiday money with it and could we lend him a few thousand until he got back? Live and learn. Eventually he graduated from begging other staff for loans that got paid back at twenty bucks a week if you made a really big deal of it and started sharking the customers. Hence the 'Is he the owner?' questions from regulars who were surprised that the owner of such a crazy-busy place would ask to borrow a few hundred dollars, but who were also strangely willing to lend money to the owner of such a crazy-busy place. It sounds implausible, but like all champion hucksters Bill was so good he left a trail of people insisting, 'But he was so *believable*.' His run of bad luck was legendary. Stolen wallets, kids' medical bills, broken-down cars. He swiped the tips a few times, too. And he was sprung putting his footy tips in on a Monday. The Eye of God had picked eight winners. Amazing.

Bill broke the cardinal rule that you don't steal from people with less than you. He had a nice house in a nice suburb, a bunch of kids in private school and a wife who liked to tell people at dinner parties, 'I could have done a lot better than him.' They deserved each other, really, but the thing was he was an okay guy when he wasn't hitting people up for money. That possum population explosion in leafy Barton Square? Everyone assumed it was the hippies but it was actually Bill feeding them leftover bread. All that Star ciabatta kept the possums breeding like rabbits.

Marcello, on the other hand, liked to keep things above board. Mostly. When he and Bill teamed up, it was like the Keystone Cops with aprons. The Star's two crack waiters were overheard one day telling diners they couldn't sit in their section because it had just been sprayed for cockroaches. The lazy buggers. But Marcello didn't steal from his workmates, and that is one thing in his favour, although he did think it was okay to steal from the Salvation Army. A bag of ties left outside an op-shop. To Marcello it was manna from heaven, a piece of remarkable good fortune unencumbered by any of the pesky sensitivities that might attach to taking something intended for charity. 'They were just there . . . no one wanted them,' he said in his defence. Maybe. They were hideous things. Brightly coloured polyester. He wore a different one every day, each more aesthetically volatile than the last. The Salvos visited the Star to shake their tin just before Christmas and Wazza claimed revenge on their behalf by handing over Marcello's nightly tips. In place of the fifty dollars he was expecting, Marcello found a note in the tip jar saying, 'The Salvation Army thanks you for your kind donation. Your soul has been cleansed.'

That was the only way to get at Marcello. Through his wallet. He pretended not to care but the loss of that money burned deep in his wretched little soul. To say that Marcello was tight is like saying the sun is hot, or water is wet. Sometimes it seemed self-evident that he was a few slices short of the family pizza, but Marcello was in fact a fully fledged, bona fide multi-millionaire. What kind of guy owns a dozen rental properties and still drives a beaten-up old Barina he bought for five hundred bucks? An old shit-box you could hear coming from half a kilometre away, the dodgy muffler scraping over every speed bump. When it finally died he replaced it with another one exactly the same. He came in beaming one day when a young woman accidentally nudged his fine piece of motoring history in a carpark. The poor lass found herself paying him more than he'd paid for the actual car, all over a dent pre-dating religion that he made out she'd caused. Staged a massive scene and everything. What an arsehole.

Marcello broke all the laws of waiterly greatness. He had no concept of discretion. He didn't possess the purported psychic abilities of Uri Geller. He was not the kind of waiter who was magically there when the customers needed him, absent when they didn't. Yet Marcello was one of the greats because of his immeasurable sense of self-belief. His zero understanding of how to read people worked crudely in his favour.

He upsold his skinny arse off, but for every customer who found themselves paying twenty dollars more than they intended for wine, he actively repelled another. That's what any spreadsheet breakdown of sales per head of staff fails to take into account— that some of those people would never come back while that snivelling Italian guy with the nipple-high apron was there.

There was a woman who liked to come in for an afternoon glass of wine. She was well-dressed, educated, classy, and it was obvious to every person working there that she wanted to be left alone to drink her riesling and read her book. Except Marcello. He thought any female sitting alone 'Sad . . . so sad' and decided she was overdue for the Marcello charm offensive. After he finally backed off she beckoned me over. She spoke slowly and evenly. Politely, even, considering the words coming out of her mouth. 'Keep him. The fuck. Away from me.'

I hear you, lady. I despised the customers who fell for Marcello's crap and left him a big tip so he danced around like a crack-smoking capuchin monkey, waving the money in the air and singing 'Marcello is the greatest'. He had an impressive following of devoted fans. Older men tended to like him, because he was so deferential. Groups of businessmen, who enjoyed the sensation of their balls being licked. Plenty of women, I'm ashamed to say on behalf of my sex, loved the flattery. Sad . . . so sad.

The whole ersatz Italian thing worked for Marcello. The food world is in thrall to authenticity, and waiters like Marcello are canny enough to serve it up steaming on a platter. *Ciao bella, grazie mille signorina, bene, bene.* Marcello was as Italian as it was possible to be yet he'd never been to Italy. He'd never been outside of Australia. He would have choked to death coughing up the money. The furthest he got was one of those islands off the coast of Queensland where he took his wife on their honeymoon and spent the whole time complaining about how much everything cost. To save money they ate sandwiches in their room every meal, except for the free breakfast buffet, which he attempted to eat clean before pilfering sausages for lunch.

We later found out—through George, no less, who'd grown up with him—that as a young man Marcello had reinvented himself as Donny and been a super-stud with the ladies. Hard to fathom when looking at this cock-a-hoop village idiot, but people often hold onto the haircut from the age they felt the most attractive—it's the tonsorial equivalent of hitting the pause button—and Marcello/Donny sported an extravagant centre-parted 1970s mop that spoke of a John Travolta-esque, disco-dancing past. It was disturbingly easy to imagine his don't-take-no-for-an-answer waiter skills being honed on a succession of neighbourhood girls. Let Donny put his hand—there.

It's no accident that so many waiters are unemployed actors. Waiters outrageously play up their accents, if they're lucky enough to have one. I once had a French waiter charmingly tell me, '*If you wear ze time, ze time wears you*,' (translation: If you wear a watch you're too conscious of the passing of time . . . I think) only to later overhear him talking in the kitchen about some bird he'd rooted. Waiters are full of it. They talk about their time living in Mexico when they went on a package holiday to Cancún for two weeks. But customers love it. Authentic waiters! Authentic food!

Marcello's florid Italian-isms aided and abetted his evil brand of suggestive selling. A sober and dispassionate 'Would you like some sides—maybe a bruschetta?' is just plain uninspiring compared to the carnival of fun into which Marcello turned it. Just try to imagine the thick-accented flourish of 'Let a-Marcello take care of some sides for you. Some a-bruschetta, a bewdiful rocket and pear salad.' Five times out of ten, or two times out of four, the people at that table would sit there thinking, 'Who is this pleasant chap who has taken it upon himself to bring us some delicious-sounding sides for free? It must be that wonderfully traditional Italian notion of hospitality.' Then of course they'd get the bill and be either so drunk they didn't notice (Marcello was

KATHY

A woman vomited into a glass and handed it to me.

equally good at upselling wine) or too embarrassed to mention a misunderstanding they blamed on themselves.

Another lesson: the customer is always wrong.

Oh Marcello. Marcello, Marcello, Marcello. King of the dining room. Scourge of the Star. The enemy of all that is right and decent in this world. Marcello, who when asked 'Why do you always talk about yourself in the third person, Marcello?', responded as if his grandmother, mother, aunts, sisters and all ancillary female relations had just been accused of prostitution. 'Marcello is not number THREE! Marcello is number ONE!' he screamed, his mop of grey hair quivering like a rabid squirrel trying to fight its way out of a bush. He stormed off to the kitchen, roaring his new mantra: 'NUMBER ONE! NUMBER ONE! NUMBER ONE!'

Can you name a celebrity waiter? Bet you can't. If you can, you're in the industry. That's different. Every industry has its celebrities. The waste disposal caper will have some crack garbologist whose peers are in awe of the way he sorts rubbish from recycling and can tell PET plastic from polypropylene at twenty paces. It just doesn't count if it's in-house.

If chefs really want to be the new rockstars—pause for laughter—then at the very least waiters deserve to be the new support act. But they're much further down the food chain. They're more like the roadies. The pit crew. Waitering has not become an acknowledged realm of celebrity. Chefs have appeared on *Dancing With The Stars*. Waiters have not.

Read any restaurant review. It's all Chef this and Chef that and maybe one throwaway line about the service. Waiters are the ghosts in the machine. I'm guilty, too, Your Honour. My reviews left the waiters more or less invisible. Disposable and unimportant. Mea culpa. I'm sorry. It's time to stand up and proclaim this state of affairs is unfair. Inequitable. Unjust. This terrible cult of chef-worship must shove over and make room in the bed for the waiters who have to deliver food to tables with lines like, 'This dish is a memory of Chef's childhood when he was forced down the coal mines to support his destitute parents and nine siblings. We call it carbon, pit-pony and tears. Enjoy.'

Sorry to tell you this, big chef-person in the kitchen thinking you're hot shit: consumer surveys consistently show that diners remember the service over the food. Okay, so a handful of customers are going to photograph each plate, bang on endlessly about the subtle use of vanilla with the marron and generally be stereotypical food wankers mocked by all and sundry. They're your elite, SAS-style of diner. Normal, everyday, garden-variety people just want to go out and have a nice time. They want to eat some nice food, drink some nice wine, have a nice chat with friends. Nice is the operative word for what they're looking for. They don't know more than nice. They can't define nice, they can't elaborate beyond 'It's . . . nice', but they know nice when they experience it. And they know that nice begins the minute they walk through the door. Ultimately, even if the food has been knitted from fairy wings and the restaurant is a high-concept take on Lady Gaga's bedroom as designed by Marc Newson, if the waiter is un-nice then the experience is going to be a dud.

Telling nice from naughty? I'm eternally glad that is someone else's problem. It's something even Santa can't pull off with any degree of consistency, so what chance does a normal person have? Further muddying the naughty/nice waters is the fact that it's terribly easy to be a good waiter when everything's going right. Even mediocre waiters can accidentally find themselves being good ones when the mood is right. A good service brings to mind the velvet click of expensive machinery. A bunch of people working together with one mind, like the legs on a centipede. Exhilarating stuff. When it's going bad the illusion of the cohesive whole shatters and each shard refracts a separate, mercenary individual who'd rather stick glass in their eye than pick up any slack from a co-worker in need.

The domino theory didn't exactly come to fruition in South-East Asia but you can witness it first-hand any day of the week in a busy restaurant. All you need is one piece to fall and it's game over. One section starts lagging behind, waiters begin hissing at each other, the kitchen keeps banging out food that sits forlornly under the warming lights at the pass while the chef, in a state of foaming crisis, rings the bell *ding ding ding ding*, but the violence of the tone transmits the message 'Never send to know for whom the bell tolls', or its modern iteration, 'Enter the kitchen and DIE'. Diners will learn more than they ever wanted or needed about the chef's semi-illiteracy or the bartender's boyfriend troubles when the game known as 'passing the buck' begins, and all the while the whole place falls into a state that looks more like the aftermath of a frat house party rather than a properly functioning restaurant. More and more patrons will start doing that universal little wave—the helpless hand flutter, like a bird in a cage—that means they're trying to get the waiter's attention without causing them additional grief, although if ignored for too long they'll invariably quit the nice guy act and raise the stakes to the full vigorous arm wave that means 'Get the fuck over here NOW'. A handy rule of thumb is that if you walk into a restaurant and there are more than two tables waiting to be cleared, do yourself a favour and leave. The scenario is unlikely to end happily.

If I ruled the world, restaurant owners would be encouraged to hook up prospective employees to a polygraph machine for a lengthy interrogation, or at the very least shine a bright light in their eyes while wearing military regalia. How else to judge their likelihood of being the weakest link in the chain—a passenger who'll need to be carried when the going gets tough? Hit them with the big questions. A table comes in ten minutes before closing time, what do you do? A large group wants to split the bill based on the exact measurement of wine consumed—do you let them?

Finding that truly great waiter is like finding the perfect pair of jeans or the ideal tropical holiday destination unspoiled by hordes of tourists. Forget it. It's an illusion. A beautiful illusion. Greatness comes but once a year, if you're lucky. Better to concentrate on rectifying the mistakes that even supposedly good waiters make every day. Things so commonplace they've become unremarkable, but no less annoying for it. Some of these things are so entrenched that the horse hasn't only bolted, it's taken the car and trailer with

MYFFY

I started off as a short order cook, but I'd occasionally wait tables if the restaurant was short staffed. I was, um, pretty unpolished. My favourite thing to do, and remember I was at uni at the time, was to try and make 'fuck you' and 'thank you' sound like the same thing.

it. But please, for the sake of all that's good in this world, let's give it a try.

HAVE YOU DINED WITH US BEFORE?

I was once asked this three days after the restaurant opened. (What to say? 'Yes. I'm a regular. I come here all the time.') I don't need to know how the restaurant 'works' or the 'concept' behind it. Even that Japanese soldier in the Borneo jungle unaware the war has ended probably doesn't need share plates ever explained again. Restaurants shouldn't need explanation. Any restaurant that does need explanation is a bad, over-thought, overwrought restaurant from which you should run away at speed. Just once I'd like a waiter to say 'Have you dined with us before?' and if someone at the table says 'No', hit them with: 'This is a restaurant. We serve food. You eat it.'

NOT A PROBLEM

The 'not a problem' waiter is one step up from the 'Hi, I'll be your waiter today' waiter or the table-croucher who thinks getting down to the customer's eye level will increase intimacy instead of making them feel they're getting a pep talk from Coach ahead of a really important Little Athletics meet. Why is everything not a problem? Why, indeed, *should* it be a problem when you're just doing your job? Do you think saying three words instead of one perfectly serviceable 'yes' will show you're working harder, or that you deserve a bigger tip? Or is it simply that if you say 'not a problem' enough, the entire restaurant will be appraised of the fact that you do not, in fact, have a problem?

DON'T KNOW THE ANSWER? JUST MAKE IT UP!

In some ways this is an unpleasant by-product of a bigger issue, in the way of pink slime in the meat industry, permeate in the milk industry, or travel allowance scandals in the political industry. Namely: chefs who make waiters too scared to ask questions. Alternatively, telling diners barramundi is a Japanese freshwater fish, cilantro is a smoked chilli, and avruga is premium caviar, could be a symptom of a waiter who just doesn't give a crap.

WHAT'S GOOD? EVERYTHING!

It's a big menu, you want to order well, how about a little bit of insider knowledge? Please, please, offer something. Anything. Even pointing to the big-ticket items involving foie gras and truffle would be preferable to the bland cop-out of 'Everything's good!'— although don't point me to the prawn gumbo on the specials list, which is a transparent way to get rid of last Friday's seafood.

THE MEMORY CHALLENGE

Wow. How impressive. You don't need a notepad to write down our order, you can do it all with the power of your mind. Honestly, we don't mind being interrupted another five times if you want to 'just check' a few minor facts such as whether there were three steaks or four. On second thoughts, how about you just buy a notepad? No one's going to think badly of you, and your memory game is making us a bit jumpy that our triple-cooked chips have already been forgotten.

THE STORYTELLER

I'm just going to get your drinks, then I'll come back and take your order. I'm just going to set your table now. I'm just going to set another table then I'll see how far off your mains are. I'm just going to clear your table. I'm giving you way too much running commentary when I should just shut the hell up and get on with doing my job as unobtrusively as possible.

THE OVER-SHARER

So you used to be married and you're studying to be a vet and you're really excited about your trip to Bali next month. Awesome. Let's keep the veil of mystery up, thanks all the same.

THE WAITER WHO SAYS 'BON APPÉTIT'

Are we in a restaurant in France or any French-speaking part of the world? No? Then please fuck off (*Veuillez foutre le camp*).

THE 'HOW IS EVERYTHING?' WAITER

How is everything? Well, you've just asked a fairly intangible question and it will take some time to formulate a reasoned and considered answer—if I was in a position to answer, which I'm not, considering I'm currently chewing a mouthful of food, and come to think of it I would prefer to eat my meal than engage in chit-chat with someone who simply requires me to say 'good, thanks' and would not know how to react should there be an actual complaint.

THE SNOB WAITER

Why so superior? I've come to eat in a hip pizzeria, you work in a hip pizzeria. We're in this together. So what if I occasionally like to get down and dirty with a bit of Hawaiian action? It's my culinary bit of rough, and I'm normally only a little bit ashamed, but then you go and say 'We don't do Hawaiian' with a little trill of a laugh, one of those fake operatic la-la-la's clinically proven to reduce the receiver's height by a foot and a half. 'But we do,' you say, brightening visibly, 'have a Queenslander.'

'A Queenslander? Why, what's that?'

'It has pineapple. And speck.'

~

And finally we arrive at the wine waiter. Somewhere in the distant past the evolutionary tree split off and created the great apes, humans, and a separate species known as the sommelier. A lot of people think sommeliers are scary but they're not—they're really super-fun guys and the most important person in any restaurant. Just ask them.

Okay, okay. It's a cheap shot to pick on the somm. Fish in a barrel and all that. It's not their fault that the average person treats dealing with the somm on a par with going to the dentist: delicate and expensive, but necessary if you want to keep eating at fancy restaurants.

It's a lonely job. Most people just want to get out of the transaction as quickly as possible with their dignity and credit card intact. A quick wham-bam, second cheapest bottle of wine ma'am kind of thing. I find it a bit sad that someone can study for years and years only to have people recoil when all they want to do is share the glad tidings of a cheeky Argentinian Torrontes that has the wicked snap of knicker elastic.

Sommeliers aren't sneery anymore. Some of them get more excited about those trendy low-intervention Orange wines with their sock-drawer musty strangeness than anyone reasonably ought, but they took the pole out of the backside some time ago. It's just taking the news a while to filter through. Diners remain on high alert. It's as if they suspect that if they relax too much the sommelier is going to reach over and start rummaging through their wallet. But a somm stumbling across someone who loves wine as much as they do will be overcome with joy. One of us! Someone they can talk to in their wine-speak mother tongue, all silky gamay this and fleshy shiraz that. God they love that shit. They'll keep sidling back to the wine-appreciating table like a dog that's been kicked too many times and just wants a ruffle behind the ears. Fair enough, too. Most of the time the job must feel a bit like looking down at lobsters dangling over a pot of boiling water, if lobsters could look panicked, instead of just lobstery.

Wine service is one of the most profoundly uncomfortable experiences a person can go through (see also: public speaking, death). It's a little bit like taking a car to the mechanic. You don't really want to know that the carburettor had to be cleaned and the throttle shaft replaced. You just want to know that the bloody thing was fixed, and that you weren't too badly ripped off in the process. Same goes for wine. Florid wine-speak just makes people squirm. They're feeling vulnerable. It's a performance for which they don't know the lines or the cue marks. They don't want to be laughed at for dabbling around the shallow end. They want to be affirmed that Sir or Madam has an eye for quality at a reasonable price.

Gosh it's awkward. But it needn't be. There's a story about the actress Cameron Diaz visiting St Kilda restaurant Circa, when she interrupted the sommelier's wordy introduction to an expensive French red with the immortal line 'Just give me the juice, baby'.

Talk about popping the bubble of pretence. Of course, a customer without the natural attributes of Ms Diaz mightn't be seen so much as a charming thespian as a complete philistine. But maybe it's a risk worth taking if you don't feel up to smiling appreciatively when the somm talks about a 'slightly feral but still delicious background note'. Up to you.

There was no such thing as a sommelier at the Star. Don't be daft. We did the best we could, and some knew more than others, but there was no designated higher authority to turn to when a customer had a real, actual wine question rather than automatically ordering a glass of sauvignon blanc.

Sauvignon blanc ruled the school. Sauv blanc, the grape derided as cat's piss, assuming the tasting notes for cat's piss include the words 'passionfruit popsicle'. The missing link between wine and West Coast Cooler. The grape whose inexplicable popularity caused both islands of New Zealand to be completely razed so that entire Pacific nation is now one giant vineyard squeezing out grapes destined for the easy-drinking aisle at the local bottle-o.

We had a competition at the Star to get it known as savvy b, much in the way chardonnay, the 'it' grape of the 80s, became derided as chardy. Dead easy. Within a few weeks half the neighbourhood was down with the program. 'I'll have a savvy b,' purred one local mid-week tennis lady in the way she might have uttered the phrase 'the young Paul Newman' or 'half-price Oroton'.

Behind the bar it was known, less politely, as Cougar Juice. A shameful feminist slur, but it WAS the drink of women of a certain age. And it was certainly more respectful than its other unofficial name of—I almost can't say it—Bitch Diesel.

Funny how you can't put something in your mouth these days without being judged for it. Fermented grapes—the crucible of class, taste and sophistication. A test set up so all but an exalted few are destined to fail. Once upon a time you would have been better off drinking beer, but the whole craft movement came along to scupper its status as a safe haven. There really is nowhere to run, nowhere to hide. But it's comforting to remember that like pretty much everything else in this world, grapes go in and out of fashion. Pinot gris is the new sauv blanc, which was the new chardonnay. Keep up, people. Or don't keep up, but don't let anyone make you feel bad for what you want to drink, unless it's one of those alcopops and you're over the age of nineteen, in which case you should be thoroughly ashamed of yourself.

We were armed and dangerous at the Star. Partly, although not exclusively, in case of cougar attack. The waiter's friend is a piece of hardware soon to wind up in a museum next to the cassette tape and the floppy disk but it was necessary, children, back in the days when wine bottles were stoppered with something called *corks*. Subcutaneous tree bark, of all crazy things, doing a pretty good job of keeping precious wine safe from the insult of air. Difficult to imagine, and difficult to use—I was never able to open a bottle at the table without having to jam it between my knees and lever the corkscrew while going red and quietly swearing. Not such a good look, which is one of the arguments in favour of the all-conquering screw cap. Purists resisted bitterly for a while. There were mutterings about an armed resistance movement. But when everyone realised that the Pavlovian response applied to the crick-crick of a screw cap as well as the satisfying pop of a cork, everyone relaxed and got on with the business of drinking.

Sommeliers' joke: 'It won't be corked, but it can be screwed.'

The screw cap isn't watertight. Well, it is, but it still has problems. The wine can be oxidised. It can be tainted with sulphur. But it's put to bed the once-common sight of three or four bartenders and assorted floor staff huddled urgently around a glass debating whether it suffered from cork taint. It happened quite often. An imperfect science at best. On one infamous occasion the bartender went to the table to deliver the collective wisdom: 'I'm sorry, sir, but it isn't corked.'

'You're wrong,' insisted the customer. 'I'm sure this bottle is corked.'

'Sir, it is not corked. My colleagues and I have tasted it and it's definitely not corked.'

To which he received the reply to which there is no comeback: 'It's my wine. I'm the winemaker. I promise you, it's corked.'

Homer wrote in *The Odyssey*, 'It is the wine that leads me on, the wild wine.' He also wrote, 'If you serve too many masters you'll soon suffer,' but that's beside the point. Even the ancient Greeks were busy judging each other over their wine choices. They celebrated some wine-producing regions, they laughed at others. They had their equivalent of Marlborough sauv blanc. But I wonder if Homer ever suffered the 250 per cent mark-up thanks to his wild wine list being stacked with unfamiliar drops? Fast-forward twenty millennia and every second wine list is bursting with exotic Spanish drops, Italian, South American. It's enough to bring on nostalgia for the simpler time when wine was a choice out of white burgundy and claret, but the handy by-product for the restaurant is that consumers don't have a price comparison at the local bottleshop.

It's a game of trust. Like Marcello with his beloved bloody Koona-kunga-kerchunga shiraz. He flogged the stuff with the enthusiasm of a bingo caller at the RSL. But should you believe the little Italian guy who promises the wine is so smart it could win a Nobel prize? More than a few cases had crossed his front doorstep thanks to palm-greasing wine reps. Was he really so enamoured of its heady blackcurrant and plum nose, its undertones of leather and cigar-box, or did his enthusiasm stem from the fact that he was getting free plonk?

Marcello was fired, incidentally. Even George couldn't take the endless Marcellos anymore. Plus he'd taken to drinking Koona-kunga-kerchunga from a coffee cup during work hours. His final words as he departed the Star for the last time: 'Tell George I'm never talking to him again.' Amen to that. But you can't keep a guy like Marcello down for long. He bobbed up sure enough, like a turd in a toilet bowl. Anyone buying a second-hand car in the greater Melbourne metro area, beware: 'MARCELLO IS THE NUMBER ONE CAR SALESMAN IN THE WORLD!'

— 14 —
WHAT LIES BENEATH

I used to sell clothes with a couple of girls who liked to go out to dinner with no underpants on. They came from traditional Greek families so there was really no option for getting frisky with their boyfriends at home. As for staying in a hotel—forget about it. Be sprung doing that and they would have been scrubbing floors in a convent for the next twenty years. Going pants-less was their little act of rebellion against parental control, as well as a cheap thrill to keep their frustrated menfolk dangling on the line.

'Got a date tonight,' one would chirp as we locked up the shop for the night. 'That new Italian place. No undies.'

'Better order the seafood platter then,' the other would offer sagely before they fell about laughing at the weirdness of being good Greek girls.

A full two decades later it's amazing how often I'll be sitting in a restaurant and the thought pops into my head unbidden: *Who in this room is not wearing any underpants?*

Someone ought to write a PhD on the sex life of restaurants. It's a rich yet largely ignored subject. Working title: *What's Not on the Menu: Sex and the City Restaurant*. That'd be a guaranteed grant magnet in any cultural studies department. I might write to David Attenborough and suggest it as a great subject for his next TV series. I can already hear his breathy introduction—'A fascinating anthropological study that reveals more about the secret business of the species known as *Homo sapiens* than most of us ever suspected'—over the opening montage of waiters unfurling white linen tablecloths. Restaurants are where a lot of the Big Stuff in life happens. Which is actually a bit . . . weird. Out there, in the open, private lives. People go to restaurants to pick up and to break up, and in between to hiss insults at each other when the official weekly child-free date night goes predictably wrong sometime around the second drink.

The waiter sees it all. Everything. And she probably overheard that bit about the strange rash. That was unfortunate.

I don't think I can be alone in finding restaurants kind of awkward. Even though they're my lifeblood, which means I spend a fair chunk of my work time feeling self-conscious. Maybe it goes back to that whole master–servant thing, which is bound to make any believer in an egalitarian liberal democracy a little itchy. Someone is being paid to bring me food and clear away my dirty plates and refill my wineglass and silently eavesdrop on me fighting with my beloved about which of us does more housework and whose turn it is to go to parent-teacher night.

It's odd, right? At the very least it's uncomfortable on top of undignified with a twist of embarrassing. Even when I'm making a match-winning point (example: 'vacuuming the house is worth three lots of unstacking the dishwasher') the sixth sense is calculating when the waiter has left the danger zone and open hostilities can resume. Possibly it stems from the fear of being judged by the servant. That extra dollop of humiliation on top of losing one's shit in front of strangers. Sadly the only thing I share in common with the upper classes.

So I'm uptight. Some people brazenly use restaurants as a sort of all-purpose pit-stop for relationship fine-tuning. They'll pack their dirty laundry in a big bag, lug it to the table and spend the meal pulling it out item by item, holding the stains up to the light to get a better look. There's something strange about people who don't have the basic human decency to sit quietly and whisper horrible things at each other. Downright unnatural. They'll be expecting the waiter to adjudicate, too. Apparently the service comes free with the meal. Or the meal comes free with the service. It's hard to tell. One minute you're a simple waiter, the next you're the new Dr Ruth, parachuted into a shockingly private conversation. All friendly like, though, as if you're old buddies just chewing the fat. 'He thinks it's okay to go on a surfing holiday with his mates when I haven't had a break from the kids for the past year—crazy, huh?' Or, 'She said she was going back to work when the children started school but now she sits around watching repeats of Neighbours and eating Twix—you wouldn't do that, would you?' It's couples counselling with a wood-fired pizza option.

Beware, though. It's a trap. A big, gaping, steely-jawed bear trap waiting to gouge the flesh of the unsuspecting waiter who stumbles innocently into the clearing. No good has ever come of playing intermediary between warring partners. Unless you aspire to be Dr Ruth, in which case, knock yourself out. Otherwise, assume defensive position. Avoid eye contact. Reply only in the most non-committal way, avoiding the use of all known words.

'Mmm . . . mmm' should do it. Just get out of there as fast as you can. Of course if they've been rude, you could always make like a stealth bomber and blow up the situation. That can be fun. 'No WAY would I be going away surfing—are you kidding, mister? My brother-in-law pulled a stunt like that. My sister left him. She got the house. And the car. But don't worry, he got the kids.' Alternatively, try to play it smart and side with the one who's more likely to tip. But if one person has a mascara-smeared nose and the other is fumbling for the car keys and there's a soft acid rain falling over the table, the likelihood of any tipping action is somewhere south of zero.

We saw some epic bust-ups at the Star. There was one woman who broke up with two men in a single night. She was having an affair with her boss. They're sitting all cosy together, holding hands across the table, and her husband turns up in a white-knuckled fury. She's drunk and in a fighting mood so she sweetly tells the husband to fuck off, she's leaving him. Husband storms off, woman and boss then get all heavy. You could hear him saying he wasn't ready to go for the big commitment, he thought it would just be a bit of fun and he never meant for her to leave her husband. So she gets her back up and now *they* start fighting. By the time the husband storms back in with a fake gun—we assumed it was fake but you never really know—you could tell the boss was rethinking the deal. Maybe not such a good idea to have an affair with a married employee with a psychotic husband after all. So he leaves. And the husband leaves. And she's sitting there at the table, drunk and alone and possibly unemployed to boot, wondering what the hell just happened.

Another couple came in for a meal and an unscripted moment of pure emotional catharsis when an engagement ring went flying through the air and landed with an expensive tinkle behind the bar. They left, ringless, still arguing, him running after her as she stormed down the street. No tip, of course.

They came back in the next day, arm in arm, to ask for the ring. They didn't even have the decency to look sheepish. They'd already mentally filed their huge scene as one of the adorable stories that plotted the course of an adorable relationship. The One Where She Threw the Engagement Ring. Something to laugh about in the wedding speeches. They were so in love. Simply glowing. Totally obnoxious. Just to rub salt in the wound, the guy gave this smug parting shot after we'd handed back the bling: 'Lucky for me. This thing cost me forty grand.' Every waiter in the joint winced and thought, 'Shit. Should have kept the bloody thing.'

You just don't get scenes like that in restaurants with no liquor licence. What you get is a bunch of bored-looking people thinking wistfully about the bottle waiting on the kitchen counter for them to get home. Sweet, sweet booze. Wicked, wicked booze. The reason restaurants are built on the invisible fault line between best behaviour and outrage. *In vino vitriol* and all that.

All you need to destroy the veneer of civilisation, built up layer by layer over many millennia by noble human endeavour and sacrifice, is (in my case) around four vodka tonics. Or three shots of tequila. Or three-quarters of a standard bottle of wine. Restaurants can be funny places to work because they're a lot like San Francisco. On the surface stable enough, but the next big quake could hit at any time.

As my undies-less former colleagues showed, the sex life of restaurants is mostly shadowy and subterranean. It's something you need to go looking for. Pop your head under the table. Go lurk in the toilets. Something will turn up. But every so often bad behaviour bursts to the surface in a spectacular display of such wonderful wrongness you half expect the whole restaurant to raise placards with marks out of ten. I recently saw a couple sitting at the bar of a Spanish tapas joint celebrating the end of the working week with a hand job. Too much sangria, I guess. First her hand

GENEVIEVE

I was sitting down with a supplier one day in the empty dining room and the chef, a notorious pants man, bolted in. I've never seen someone look so terrified. He was so scared he was completely oblivious to the fact he'd run out of the kitchen clutching a bunch of dried spaghetti in one hand. He ran up to me and just kept saying, 'Please help me . . . you've got to help me.' He could barely talk. He was just stammering and shaking, and all the while holding so tightly onto this bunch of spaghetti. So it turned out that he'd been having an affair with the girlfriend of the sous chef. He'd even sent the sous chef home early so he could have sex with his girlfriend—all matey, like 'Why don't you take the rest of the night off?' Evil. So the sous inevitably found out and came after him with a big knife. He really would have killed him, I have no doubt about it, if he'd managed to catch him that day. It was almost unfortunate we had to fire the sous chef instead of the head chef. It was kind of unjust, although I guess that's what happens if you pull a knife on someone.

disappears in a crotchward direction then her arm begins doing the old piston action. Better than a floorshow. He looked like he was really getting somewhere, too, until the waiter turned up with their food. It was pork, which seemed fitting.

~

The chef's change room at the Star saw its fair share of action. It was next to the functions room. A celebration, an open bar tab . . . the perfect recipe for drunk shenanigans. Two women got more than they bargained for when the entire kitchen crew burst through the door just as they were getting to third base. News of Sapphic action going on where they stored their smelly street shoes had filtered down to the chefs, so they downed tools in the middle of service and charged. The battle scene from *Braveheart* had nothing on Damien and the gang hoping to see some girl-on-girl action. It was a happy hunting ground for the bartenders, too. Waz was caught going down on some girl—I mentioned earlier he was always a very giving kind of guy—and Robbie took an unscheduled break from a twenty-first in the functions room to shag the birthday girl. No extra charge, either.

It's an unofficial part of the job to be complicit in sexual misadventures. Not as a party to them, necessarily, but—for example—a practised waiter can tell where people want to sit the minute they walk through the door. People automatically look at the table they want. Businessmen will want the biggest table, to accommodate their enormous bollocks. With couples, round tables are more popular than square. Maybe roundness suggests intimacy while sharp lines are too brisk to be romantic. People carrying on *in flagrante delicto* will want to sit somewhere secluded, naturally enough. It can be a surprise exactly who wants to be *in flagrante,* whether *delicto* or not. The most unexpected people. It's one of the follies of youth to imagine elderly people as uniformly sexless. It's unfair and untrue, but even Dr Ruth would forgive the assumption about this old gent—yes, a gent—in his uniform of grey flannel pants, blue blazer and trim white moustache. Once a week he'd eat lunch at the Duke with a woman about a decade younger, which would have made him around seventy-five. Forgive me if I describe her as a 'librarian type'—librarians are sexual deviants by and large, but it's a lazy shorthand for describing her cardigan and pearls, court heels and sensible permed 'do. A right proper gent having lunch with his lady wife, discussing the grandkids while planning their next European river cruise? Not exactly. We ran into him one night at a different restaurant. He came in with another elderly couple and a woman who looked like the Dowager Empress of India. It couldn't be, could it . . .? Oh yes. His wife.

It was a pompous restaurant but it was worth the $40 mains when he caught sight of us and turned an interesting shade of lilac. Really, what did he think was going to happen? That we were going to yell across the room: 'It was so lovely to see you and your girlfriend at the Duke the other day. She's a babe! See you next week?' Please. But he was worried, so when Ben went off to the toilet he followed. Cornered him in the corridor, jabbed his finger solidly into Ben's sternum and breathed close to his face: 'Not a word of this, boy-o. Not a word.'

He was never seen at the Duke again.

I ask my waiter mate Vicky what she would like to make a capital offence when we rule the world and can smite customers as we please.

'The mobile phones,' she replies. 'The bloody mobile phones. Every time I have a bunch of plates to put down, it's like bloody Silicon Valley. If they're so precious, why put them on the table? If I even nudge one they carry on as if I was giving their child a tribal tattoo. It's insane.'

Underpants? Not such a big deal, as it turns out. As Vicky says, 'Wear underpants, don't wear underpants . . . just so long as you're not hurting anybody.'

Waiters are a kind and understanding lot, on the whole. They don't care about the sexy times you're having underneath the table or in the chefs' change room, although they may very well try to have a perv. What they do care about is the little things that make up the flip-side of the social contract. The death by a thousand annoyances that can turn a great profession—well, apart from the drugs, the alcoholism, the health problems, the hard work, the low pay and the bad hours—into a compete shit-fight. On the subject of phones, I'm with Vicky. They're wonderful devices for uploading pictures of the food you ought to be eating instead of photographing, but they have no place sitting on the table. The table is a sniper's alley of drinks and sticky condiments and hot plates waiting to put a bullet in that expensive communications device. Putting a mobile phone on a restaurant table is like leaving a baby on train tracks.

Get drunk if you want, but be a nice drunk. And be sure to observe the line between drunk and *too* drunk. 'There was a real lush at a place I used to work,' says Vicky. 'He'd come in and basically just pass out at the table, face down. So we'd put a dirty plate and used cutlery down around him, wake him up and give him the bill.'

What else, Vic?

'Anyone who leaves their chewing gum on the plate. Or under the table. It's disgusting.'

And? 'And people who rip up coasters and leave the bits all over the table and the floor.'

And? 'And those women who order skinny lattes and chocolate cake. They're just so annoying. I always feel like shaking them and yelling, WHO DO YOU THINK YOU'RE KIDDING?'

And? 'Oh god, and those people with allergies who have to remind you every time something lands on the table that they have an allergy, just in case you forgot the five times they reminded you in the past half-hour. And they have you totally freaking out that they're going to die if they breathe in a miniscule particle of gluten or dairy or whatever floating around in the air and hold you personally responsible for it.'

And? 'And then they all go and order the cheesecake anyway. Seriously. Kill me now.'

I'm with her. Misty-eyed with nostalgia for the good old days when people either ate the food that everyone ate or politely died. How much simpler it was. A clear-cut choice that would make the modern army of the gluten-intolerant think: 'Hey, maybe pasta, bread, beer, couscous, soy sauce, tomato sauce, commercial salad dressings, some ice-creams, certain cooking oils and various imitation meats aren't such a bad option, after all?' Speaking as a concerned member of the herd, pandering to this dietary business means that we're going backwards, evolutionarily-speaking. We've opened the door to dietary failure and said 'welcome'. We've broken Darwin's fundamental rule: adapt or die. Tattoo it on your wrist, if you're not allergic to tattoo ink.

Food allergies are little more than a hobby of the bored elite, anyway. Allergies and their bastard cousin, the intolerance, cluster in wealthy areas. Poor people can't afford allergies. They have to save up to be gluten sensitive. For so many people around the world, gluten sensitivity is no more than a dream. If they work really hard, maybe their children or their children's children have a chance at gluten intolerance, but they'll have to be content with reading about how difficult it is to choose from the thousands of gluten-free products on the market and fondly imagine a life of loudly discussing flatulence and bowel irregularities like half the customers in my local health food store. Staring into a toilet bowl is the modern urban elite's answer to reading the tealeaves. Maybe they don't realise that only one in 100 people is truly allergic to gluten, which means that they'll go on and develop an auto-immune disease like Crohn's. (Darwin, incidentally, may have died from Crohn's. Vive la irony.) But a staggering one in ten Australians (and one in seven Americans) now claims to be gluten intolerant. That means that at least nine out of 100 people are either lying or stupid enough to confuse toast binge discomfort with a legitimate medical condition. Let me reassure you: feeling like a boulder has taken up residence in your stomach and all major organs have been evicted from their usual addresses to make room is perfectly normal. It's a by-product of something called 'enjoying food'. It doesn't make you special.

I really wouldn't care a jot if these people stayed home to eat their miserable cuisine of denial. Really I wouldn't. But they won't rest until they get anything less than world domination. Every time I make a restaurant booking and get asked the simpering question about dietary requirements, I'm reminded they've bent an entire industry to their will.

So here's my ten cents' worth. The rise of faux food allergies is a reaction against a culture of plenty. Until the twentieth century it was fashionable to be plump. In some ages (the voluptuously dimple-bottomed maidens of Renaissance art who 'loved their curves' in modern women's magazine parlance) and some cultures, it was fashionable to be positively obese. Being fat was a sign of wealth. Then food inconveniently goes and becomes abundant thanks to modern farming techniques and industrialised food practices, and waddya know: now it's fashionable to be thin. Gosh we're a contrary bunch. Being thin shows you have willpower (and a personal trainer, another domain of the wealthy) and that you're not one of the plebs jamming fast food down your gullet faster than you can say 'Would you like fries with that?'. Food allergists are simply following in the steps of a well-established tradition.

I feel revoltingly sorry for any real allergy sufferers. A life without pasta or cheese is a life half-lived. One can only offer sympathy to people forced through no fault of their own into the arms of mock products like cheesley (actually, I *can* believe it's not cheese, and I'm more than a bit horrified that it's also known in the trade as analogue cheese). The legitimate sufferers ought to be mounting a class action against the fraudsters who've tarnished them with the picky-eater brush. As for the new-age nostrums about respecting everyone's choices and—shudder—'lifestyles'? Well—no. I will not. Entertain your food neurosis in the privacy of your own home but please don't burden waiters with your faddishness. We are intolerant of your intolerance.

As I was telling my mate Vicky, when I become President for Life, anyone claiming 'dietaries' in a cafe or restaurant will have to produce a doctor's certificate on demand. A bit like getting a concession fare on public transport. Alternatively, they'll just have to go sort it out with the chef themselves. That'll separate the real gluten intolerants from the shammers. If you want to be a picky, annoying, sanctimonious, self-righteous, change-the-menu-just-for-me kind of a customer, be my guest: go into the kitchen for a chat. Door's that way.

∽

Being a good customer is a pretty straightforward mix of common sense and uncommonly large tipping. Actually, saying please and thank you is a good start, although that can be problematic enough. I still haven't figured out if it's polite to say thank you every time the waiter performs a task or if there's such a thing as politeness overkill. These days I prefer to save the thank you's for the big-ticket items, like ordering food and being stiffed on wine but not for things like cutlery changes and water top-ups. It was a hard decision to make but table conversation was starting to sound more like a text war. 'And then he—thank you—fell over when he was getting out of the taxi—thank you—and Kev was all like, wassup bitches—thanks—and that's when we—thank you—decided never to eat muffins—thank you—again.'

Indecision is another restaurant curse, due to the medically recognised condition known as food envy. Some diners are so terrified of comparing their meal unfavourably with their companions' that they'll keep the waiter standing tableside for five minutes while they hear everyone else's orders then change their mind two or three times before finally reverting to their original order and later regretting it. Annoying, yes, but not quite as annoying as people who forget what they ordered and leave the waiter holding hot plates and developing full-thickness burns while they argue about who ordered the veal involtini and who regrets ordering the veal involtini when the rotisserie chicken looks so much better.

While we're lining up annoying customers against the wall, let's add the soy skinny decaf latte crowd. The universal consensus is just in: why bother? See also: people who order their coffee 'hot but not too hot'. (Memo to anyone who does this: it might be a quantifiable temperature inside your head—as scientifically precise as 'spicy but not too spicy', am I correct?—but to the barista . . .

not so much.) Bill splitters who dither over who ate dessert/ordered the expensive wine/ate two more chips. Anyone who turns up just before closing time expecting a three-course meal and polite service. Menu reciters. You don't have to say, 'I'll have the pan-fried salmon with wilted spinach, cherry tomatoes and balsamic vinegar glaze.' Just 'the salmon' will do, thanks. The doggie bag crowd. Nothing wrong with the doggie bag, but try to make it count. Don't be a pain in the bum and ask to bag up one prawn, even if it's just a naked ploy for an aluminium foil swan. As for people who try to involve their server in a light-hearted argument over who's paying the bill—don't try to force a credit card or wad of money into the waiter's apron pocket like they're some sort of food-carrying stripper. Sort it out among yourselves, please.

Serial complainers. You know, the ones who always preface their complaint with 'I don't normally complain about anything, but . . .' An alarming degree of overlap with people who think things are the waiter's fault which are not the waiter's fault. Like food that's taking a long time to come out of the kitchen. Tardy food is generally not the waiter's fault. Being angry with the waiter about food that is slow to arrive is like blaming the airport newsagent for a delayed flight. Nor is it the waiter's fault that everyone loves to eat at 7 p.m. but no kitchen can handle an entire restaurant's worth of customers arriving and ordering at the same time. That might explain why you were denied a 7 p.m. booking and arrived at the unfashionably early time of 6 p.m. but there are still empty tables *at 7.30 p.m.* Outrageous. Dial triple-zero.

Everyone's an expert about food these days. The number of hours spent debating whether a steak is rare or medium-rare could solve the whole Israeli/Palestinian conflict with time left over to catch a movie afterwards. And so what if you could make the dish at home for a quarter of the price? Well, maybe you should.

When making a complaint about the food, it really does help to know your shit. There was a woman at the Star who complained the bouillabaisse was too fishy. Indeed it was somewhat fishy, because it contained fish. And prawns. And mussels and maybe even some crab. Bouillabaisse is funny like that. She also complained that the onion in the bouillabaisse was too crunchy (it was fennel). And it had taken her three-quarters of the dish to decide all this. But she won. She was a hairdresser across the road. She could have bitched to half the neighbourhood about it. So the fishy bouillabaisse was taken off the bill. And instead we bitched about her to half the neighbourhood.

∼

Contrary to all admissible evidence, people continue to think it's a good idea to take children to restaurants. These are the same people who, during the heady, hormonal optimism of their first pregnancy, will declare, 'Life isn't going to change for us—the baby will fit into our routine, not the other way around,' while all existing parents in earshot nearly pass out from smirking knowingly at each other.

They're the same people later seen at restaurants taking it in turns to do the walk-and-jig routine with a screaming infant while the other shovels food down as fast as possible so they can get the hell out of there and whose damn idea was it to come here in the first place.

Parenting is the death of cool. That's why adults tend to break into children and no-children factions. I haven't seen my childless friends since 2008. I miss them, but it's totally worth it not to hear about their lazy weekend spent doing nothing more than reading novels and binge-watching *Game of Thrones*. And I get to keep up with all their news on Facebook, anyway, where their tales of overseas holidays and spontaneous mini-breaks to sweet B&Bs in the country on blackberry-picking weekends are punctuated with lengthy complaints about unruly children at restaurants making like the brownshirts at Kristallnacht and pretty much fucking up the night for everyone.

Like Whitney Houston, I believe the children are our future. The old people certainly aren't. Yet it's been a very long time since it took a village to raise a child. Parents these days are terrifyingly alone. My childless friends should be thankful no one is knocking on their croft door at 4 a.m., asking them to look after three small children while mum goes off to milk the goats and weave some sackcloth. It would be nice if they could take some of that gratitude, and uninterrupted sleep, and roll it into a whole-village approach, if only for the highly specific instance of being in a restaurant where a wee one is busting a few moves from the brat handbook.

Because you know what, childless people? Parents can't win. The individuals criticising them for letting their kids run wild in restaurants will be the same ones going tsk-tsk at kids in front of an iPad, brought out by the desperate parents to get their kids to shut up so strangers don't judge them. It's sad seeing a table of youngsters with their faces buried in small glowing screens, but I choose to regard it as a silent cry for help from forty-somethings who just want fifteen minutes to drink their chablis in peace.

Returning to my original thesis, children are like puppies. They need to be socialised. That means they have to learn how to behave in restaurants or they'll wind up piddling on the dining room floor when they're eighteen years old.

You've probably twigged that this is pure personal interest wrapped in the decoy of a greater-good argument. Well done. For my part, I'll concede that if you can afford to go fine dining (or *fayn dayning*, for any readers from the leafy suburbs) you can probably afford a babysitter. But my selfish desire not to be stuck staring at the TV every night has forced me to re-evaluate some earlier prejudices. Hence the radical reappraisal that lower down the food chain, restaurants and cafes should be child-friendly.

I'm not saying this because I love kids. I love other people's crotch-spawn about as much as they love mine—that is, not at all. I might admire children's adventurous spirit, but as a waiter I did not enjoy the exercise of that adventurous spirit when they ran behind the bar or stood right in front of the kitchen swing door so next time it opened they made like a pancake. I did not enjoy the way parents left wet, wadded-up tissues in cups, and empty yoghurt packets and banana peels on the table. Children are innately disgusting. Hold hands with one and you might as well be making out with a petrie dish. It's not the parents' job to make it even worse by scattering their disease-riddled rubbish everywhere. Take the national park approach—carry out what you carry in— and everyone will be a lot happier.

I'm not advocating spending any discretionary dining dollars at the *really* child-friendly places. Generally speaking, any business specifically geared towards children is to be avoided like anthrax. That way lies the bewigged charlatan known as Ronald McDonald. Or the old man who used to roam the streets near my house with a bag of boiled lollies looking for children to drug and boil into soup. Actually, he was probably a very nice man who wondered why a bunch of tiny, suspicious faces always rebuffed him with the severity of Romanian border guards, but our parents had done a very good job of warning us about people like him.

I quite like the IKEA approach, where you can throw the youngsters into a pit of multicoloured plastic balls and go on your merry way to the $1 hotdog stand, despite misgivings that at the bottom lies the body of a toddler who's been missing since 2011. But it's important to aim higher if the family is to break out of the primary-coloured ghetto. It's not a mission for the faint-hearted. It's only for those armed with comforts and distractions: colouring pencils and paper, small boxes of sultanas, an economy pack of wet-wipes. It requires enlisting the aid of a waiter who understands that children are just tiny little drunk people and that it's not their fault they don't understand reason. Cause and effect will come later and it will prove a great tool for threats, bribes and intimidation. For the little 'uns at the very start of their restaurant socialisation, it's best to target their natural fear of authority. This is where the waiter comes in. Start by referring to the waiter as 'the boss'. Every time the kid does something naughty, tell them that 'the boss' saw and was really unhappy, and you're going be thrown out if it keeps happening. Plus you can get the waiter to pop by occasionally to check sternly if the greens are being eaten. What can I say? It worked for us. If that fails, try the trick where it looks like you're pulling off your thumb.

One last thing. Don't change your baby in the dining room. Not even if it's 'only' a wet nappy and the baby is in its pram and you can do it more or less discreetly. It's the principle of the thing. Bare genitals do not belong where people are trying to eat, unless you yourself have gone discreetly underpants-free— *discreetly* being the operative word. On the other hand, breasts— or boobs, or knockers, or cans, or whatever semi-satisfactory but still slightly wrong term you want to call them—are fine. They're more than fine. They're desirable. Just so long as they're lactating. It's amazing the number of nursing mothers who ask permission to breastfeed at the table. As if it would be reasonable to say, 'No, I demand you go to the toilet and lock yourself in a cubicle. You and your baby should be comfortable there. The acoustics are quite nice—all that tile.' It's a sad indictment on society that boobs are considered all porn-y and lascivious when they're doing what they were designed to do. Anyone who asked my permission to breastfeed at the table paid the price of being subjected to my joke: 'Well, usually we don't allow BYO but in this case we'll make an exception.' Ha. Hahaha.

~

In 1918 more than 100 waiters were arrested for poisoning bad tippers in Chicago. The internet told me that. The internet also told me Hitler escaped his bunker in a submarine and ended his days living in the Arctic, so I'm not sure it's always a reliable news source. But in this case I choose to believe it. Except for one thing.

One hundred waiters. So few?

Let me tell you about someone I gladly would have poisoned.

I was working at a bona fide celebrity chef's restaurant during the brief interregnum after Ben had fired me from the Duke for insubordination and general crapness and before I started at the Rising Damp. I was working the function one night. The functions room was upstairs. They generally are. That's part of the reason working functions sucks (unless you're one of the Damp's barmen) because it involves a whole lot of running up and down stairs carrying heavy trays. It's like doing four or five back-to-back step aerobic classes. Great if you're Michelle Bridges. Not so great if you're a committed smoker. Even worse, people rarely think to tip at functions. It's called the bystander effect. The herd mentality kicks in. Someone else will have taken care of the tip, right?

It was a function of cardio-thoracic specialists. Probably not short of a coin. A sedate enough dinner. Wine consumed in mindful moderation. Salad playing yin to the roast pork's yang. Conversation treading a professional line peppered with the odd cardio-thoracic joke (punchline: 'and then I explained to his wife that he died of a myocardial infarct and she thought I said fart!')

Party on. They decided when I was clearing the cheese course that they'd split the bill and leave me a tip of $100. Nice one. That was enough to pay the rent and the phone bill that week and more than enough to make the stairs feel a little less steep. They'd come prepared, too. Everyone must have stopped at an ATM en route to the restaurant to ensure there was none of that 'just give the cash to me and I'll put the whole lot on my credit card' funny business. Possibly not the world's most trusting lot, the cardio-thoracic fraternity, but I was stiffed anyway. A woman wearing a twinset handed me a single $50 instead of $150, right in front of the whole table, and that was the end of my tip. The look on her face made it clear it was design, not accident. She knew exactly what she was doing. But something underneath it was pleading and apologetic. A look to make me think, maybe she's broke. A gambler. Alcoholic. Messy divorce. So I held fire. All I did was glare at her with the heat of a thousand suns as she and her fellow cardio-thoracic specialists filed out into the night.

If Twitter had been invented back then I would have gone home, logged on as AngryServerGirl666 and let rip with pictures of sad pandas captioned with things like 'EVERY TIME YOU STIFF A SERVER A PANDA COMES CLOSER TO EXTINCTION'. Twitter was invented by waiters needing an anonymous forum to bitch about bad tippers. It provides much-needed catharsis, especially in America where the average waiter earns a base wage of $2.13 an hour.

In the States, tips are the difference between survival and starvation. In Australia, where the living wage is more generous without being anything to hold a ticker-tape parade about, it's not so urgent.

So why tip, then? I could give you a hundred reasons why you should tip, even when the waiter is being paid enough to afford a new toothbrush every once in a while. I could go on about tipping being appropriate because it's thanks for an enjoyable time, or polite acknowledgement of a difficult job, or simply because it's a noble tradition.

But the clincher is this: just think of who *doesn't* tip.

Mean people don't tip. Hitler wouldn't have tipped. The Manson family didn't tip. Parking meter inspectors don't tip. Genghis Khan? Not a tipper.

There's a general rule of thumb that you can judge how well a person will tip based on how they want their steak cooked. The well-done crowd are misers who wouldn't tip even if there was a gun to their head. They'd be arguing with the gunman about the unfairness of waiters expecting a tip when pretty much every other service industry (except, they'll announce triumphantly, STRIPPERS) goes tip-free and if we head down this path we'll fall into an economic hole like America where a huge underclass is forced to scrape by on their tips. Little do they realise that no one's fooled by their smokescreen of political concern. They're just cheap. The whole post-industrial construct will not collapse if someone leaves a measly five bucks on a saucer.

Speaking of which, tips should ideally fold, not tinkle. As Waz used to say, handing back a generous twenty or fifty cents to a startled diner, 'That's not a tip, that's an insult.'

The worst are the people who leave notes instead of a tip. The fey: 'A hummingbird's heart beats 1400 times a minute.' The righteous: a Jehovah's Witness pamphlet. The nasty: 'You suck.'

It helps to be a regular if you're a big tipper. Why tip big if you're never going to the place again? Where's the incentive? Return for the glory. Being known as a big tipper, or a big-enough tipper, means you will be looked after. I'm proposing a national database so that tipping generosity doesn't just evaporate into the void and instead follows the generous tipper from establishment to establishment, laying down a soft carpet of anticipatory gratitude. That said, everyone should know at least once in their lives the comforting certainty of being a regular. Regulars are the butter to the waiter's bread. They can be a solace. A confidant. Sometimes even a friend. Unless of course they're gluten-intolerant mobile-phone addicts morally opposed to tipping but in favour of letting their children run wild. Then you're screwed.

COLIN

It's really irritates me how often people don't listen while the menu is being explained. This was in a degustation restaurant that had quite a few vegetarian offerings. Are there any dietary requirements or allergies? No response. At the end of a fabulous meal one vegetarian guest said she thought the kitchen was doing amazing things without meat and what was that delicious creamy mid-course? Um, that was foie gras. What's foie gras? It got pretty ugly after that.

— 15 —
AN UNEXPECTED REVERSAL OF FORTUNE

It is a source of general wonder that I transformed from a connoisseur of instant noodles into a professional restaurant reviewer, so here is the story in full, beginning at the start and finishing close to the end and in between featuring approximately 1400 restaurant meals about which I was paid to write. In addition it involves an ongoing battle with 5 kilograms that came along for the ride uninvited and proved so tenacious that a few weeks or a month after their last defeat I'd look down in surprise and exclaim 'YOU AGAIN! HOW THE HELL DID YOU GET BACK HERE WITHOUT ME NOTICING?' Always the same 5 kilos. I knew them by sight.

I promise not to chunter on about my CV. It's an inglorious document, with a notable absence of awards and commendations.

The simple matter is this: I got a job on a newspaper. Remember newspapers? Me too! A career chosen on the rigorously scientific basis of realising my favourite part of the day was reading the paper while drinking coffee. Ergo, I should write for a paper while drinking coffee.

Jobs in newspapers aren't that easy to come by, even back then when they still existed. On getting an interview at *A Well-Known Daily Broadsheet* I celebrated with Ben in world's best practice style by getting shickered at our favourite Thai place. The hangover the next day when we woke up, fully clothed and sprawled haphazardly across the bed like the victims of a violent home invasion, can only be described by resorting to the German. Germans have a word for every occasion. Their word for hangover is *katzenjammer*, which translates as something like 'a cat in the head'. What an admirable facility for language. This was a three-cat hangover.

I was interning at the time on Australia's *Only Daily National Financial Newspaper*. To say any more would be to risk revealing its identity. Suffice to say you did not call in sick when trying to get a foot in the notoriously heavy door of the media industry—with or without a cat in the head—so, feeling like Ernest Shackleton confronting the soul-destroying wastes of the Antarctic, I summoned every reserve of courage and embarked on the perilous journey to Collins Street. I sometimes wonder if the great man ever faced a similar dark despair to the one I experienced when dashing off the 96 tram to vomit behind a Moreton Bay fig in the Carlton Gardens. Or whether the Shack ever temporarily escaped his world of pain by entering a place deeper than sleep—a refuge known as unconsciousness—as I did later that morning in the Telstra annual shareholders' meeting.

The plush seat at Hamer Hall was a kind host. Far kinder than I deserved. It proved so comfortable I wound up with my head flung backwards, mouth open, and snoring like a narcoleptic warthog. The reason I know I was snoring is because one snore was so loud it woke me up. At least the hangover anaesthetised the humiliation. 'I have to go . . . to the dentist,' I announced to the bemused journalist assigned to show me the ropes as the shareholders argued about their annual dividend. A clever ruse indeed. I went home, slept for two hours and went back to the office as if nothing untoward had happened.

Word of that misadventure thankfully didn't spread. I was given a job as a cub reporter and sent off on the merry hell of news reporting, chasing ambulances, police, politicians and, for a brief but thrilling time, an errant gang of private-schoolboy hedge-burners. There were several long months on the graveyard shift desperately hoping for some terrible crime to be announced over the police scanner to alleviate the boredom, but sadly I was denied the gangland murder for which my compatriots all prayed. The only lasting lesson to emerge from the carrier wave's electromagnetic fuzz and crackle was the depressing number of people who deliberately overdose on paracetamol. Especially on a Saturday night.

I'm getting to the food. As usual, it is Ben's fault. At the very least, an open-and-shut case of accessory to the crime. For it was he who drew my attention to the newspaper's cheap eats guide, whose kind editor was known as willing to take a chance on a greenhorn. Hey, I'm cheap, I reasoned with unflappable logic. And I eat.

My first review was a trembling disquisition on a St Kilda cafe, full of praise for the 'heady aromas' of baking bread and the virtues of sitting in the window to 'watch the passing parade'. Clearly a talent to watch. To bookend those crimes against the cliché, I'll declare it was the first step on a journey of discovery. I'm petitioning for leave to use the word 'journey' here, on the undertaking it be used strictly in the pre-food TV sense. These days a terrine can constitute a journey, which makes a twelve-hour lamb shoulder an epic adventure. Hyperbole has taken its place on the table next to the pepper and salt.

Among the many clichés of food writing—or of food writers— the hoariest is that one must have been raised on good food in a family well versed in the pleasures of the table. Not like the Junior Gourmands in their expensive restaurants. They are a breed apart, an exotic butterfly of a diner. What I'm talking about here is 'honest' food. That's the telling word. I'm not exactly sure what constitutes 'dishonest' food, but honest food evokes a vegetable patch, a lemon tree, an apron-wearing mother with freshly baked things for the children's return from school, the sticky glee of the pasta dough that Nonna would lovingly make using the rolling pin smuggled through enemy lines in World War Two. This is the clay from which food writers are formed. It's the very blood pumping through their veins, making their career path as pre-ordained as eye colour.

My family, by way of shuddering contrast, was prone to panic when it came to food. Food was essentially fuel, a base requirement of survival, but it was also tied up in a measure of failure. A deep well of insecurity about the pleasing of others. Food was a display of love we felt somehow unsure of giving, which turned family occasions into little more than an opportunity to sit around the table passive-aggressively apologising to each other.

'I'm sorry the chicken's dry.'

'It's not dry.'

'No, it's dry. I left it in too long. Damn.'

'It's fine.'

(Small voice) 'It's . . . *dry* . . .'

'I SAID IT'S FINE NOW WOULD YOU PLEASE SHUT UP AND LET US EAT.'

Eating at our house was not relaxing.

Oh, my father did his best. He was the one who really loved food, despite some legendary failures. He once served up an all-white meal—chicken, cauliflower with white sauce, and mashed potato. Everyone who witnessed it couldn't help but deflate a little, like a day-old party balloon. An early lesson in colour being integral to the enjoyment of food. Poor Dad. He didn't stand a chance in a family of three sanctimonious women hell-bent on his eternal salvation through the eating of Fibre and Green Things. 'Only you understand, don't you, mate?' he'd say sadly to the dog, his sole male ally. The dog would wag his tail and slobber happily, because he was in on a secret.

Being a complete wog, my father had it ingrained in his DNA to love all meats that had been smoked and cured into salty bliss. Items verboten by us, the ones who loved him most. He and the dog would often disappear on long walks to the park, an activity approved by the House Committee for Healthy Activities, but their idyll was busted when my sister went fossicking in his man-bag and turned up an indictment of deli wrappers bearing exciting labels like 'salami' and 'prosciutto'. If only we'd known he wasn't going to make it past the age of sixty-seven, we would have said, 'Go on, Dad, knock yourself out. Eat the mortadella . . . Enjoy it. Please, please enjoy it.'

Dad would have loved my job.

Mike Dubecki would have been waving pompoms in the grandstand as I graduated to the proper restaurant guide—farewell, abject land of the cheap eat—and then scuttled up the ranks from the merest, cling-on, entry-level restaurants to the gastro-temples where people genuflect to the chef as a modern genius and nervously ask to take a snip of hair for their home shrine. An edible education. Maybe the more you get to know, the more you love to eat: a very clever chicken-or-egg food metaphor for you there. Or maybe simply it's the more prosaic result of the stomach gradually stretching through overuse, eventually requiring the purchase of several pairs of control underwear. I certainly discovered I shared my father's prosciutto gene and cheese chromosome. I also discovered that food isn't a quasi-mystical subject but something that can be learned using the forensic approach of the rounds reporter who is thrown into transport, or health, and starts off knowing very little and ends up knowing quite a lot. As a wise colleague said when I dithered nervously in the face of the offer of the top, bees-knees, full-time reviewing job: 'It's food. It's either delicious or it's not.'

He was right. Start at delicious and go from there.

Along the way I've learned plenty of stuff. Stuff by default and by accident and very much on purpose. Stuff the conspiracy of food books, magazines and newspaper supplements will not explicitly say. A lot of it feeds into General Revelation 101 that the main reason restaurant cooking shits on home cooking is that chefs are on very cosy terms with all the evil things that make food taste good. Even when they're pretending to be concerned for your blood pressure and glycaemic index, it's usually little more than a sneaky bit of PR spin. So much restaurant cooking is like the moment in *The Wizard of Oz* where the curtain is pulled back to reveal the little man with the levers. It tastes good because—oooh, all that butter. All that salt. It's not rocket science. Even salad. You learn that salad should be seasoned. That's why restaurant salad tastes better than home salad. It's the salt. Salt makes things delicious. More of those addictive little white crystals.

You also learn that you shouldn't be afraid of heat. In restaurant kitchens there are flames sheeting for the sky, like a test-run for hell, which sadly means trying to get restaurant results on a domestic burner can be like trying to win the Indy 500 in a go-kart. You learn that the better the restaurant, the more tepid the food. Especially the meat. You learn the fundamental rules of ordering, such as not ordering risotto in general, or seafood on a Monday, especially when it's on the specials list, and that it can actually be surprisingly difficult to find a really good steak—particularly when what you want, above all else, is a really good steak. You learn the importance of acid to a dish, that chicken is generally a meat for boring ditherers, that most kitchens overcook swordfish, and that a jus by any other name would still be gravy with tickets on itself. You learn that anyone who cheats by putting crackle in a deep fryer should be publicly flogged, that duck fat is generally wonderful, and that all good pasta is ugly in a beautiful way.

The list goes on. There's plenty of bullshit, too. Not all truffles are created equal, although they are all presented with hilarious solemnity at the table (partly to justify the $30 'supplement'). You could argue that instead of being a by-word for luxury, foie gras is just liver that's gone to fat camp, that the whole wagyu thing has well and truly jumped the cow shark. But in the end, the only three prerequisites for the job are to love food to the point of gluttony, to keep an open mind, and be prepared to eat the head cheese. Mmm . . . *head cheese*.

~

My daughter, when she was a three-year-old developing the kind of observations that put parents terrifyingly on notice, used to say accusingly, 'You're not going out to work, you're going out to *dinner*.' She was on the winning team with that one. Nine-and-a-half out of ten people will agree that eating for a living does not count among the most taxing occupations in the world. Not even

EWEN

I was starting a new job and getting the tour of
the restaurant from the manager. We walk into the
kitchen and there's a chef running around with his
pants down with a carrot stuck so far up his arse
only the feathery top is poking out. The other chefs
are killing themselves laughing and they all look
at us in surprise—I guess they weren't expecting
any visitors—but the guy with the carrot manages
to collect himself enough to pull it out and say,
'Welcome to (X).' The funny thing was the head chef
was an absolute Nazi about produce, so when he
came into the kitchen a few minutes later he spies
a whole carrot in the bin, pulls it out and waves it
around while lecturing everyone about not wasting
anything. They had to secretly throw it out again so
some poor customer didn't eat the arse-vegetable.

among the top 100,000. Many will argue whether it is work at all,
or if it is in fact leisure time with a dollar value added to it.

But you try it. Please, be my guest. Put what you eat into words.
Stick something in your mouth then describe it. Only first you have
to eliminate 'yum' as an adjective. Yum is for children and television
hosts. So is 'beautiful'. TV chefs use beautiful as a rapturous catch-all
when they don't know what else to say. It's important to pronounce
it *beauuuu-ti-fuuuul*, with a crisp 't', rather than 'bewdiful'. I think
the intention is to show something is so gobsmackingly delicious it
deserves the extra effort of correct pronunciation.

On paper it's a little trickier. You should not—really, you CAN NOT, under pain of death—describe meat as moist, or dessert as sinful. However hard a brownie tries, a combination of sugar, flour and chocolate cannot be wicked in the classic jurisprudential sense. You can't write about wafting aromas and succulent anything. Succulent is on Interpol's watch-list of banned food words. They'll send their crack squad of assassins to neutralise the culprit without a second's hesitation. See also: tender, melting, decadent. In fact, the English language is shockingly ill-equipped to describe food in anything except the most ham-fisted ways. The Germans would probably have a word for the perfect briny slap of a good oyster. Food writers in English have been known to reach for 'ozone'. Personally, I have no idea what ozone tastes like—I prefer it much higher up in the atmosphere, protecting the earth from the sun's shattering rays—but a good oyster will taste like high tide and the fresh salt of an ocean gale rather than the seaweed dankness of a rockpool at low tide. But perhaps it's better just to say the oysters are fresh, and good, and be done with it, although if all food writing were reduced to good and bad, fresh and not-fresh, the bottom would fall out of the restaurant reviewing market. Until the language police come a-knockin' to really put the frighteners on dweeby food nerds getting all poetic with their dinner, we'll be stuck with writers falling into the abyss of their own critical conceits like this: 'Pickled and roasted quince plays support in a simple but totally convincing duet of two simpatico bandmates.'

Ugh.

Actually, I wrote that. It seemed like a good idea at the time.

To steal a quote and poke it with a stick, writing about food is like dancing about architecture. Elvis Costello said that, the interweb tells me, although it was music that struck him as an impossible subject to put into words. He's obviously never been struck by how difficult it is to describe mashed potato without resorting to 'creamy' or babaghanoush without 'smoky' or crackle without 'crackly'. Writing about food is all about donning a leotard and doing a representational dance about salt cod croquettes, or mustering an impassioned Dying Swan in response to a Peking duck where the pancakes are just slightly too thick and the cucumber slips out thanks to a heavy hand on the hoisin.

Don't get me wrong. I go innocently about my line of work most of the time, even pausing to cheer inwardly when a particularly good phrase pops into my head. (Can I say the panna cotta trembled like a bird in a cage? Like Obama: Yes we can!) But every so often the crushing absurdity of the job creeps up and thwacks me over the head with a rubber chicken. Usually when I've been sweating for two hours on how to describe yet another panna cotta. That's when the inanity of describing the process of chewing, tasting and swallowing forces me to go and lie down on the couch until the shadow passes.

I guess no matter what you do for a crust, no matter how thrilling it seemed at the very start, one day it simply becomes work. Work with notable outbreaks of enjoyment, but still work. The spray-tan specialist at Paris Fashion Week sighing as he adjusts yet another supermodel's G-string—work. A tennis pro-slash-Rolex 'ambassador'—work. The Queen of England—work.

Writing about restaurants is work, too. Not just the writing bit. Even the chewing, tasting, swallowing bit. I'm not asking for a violin to hit a mournful low note or anything, but even when my bum is perched on a plush seat, a napkin in my lap, a drink in my hand, it's still work. I just get to work in a nicer place than most people. And drink on the job.

It might seem strange to introduce dolphins at this point—I swear I would never dream of grilling one over charcoal after a brisk lemon-and-oregano Greek-style marinade with a whisper of garlic—but I often think of dolphins when I'm in a restaurant. They're a remarkable species that can shut down half their brain at a time to let it take a break from all that thinking business. Seated at a restaurant table, the average reviewer will feel a bit like Flipper (hopefully minus the high-pitched squeaks and bottlenose) with half a brain focused on some gossipy conversation with a friend and the other half trying to figure out what the hell is in the aioli.

Add to the half-brain affliction the fact that the job leaves the reviewer semi-catatonic by the time the bill arrives. Metabolising all that food and alcohol is hard work in itself. I've heard of some reviewers who manage to achieve the Platonic ideal of simply tasting each dish then pushing it away, rather than hoovering it up as though the food is carpet lint and their mouth is a high-performance vacuum. I know of one who uses allergies as an excuse to send food back after taking a few prim bites. I can't decide if it's admirable or pathological. People generally get into this food caper because they love food, so pushing it away makes about as much sense as a pacifist going into arms manufacture. Plus I can't live with the look on the waiter's face when a dish is only half-eaten and they know it's a reviewer's table, because when they take that plate back into the kitchen they're going to get a grilling from a panicked chef that would make the opening scene from *Saving Private Ryan* look like a beach picnic.

Forget the dolphins. Here's another analogy. It's like piloting a commercial plane. There are people's lives—well, their livelihoods—at stake. Yet the critic is being asked to think critically while filling up to the brim with food and booze. They're flying at a blood-alcohol altitude of 0.05. The cabin is depressurising. The oxygen is dipping into the red. A crash is imminent. Here's an interesting factoid for you: the first sign of oxygen deprivation is the iron-clad belief that you're NOT suffering from oxygen deprivation. That's why most restaurant reviews become a little fuzzy by the time they get to dessert. Or, at least, mine do.

One of the most rewarding parts of the job, apart from the subsidised eating and drinking, is the correspondence I share with readers. An example:

Dear Ms Dubecki,

Your review sucked. I recently tried the pork belly you thought was 'so disappointing' and it was WONDERFUL. You clearly don't know what you're talking about. Furthermore, you didn't start writing about the food until ONE-THIRD of the way down. You seem to be much more interested in the music they're playing and the chairs you're sitting on than what's on the plate. Are you a food reviewer or a décor reviewer?

Yours sincerely, Anonymous Self-described 'Foodie'

P.S. You cannot use words like 'leitmotif' in a restaurant review. A leitmotif is exclusively a term for music. You are responsible for the pollution of the English language and the decline of Western civilisation.

Dear Anonymous Self-described 'Foodie',

I am glad you liked the pork. At $38, it would be a very good thing to like it. But have you ever stopped to consider the basis for your belief that one person's restaurant experience will be the exact equal of another person's? I struggle daily with the idea that something as protean as a restaurant can be quantified on an objective scale. On the other hand, maybe the French philosopher Descartes and the *Matrix* trilogy were right and we're really only brains in vats—in which case this restaurant thing is just a very expensive illusion.

Yours sincerely, Larissa

P.S. I hope my vat isn't next to your vat.

Maybe I should simply have written, 'It's my review and I can do what I want with it, so YA BOO SUCKS!' but I won't sink to the level of Urbanspoon and TripAdvisor, where a ragged consensus is crowd-sourced from anonymous contributors with an axe to grind, a barrow to push, and crimes against syntax to commit in Randomly Capitalised screeds: 'We were Kept Waiting for half an hour and then the Eggs were OverCooked and only ONE Peace of Toast this should nevr happen Ill Not return Again.'

I'd like to get my hands on the brainiac who decided the criticism business could be reduced to a popular vote like the Logies. Democracy be damned. There's no fun in being a critic if it doesn't come with official Voice of God status, preferably read in the voice of James Earl Jones as Darth Vader although a classic Charlton Heston would suffice. I'd be far happier if the job came with a gold badge that said 'Voice of God'—even VOG would do, at a pinch—but am prepared to settle for acknowledgement that it's more valuable than the wisdom of the huddled online masses.

Just for example, if someone going by the name MadDog64 sees fit to alert consumers to a Sichuan restaurant where 'If you order something spicy it comes with a lot of spice' and 'The service is absolutely terrible', he (assuming *he* because surely a woman would follow gender protocols and call herself MadBitch) is missing two points. Firstly, the name 'Sichuan' is dialect translating from the Mandarin as 'before the hotpot is ended you will beg for death'. Secondly, experiencing cheerful, upbeat service in a place like this would be like seeing a Chekhov play adapted by Andrew Lloyd Webber with lots of high-stepping song-and-dance numbers.

I visited the same Sichuan restaurant as MadDog, and indeed it did have the kind of service Marxists fondly imagined when they talked about the dictatorship of the proletariat. We asked our waiter for advice on the encyclopaedic menu with photos of dishes all bristling with a thick forest of angry red chillies so it looked like the same picture reprinted 200 times. 'Here,' he whispered, pointing discreetly so no colleagues would report him to management for being helpful. 'This one good.'

He was right. It was excellent. We even tipped. I hope he wasn't punished for our indiscretion.

I've long harboured a soft spot for these laminate, fluorescent-lit places that evoke parts of China only heard about here if an earthquake wipes out 50,000 people. The food can be outstanding (and outstandingly cheap) plus they don't give two hoots if they're serving a restaurant reviewer or the person who puts the stickers on fruit. Everyone is treated equally as a complete and utter annoyance. Only high-ranking Party officials and Canto-pop stars have a chance of getting service without setting their hair on fire; sometimes you even see diners get so tired of waiting they go foraging for their own drinks and cutlery. It's good to feel part of a noble and proud tradition of non-service stretching back into the fog of history, honed into comfortable recognition. For a reviewer who is used to being given the Rolls Royce, ridgy-didge, here's-something-Chef-prepared-especially-for-you treatment, it's a spiritual detox to be treated with withering contempt.

The places that really annoy me—by 'annoy' I mean 'make me want to return under cover of darkness with a tin of petrol and a lighter'—are a sneaky new breed of restaurant that poses the biggest threat to eating norms since the Chiko Roll. Ladies and gentlemen, introducing . . . the Gen-Y restaurant.

The Gen-Y restaurant—generally opened by older svengali types to bleed money from a target audience still thrilled that they can legally drink—is essentially an edible business model set to a retro-ironic soundtrack. Not so much a restaurant, truth be told, as a cafeteria with a high opinion of itself. You'll find none of the outmoded 'luxuries' like linen, or cutlery that isn't jumbled in a box on the table, or things quaintly called 'entrees' and 'mains'. Basically the model is: get them drunk, chuck a bunch of food on the table in no particular order, and get them out thinking they've experienced the final word in hipness.

It sounds like I have an axe to grind against Gen-Ys in general but I assure you it's not the case. Some of my best friends are Gen-Ys. I can forgive them their rampant me-ism because they're the first generation set to fall behind their parents in fairly significant things like healthcare and education and housing. I'm totally prepared to cut them some slack in terms of the global economic clusterfuck.

Just not when I'm out to dinner.

You could argue the Gen-Y restaurant is all about distilling the contrary spirit of youth into restaurant form. They don't like the term 'restaurant' for starters, which is too old-timey and prescriptive. They'll usually tack an 'eatery' onto their name, although in the end it matters not a jot because on the first visit you'll walk up and down the street half a dozen times until you spot the sign in twelve-point on the underside of the window frame.

As for service at a Gen-Y restaurant . . . how to explain . . . think of Manhattan, and then think of Brooklyn. See what I mean? You'll be thinking of beards and tattoos and piercings and old-man fashion—brogues and braces and fedoras—mashed up with lace singlets and T-shirts bearing the logos of long-forgotten 1970s electronics brands. In other words, they're all about the style, not the substance. They'll have one or two circus ringmasters—mature waiterly types who know to serve from the right—but otherwise the floor will be buzzing with waiter pre-schoolers hired because they have pink hair and arms full of tattoos.

I realise it's hypocritical and indefensible to be charmed by certain restaurants' lack of charm, and annoyed by others. But the Gen-Y restaurant, like New Coke, promises a whole bunch of stuff it doesn't deliver. It shamelessly pretends to uphold the pillars of the restaurant as invented in post-Revolution France—things like comfort, and service, and napkins that aren't an anorexic piece of one-ply that go soggy if someone so much as breathes heavily near them. The laminate Asian places I love simply say, 'This is what we are—take it or leave it. Option two better.' See the difference?

Honestly, I don't give a *pad kra pao* if a table of diners wants their waiter to jump into a selfie to post on Instagram. I'll even move so they get better light. What I object to is the attitude dripping from these places that they're doing you a favour by letting you have a table, although I realise I'm totally out of step with the rest of the world on this one. 'I remember when restaurants had values,' I'll say sadly, looking around at some heaving joint like a grizzled war veteran with post-traumatic stress disorder. 'When they used to seat you at a time pre-ordained on the telecommunications device, and the tables weren't rammed so close you wind up sitting on a complete stranger's lap when you're just trying to get to the toilets, and maybe even have carpet so you could talk to each other in normal conversational tones instead of having to crack out the semaphore flags . . . What this generation needs is a good blooding.'

I have a mate who owns a tragically hip no-bookings place where a queue forms even on Sunday, when it's closed. He gets in the next day and the answering machine will be clogged with plaintive messages: *'We're out the front, why don't you open the door and let us in?'* It's a terrifying window into how the modern psyche has been trained to believe the coolest restaurants are more like an abusive partner.

My number-one tip when visiting a no-bookings restaurant-cafeteria-eatery is simply this: take a book. I've read the first chapter of *Ulysses* more than fifty times thanks to arriving ridiculously early to grab a table for my friends. That's my new status in life— Reconnaissance Girl—because most of my eating partners in crime quite rightly believe queuing is an affront to human dignity. At the first sign of a wait, they'll abandon me to get poundingly drunk in the bar on my own until a table becomes available three hours later, by which time I'm not hungry anyway because I popped out after the third cocktail to get some chips.

Maybe it's because I have a personal history with no-bookings restaurants. I've been hurt too many times before. I fell victim to the social humiliation of queue rage at the first restaurant I ever reviewed at length. There's me, nervously carrying my brand-new Spirax notebook and blue biro, and there's the man in the orange T-shirt who storms up to accuse me of pushing past him to take the last table. What's a girl to do except be very polite in case he's carrying a concealed weapon? The staff were lovely, though. They sided with me, but do you see what's wrong with this sentence? The staff shouldn't have to side with anyone. It's a restaurant, not Ultimate Fighter.

Ruth Reichl ruined it for everyone. She's the former *New York Times* critic whose shtick was to visit restaurants in disguise. Once she even dressed up as her dead mother, which makes me hope desperately she ordered oysters so everyone could cluck knowingly and mutter about Freud. But gosh, so much effort. I can't even remember the fake name I booked under half the time. I wouldn't want to compound the stress by worrying that my prosthetic nose was about to fall into the soup. Apparently a lot of critics feel the same about hiring make-up artists and dressing as their late relatives just to go to work, because the needle has swung the other way. In most quarters anonymity is now seen as essential to the job as an ABBA pantsuit and moon boots. Common wisdom holds it doesn't matter if the critic is recognised because they will use their extraordinary powers of perception granted by the Guild of Reviewers' Secret Wizard Council to cut through the swirling vapour-cloud of special treatment.

It's true you can't polish a turd, as the poet says. An ordinary chef can't suddenly become a better chef. The menu can't go from bog-awful to WOW in the blink of an eye just because someone armed with a notebook and a full quiver of adjectives walks in the door. It just can't.

You can, however, roll a turd in glitter. Restaurants give critics bigger servings, the best produce, the nicest table and the most attentive service, even though it can be so tortured and stiff it's like being stuck in an elevator with the cast of *Home and Away*.

I might have to go into witness protection for admitting this. It's like selling out the Masons' secret handshake. But OF COURSE it helps to fly under the radar and avoid the fuss and bother that can nudge an opinion in a favourable direction. To put it more scientifically: well, der. A restaurant spots a reviewer, they activate the Cognitive Dissonance button and glitter-bomb the entire area. Even after the meal the onslaught continues. I once had a chef call me the day after a meal to tell me he'd been upset because his dog died. Reviewers are—sob—only human, after all.

That's why it's a natural high to rival sky-diving to occasionally sneak through a restaurant's defences and land deep behind enemy lines without being spotted. Especially when you're not dressed as your dead mother. It doesn't happen often but it's worth pursuing with the steely idealism of a Young Liberal think-tank. At the very least it's crucial not to alert them you're coming. I look at booking under a different name as a good chance to try on different identities. I've always felt like an Astrid trapped in a Larissa body, so it was nice to try it out before committing to the full transition. I've used my children's names, too, so when they inevitably accuse me in their teenage years of ruining their lives with Ezekiel and Aloysius[3] I can say I've walked in their shoes a little.

There used to be a photo that ran with my reviews that uncannily resembled Sissy Spacek in *Carrie*. I loved that photo because I believe—or want to believe—I look nothing like that in everyday life except when I'm yelling at my kids for leaving Lego pieces in the shag-pile rug. The Spacek era was notable for several sleight-of-identity coups. At one banging Mexican joint I slipped

---

3 Not their real names.

through unrecognised the first time and got a few burnt end-bits of lamb for $33 frisbeed at my head by a waiter who was waiting on an important call from his agent. The second visit they clocked me immediately. The same dish was an extravagance of perfect pink meat, pouting and ready for its close-up.

There are other benefits to realising with a sigh that they know who you are, and that they know that you know that they know who you are. You can relax and stop talking in that Russian accent. Your dining compadres can quit referring to you as Svetlana. And you can scribble away in your notebook at the table instead of having to scurry off to the loos to write notes after every course, making everyone in the place assume you're suffering from a scorching urinary tract infection.

All critics have their peccadilloes. I'll generally fall into a deep, trance-like state when eating proper, authentic, rustic Italian food. A chef could put a marron on a piece of nuclear waste and I'd probably call it beautiful. *Beauuu-ti-fuuul*. I also love, in no particular order, a really good French baguette with sour butter, those incredibly soft leather banquettes that feel like the underside of a mushroom, and pop songs involving bagpipes. Combine them into one restaurant and I'd be a very happy person indeed.

And when it comes to service? Well, I don't need to feel clean on a spiritual level when eating at your restaurant, so please put salt on the table. If I hear one more waiter say, 'Chef says everything is properly seasoned,' I'll start attacking everything in sight with one of those oversized peppermills. I don't like a napkin unfurled into my lap. It's infantilising, although I understand it's an expected norm so it's my responsibility to cover my crotch before the waiter does.

De-crumbing. Another fine ritual guaranteed to elicit the old nervous joke about who's the messier diner, and a bit like nursey wiping the table before naptime. At some of the really old-school places they'll lay a napkin on top of the tablecloth ahead of dessert, so diners aren't affronted by any unsightly stains while they're eating their peach melba, but it reminds me too much of what desperate parents do when they have a toddler who's been vomiting all day and there's no more clean bed linen. I'll pass on that one, too, thanks.

Above all, I'd be utterly thrilled if I could write what I think. Some readers think I'm a chippy bitch but half the time I'm only saying half of what I'd like to be saying. In England reviewers can get away with writing the chicken curry tasted like stale toes. Thanks to Australia's defamation laws, unless physical proof of the eating of stale toes can be produced, it could easily wind up in court with the judge trying to quantify what stale toes taste like, exactly how stale the toes had been, and then where the curry ranked on the official stale toes scale. It does tend to muzzle criticism. Only the other day I had lamb ribs that could have been the fossilised remains of a small dinosaur thrown into a deep fryer. Unfortunately, however, due to the lack of evidence that I've eaten dinosaur, I had to make do with a fairly toothless 'The twice-cooked lamb ribs could have been cooked half as much'.

They didn't know who I was, by the way.

You can always tell if they've spotted the reviewer because a flare goes up from the kitchen while a siren starts wailing and staff start running around yelling, 'CODE RED!' Actually it's nothing that exciting, sadly. Everything just gets a little more awkward. It's a bit like a very polite blind date where neither party is sure they want to stick around for dessert.

The most disappointing meal of my life was in fact two meals that happened on the same day. Lunch and dinner. Back-to-back.

Human foie gras. Don't tell me it's a job without challenges. A work experiment that involved flying to Sydney for the weekend to hit its top restaurants safe in the knowledge they would treat me as a regular diner. The results were fairly depressing. Apparently, even if you want to spend half the average weekly wage on a single meal, restaurants still reserve the right to treat you as the bacteria that feeds on pond scum. The food? I can't really remember. It was ... nice. Mostly. But the service—oh god, the memory of the service to this day makes steam belch from my ears like I'm spontaneously combusting. Lunch was at that rather famous restaurant where the barman got busted for dealing coke back in Chapter 12. The young woman at the front desk sat chatting on the phone and chewing gum while we stood awkwardly in front of her for four minutes. I timed it. Later we asked the sommelier about the difference between two wines on the award-winning list. 'This one,' he said, pointing at the Alsace riesling, 'costs twenty dollars more than this one.'

Dinner was at a corporate titan hangout where each one of the flower arrangements must have cost more than the annual GDP of Mozambique. The air shimmered with wealth. The dessert was burnt. Not just Paris Hilton perma-tanned—proper, desolate landscape-after-a-bushfire black. It was so obvious that my immediate thought was, 'Oh, the chef must be playing some clever visual games. What fun.' But no, it was just burnt. The waiter cleared away the uneaten, obviously burnt dessert without a comment. We paid our $550 bill and left. None of the staff said goodbye. Maybe that cost more.

It pains me to admit it but I think any reviewer who doesn't secretly enjoy the recognition—or at least what the recognition can get them, which is a related but different thing—is lying. I like knowing my $30 dessert isn't going to be a burnt piece of shit.

I like someone saying hello the minute I walk in the door and being farewelled properly—even the times when all the staff are awkwardly lined up at the door and I can pretend to be Prince Charles backstage after the Royal Variety Performance. Above all, I like not waiting for anything because I have been unreasonably impatient since birth, although I am trying very hard to be a better person.

On the other hand, things can sometimes get a little freaky. The waiter who hovered outside the toilet so I could get a personal escort back to the table—that was a bit unnecessary. Ditto the

LENNY

I was the manager at one of the city's best restaurants. It was an open secret the restaurateur had numerous relationships with waitresses, although his then-wife worked alongside him. Until one particular event ... There was a petrol strike and a TV crew descended on a petrol station to interview motorists waiting in a quickly forming queue. It was late afternoon on a day he was supposedly flat out in the restaurant, and randomly the TV presenter chose his car. Unfortunately his wife saw the interview and the very attractive waitress sitting beside him. She quickly rang the restaurant, asking where her husband was. I replied nervously that he was standing in the restaurant deep in conversation with some customers and couldn't be interrupted. It was a pretty good effort, I thought, but she's now his ex-wife.

young man who told me pompously, 'We reserve this table only for VIPs and tonight it is *yours*.' Then there are the diners who like to come up and stage whisper, 'I know who you are but don't worry, I won't blow your cover,' thereby guaranteeing any cover officially blown. But the oddest one happened during an internal ultrasound for my second pregnancy. I've become fairly used to people saying, 'You're the restaurant reviewer, aren't you?' but it was a first to have it said by a doctor wielding an ultrasound wand (a medical term for a hospital-grade dildo) as she looked up from between my splayed legs. She loved restaurants. Loved them! Where would I recommend for her birthday dinner, twenty people, somewhere fun, etc, etc. Now, I'm not normally Miss Chatty-Pants when strangers are poking around my equator but I know my manners, and after we'd exhausted the possibilities of Mexican and moved onto Spanish she suddenly fell into the kind of heavy quiet that precedes bad news. And then she took my one hand in her two and told me the foetus had no heartbeat.

Paella one moment, dead baby the next. Quite the turnaround. It was probably only a minute, looking back, although at the time it felt like hours, what with all the weeping and despair, when suddenly she exclaimed, 'Oh my lord, I'm so sorry. There it is! I was looking in the wrong place. I really should have been concentrating on my work instead of talking about food!' And indeed, there my little boy was. A tiny pulse of light emerging from the screen's fuzzy gloom, winking at me as if to say, 'Mum, this restaurant thing is BONKERS.'

— 16 —

RESTAURANT OWNERSHIP AND OTHER BLOOD SPORTS

Despite having no previous history of self-harm, many people still want to open their own hospitality business. On hearing of such things, wise industry elders will sigh deeply and lay aside their peyote tea and ceremonial pipe to invite these individuals to their fireside. They will proffer hard-won pearls of wisdom such as: 'You'd be better off putting your money in a nice, safe term deposit.' Or, 'The average restaurant lasts a couple of years . . . if you're lucky.' Perhaps they'll get all technical and tell you there seems little point risking hundreds of thousands of dollars starting a business that, if everything goes well, will make somewhere between 5 and 10 per cent profit a year.

To no avail. All the lectures and spreadsheets in the world have yet to shift public suspicions that the restaurant game is primarily about sampling Champagne vintages, quaffing oysters and showing Veronica Lake to the best table in the house.

Even those who breathe the super-oxygenated air of the obscenely wealthy are caught up in the excitement. Restaurants have triangulated vineyards and racehorses as a must-have badge of success, which pretty much sums up the only circumstances under which I'd like to own one: strictly as a hobby, on a par with owning a polo pony named Charley and a 'sweet little yacht' that sleeps twelve. A casual side-project for my egregiously wealthy alter ego, designed primarily to show off to my equally wealthy friends while solving the dilemma known as 'what to do with the spare change down the back of the couch'. And if it all goes belly-up then I can just say, 'Well, no harm done then, old chap. Now who's up for a round of golf?'

It's far scarier that normal, everyday people who boast neither a stock portfolio nor a working definition of a chukkah still chase the Great Australian Hospitality Dream. Anyone without the luxury of being able to install a general manager before they jet off to St Barthes will quickly discover the reality that it is about as sophisticated as the exercise yard at an Indonesian prison. Only to people lucky enough not to work in them do restaurants remain ineffably glamorous. You will work like a navvy, earn much less than everyone thinks you earn—you will be judged cruelly for taking a $20 bottle of wine to a dinner party—and you will worry. And worry. And worry.

It's quite heroic, in a way. These hospitality dreamers are the inheritors of the impulse that launched people into the skies in the early days of aviation, or sent explorers to take on the Arctic in home-knitted jumpers. Everyone thinks THEY will be the one to make it work. THEY will be the one to have the whole town talking, THEY will be the insta-success that results in newspaper articles and queues down the street that necessitate the ultimate accessory: a doorperson with a clipboard taking names. You know how when the TV goes on the blink every family member wants a turn pressing the button on the remote control because they alone possess the special powers that will bring it back to life? Opening a restaurant is a lot like that.

Some people are going to do okay out of it. Some are going to do more than okay. They'll have a nice life, a great community and plenty of perks. But to those who've never put much skin in the game, the only conscionable advice is: don't choose restaurants. Choose life. Choose decent hours and an existence untroubled by staff members who phone in sick on your first Saturday off in three months. Choose a regular income and freedom from grease traps that bubble up and leave the chefs working ankle-deep in rancid fat and the dining room evacuated like Dunkirk as customers gag into napkins. Choose the sanity of a profession where colleagues treat each other with courtesy and where marriages don't break under the strain and you don't fall asleep on the couch while the kids beg for a game of hide-and-seek because they haven't seen you in a week.

And after all that, if you still choose restaurants, if you are truly committed to consummating this union, then please do yourself and everyone you know a favour and just make sure you really, *really*, love them.

Alternatively, you could take the halfway-house approach and encourage someone you know to open a restaurant. It's

GUY

A table of four pre-ordered a bottle of Grange so it could be decanted to allow it to air. They're the kind of customers sommeliers appreciate. But when they arrived they asked for four glasses of lemonade, then emptied their lemonade into their glasses of Grange, making it the world's most expensive cheap-arse lambrusco.

pragmatically evil and ruthlessly self-interested but not a bad compromise. Sure, you'll be going straight to hell but at least you'll be taking your money with you. Remember how when you were in Year 9 you pushed your best friend into the arms of a questionable dude so you could get off with his much better-looking buddy? It's like that, although to allay concerns about karmic payback, maybe it's best to choose someone you don't really like. A frenemy. An individual you secretly despise because they love being the big guy. They can't afford slaves, or they live in a jurisdiction where slaves have been banned, so bossing around a bunch of waiters is the next best thing. You cook a mean dinner party, you tell your 'friend'; you are preternaturally learned in the ways of fine wine and third-wave coffee. There has never been anyone in the history of the world more suited to opening a restaurant. A little encouragement in the right direction and soon you'll be among the chosen ones sitting at your favourite spot at the bar, watching the yuppie hellstorm as people wearing I'm Friends With The Owner T-shirts materialise out of nowhere for their free slice of the action.

Statistics that I have just made up but am pretty sure are correct show restaurant owners are 40 per cent more popular than people who don't own restaurants. Until they go out of business and then they're 40 per cent less popular. People don't like being around failure. It makes them feel bad.

You should have seen the Rising Damp being cannibalised by hangers-on until it was a skeleton with little chunks of flesh clinging onto it. God it was beautiful. Even the owners were in on the action, because they trusted each other about as far as they could kick the ice machine. Each was convinced the others were getting more in the way of largesse so they upped their ante accordingly. It was like there was some sporting trophy at stake the way they gamed the place, bringing in friends and friends of friends and friends of friends of friends to eat and drink and grandiosely announce to the waiters to 'put it all on my tab' (the owners' tab was known as table 69, naturally). By the end they were hardly on speaking terms with each other. But they sure as hell had a lot of grateful buddies.

What's that? You're not going to shove your friend under a truck and I'm a bad person for suggesting it? Well, moving briskly along then. If you're determined to go ahead and enter this restaurant caper and would like to ask my advice, gleaned from dispassionate professional observation over the past decade-and-a-half of the types of businesses that succeed versus those that fail, then it is only polite to spill my secrets and answer honestly.

I have absolutely no idea.

As far as I can see, the places that fly versus the places that thud out of the sky are a simple matter of dumb luck. Not even dumb luck. Dumber than dumb luck. Imbecilic luck. The kid-who-sits-in-the-sandpit-eating-his-own-snot luck.

I will simply say this: figure out your thing and stick to it. If you have a healthy little French bistro, for example, it's probably best to treat little French bistros as your blood type, as the very nucleus of your being, instead of trying to develop a diverse empire of bars and nightclubs and food emporiums and all the rest.

One of the typical yet reliably horrific casualties I've witnessed involved a man who had a very successful cafe that spawned a hundred imitators. It was a heart-warming rags-to-riches tale: one minute he's scraping by thanks to a close relationship with Centrelink, the next a small loan from relatives has turned him into Mr Unexpectedly Successful. For a number of years he could hardly believe his luck, but eventually the glow wore off and he started getting restless with his sweet little set-up that was busy from early morning until late at night. Now, the obvious, risk-averse move would have been to open another cafe much like the original in a suburb twice removed, but of course he decided to treat cafe number one as a gateway drug to bigger and better things. It's the human impulse to trade up. Cars and houses; spouses and businesses. In his wisdom he decided to open a fancy-pants modern restaurant in an empty warehouse shell with the help of the expensive designers du jour. Even the tiles had to be made specially which, quite frankly, seems like overkill—unless, of course, they conducted a poll and found the target market wouldn't visit a place without bespoke tiles.

But wait, there's more. Because he was determined to make it a Restaurant That Counts he signed up a well-known, highly respected and therefore expensive chef before the tradies were even on-site. So the chef's on a massive wage while flipping eggs over at the cafe, the build's delayed, as builds invariably are, and the owner's bleeding money from every orifice to the point where he's now camping out upstairs. But the dumbest thing he did in a very long line of dumb things was to sell the cafe, which was still pulling a healthy, dependable profit, to try and save his vanity project. It was a decent restaurant but it only managed to limp past its first birthday and in its passing left a long line of angry creditors screaming impotently about the money they've probably kissed goodbye forever. The last conversation I had with him was completely one-sided: 'The number you have dialled has been disconnected. Please check the number and dial again.'

I've been looking over the fence for a long time now and I still can't figure out the economics of these massive restaurants—these visual, tactile, audio-phile wonderlands that seem to be opening every other week with grand parties and PR fluff tailor-made to actively discourage people from going to the restaurant. ('Imagine the night stars glimmering through a canopy of trees as a young woman in hip-hugger jeans sips a Dolce Flirtini on the patio'— I cannot believe people are paid to write this stuff.) I'll sit at a table feverishly calculating that the owners have conservatively dropped northwards of a million on the fit-out and with X number of seats that means they need to sling a hell of a lot of green papaya salads or crusted scallops or tuna tartares just to pay for the actual space before you even factor in wages and stock, and that's assuming that the place is a success, which given the high rates of restaurant morbidity is a very risky assumption. The only reasonable response is to think: 'Shit. The wine mark-ups must be pretty high.'

Really, I'd love to tell you that a Mexican-Japanese fusion restaurant with an oyster bar will be THE sure-fire thing you should plow all your borrowed cash into, but I can't. Please don't think I'm keeping the good oil to myself. The same principle underscores why business journalists aren't all driving around in Ferraris despite writing about stocks for a living. It's a fickle market, and unfortunately the job doesn't come with a crystal ball.

I do have a pretty finely calibrated sense for when a place isn't going to fly, however. The X-ray goggles of doom. Not such a fun party trick when a nervous restaurateur is asking for feedback on the place he's tipped his life savings into.

Food is the art of the twenty-first century (one of the peyote-drinking elders told me that and I'm stealing the line, with thanks). It's culture high and low, in edible form. What's not to love? Sure, it's the only branch of the arts that leaves a legacy no more valuable than fertiliser but that's proven no hindrance to the grand, sweeping food statements that blow through with the drama of a chill southerly cutting inland on a scorching hot day. Things like molecular gastronomy, once so revered as the very essence of avant-gardism, now looked on with the fond bemusement reserved for the big-haired band posters papering a long-ago teenager's bedroom walls. The smears and swooshes, the spheres and foams, the movement's faithful handmaidens, now so witheringly *yesterday*.

Or how about the foraging era which followed it, in which chefs muddied their clogs traipsing through fields in order to feed their customers weeds—so very *real*, as opposed to the lab chefs with their test-tubes—but ultimately so drippingly *worthy* it gestated a Tourette-like reaction in the embrace of street food with a devil-may-care attitude towards the local, sustainable, organic orthodoxy.

And how about that street food? A movement that started off as legitimately exciting and then became a handy excuse to soak dud produce in trans fats and cheap commercial sauces and charge a motza. From sexy to sleazy, almost overnight. So disappointing. Most of it is like bondage with vinyl instead of leather. But it goes to show that where one place succeeds another hundred will follow. One establishment does well with southern-US barbecue and all of a sudden there's a contagion of southern-US barbecue joints pumping out sliders and Buffalo wings with blue cheese sauce. There's another one, and another one, popping up like mushrooms after rain, until everyone has their fill and suddenly their stocks tumble like it's Black Tuesday for smoked brisket and 'slaw.

Same goes for fit-outs. Depending on whether you were a Beatles or a Rolling Stones kind of person, the 60s were over either: a) when Woolies started selling Beatles wigs, or b) when the Hells Angels stabbed a hippy to death at Altamont. In a similar vein, the neo-industrial-handmade-reclaimed design ethos that has dominated the market over recent years perished the minute Kmart started selling jam jars for drinking glasses or when the McDonald's 'testing lab' served burgers on wooden boards. Eat your hearts out, hipsters.

The next big thing? Peruvian. Part of any food writer's job is to pen the annual piece predicting upcoming trends and for the past five years everyone has been pointing to a South American country known best for ceviche (fabulous) and barbecued guinea pig (can't comment). If we keep writing it with confidence long enough, it will come true, right?

I'd be happy if it was Peruvian, mind you. Peruvian is easy to grasp, except perhaps for the guinea pig bit. Too many restaurants are a clutter of fascinating ideas that make no thematic sense. They might try very hard to sell their broad, sweeping technicolour ambit (Pacific Rim, I'm looking at you) but I'm old-fashioned. If you can't explain a job in a single word—journalist, engineer, lawyer—I don't want to know about it. Same goes for restaurants.

But don't listen to fusty old me. The types of restaurant are limited only by the imagination. Korean's pretty scorching right now. Mexican isn't cooling its boots anytime soon. Sichuan's hot (get it?). Cambodian has surely got to get a few runs on the board soon, especially with insects featuring in my most recent list of the next hot dining trends. What about Inner Mongolian,

Outer Mongolian, bars that seat ten people in a reclaimed firehose cupboard? You could open a breastaurant. They're a thing. Hell, even a few brave Peruvian joints have popped their heads up, although not enough yet to constitute a bona fide trend. We shall see. The churn and burn of food fashions means some will wind up in the chumbucket before they've had a chance to stake their claim. Some will do well for a while then struggle to keep traction as the crowds go galloping after the new. (Blame the media cycle— 'Three-year-old rather good restaurant remains rather good' doesn't make a particularly compelling sales pitch to the food supplement editor.) Hysteria has taken over—restaurants open amid scenes reminiscent of a military coup in Central America, then struggle forevermore to appear as relevant as they first did. Some will do okay. A select few will have more Instagram followers than the Pope, and they will be truly blessed.

On that subject, be sure to follow the cardinal rule of hospitality: if you succeed, take all the credit. If you fail, blame external forces. Look no further than George, who took the Rising Damp's success as acknowledgement from the heavens of his rare gifts. His ability to read the market, predict the future, blah blah blah, although underneath the swagger of the self-made man you could occasionally get a whiff of the fear that led to outbreaks of weirdness such as the nacho machine on the bar. A gastropub pretending to be a classy Italian joint and there on the counter materialised one of those perspex boxes with interior warming lights usually seen at foreshore carnivals. On seeing it for the first time, the regulars would get a look on their faces like they'd just seen a cyst pop. It didn't last long. Someone must have had a quiet word that such a thing was not a good look for leafy Barton Square.

As for the Rising Damp, after the Cold War between George and the other owners had raged silently for many months, it was decided through their emissaries that they should sell. A couple of thoroughly decent fellows bought the place for a fair market price (translation: not a bargain). They spooked everyone at first when they insisted on things like decency and respect, but it caught on.

As for George, well, he believed his own press so much he thought he could walk on water. He put his hospitality superpowers to work on another pub. This time he chose a fixer-upper a few kilometres away. He renovated it with the help of Jimmy and started the hard slog of winning the hearts of the local business crowd, but unfortunately his chef overdosed five minutes before their first big lunch service. With the chef carted off to hospital, there was nothing for it but for George to get in the kitchen, apron round his fat waist, cooking and swearing. I love that story with all my heart. The business didn't go under immediately, but it did go under.

I guess the lesson is a simple one. Go and workshop your high-falutin' restaurant concept all you want. There's no alchemy. Smarts count for some, but there are so many variables clanging around it's more like a game of pinball. The fates may be kind or unkind. If you're successful, count your lucky stars. Go and say a few hosannas or lay freshly harvested sheaves of wheat at the Temple of Artemis or whatever it is you do to say thanks. Just remember that whatever your circumstances in life may be— rich or poor, kind or mean, generous or tight—there is one great equaliser and it is quite simply this: no one knows what's going to happen tomorrow.

∼

So Ben opened a cafe. His own place. He did it. After fifteen years working at the Duke, he got the hell out of Dodge and bloody

OLIVER

A customer brought her double-cooked duck and mushroom risotto to the counter and showed me a small foreign object and her chipped tooth. It was actually a rock, but I told her it was a duck gallstone that had snuck through the system in processing. She seemed happy with the explanation and the free risotto, and we never heard from her—or, more importantly, from her lawyers—again.

well did it. I cheered him all the way, being the kind of endlessly supportive, quietly encouraging and generally wonderful wife you read about in nineteenth-century novels. Actually, I wept. He and his chef buddy Matt took the lease on an old, run-down milkbar on a semi-industrial stretch of road and I didn't sleep for six months.

I am temperamentally ill-suited to being the owner of a hospitality business. I break out in hives at the week-to-week fluctuations of profits and losses and—shudder—projections. Which makes it a very good thing that I am not an owner of a hospitality business. I no more own Pope Joan—for that is the cafe's name as well as my one small contribution towards it—than Ben writes restaurant reviews. I leave it up to him. We've adopted our own version of the US army's 'don't ask, don't tell' policy. How's business? Dunno. I figure if it has burned down, he'll let me know. Otherwise, I'd rather be left out of it. Too stressful.

It's been a real bitch for my work. It's so much harder now because I have first-hand, close-up and terrifying insight into the hard graft—the endless, arduous slog—that goes on behind the scenes. Even getting the doors open is like running three marathons back-to-back in 40-degree heat with no visor or sunblock. The endless lonely miles of red tape. The regulations governing everything from how far up the wall the tiles in the kitchen have to go, to the distance from the kitchen hand basin to the prep areas and the size of the sinks. For the uninitiated with no experience of dealing with local councils and government departments, the vagaries of liquor licensing, building codes and many, many more officious pieces of officialdom, it's a pretty close simulation of parachuting into Turkmenistan without a guidebook or map, praying that the locals are helpful and don't rip you off too much. And then if it's an old building you'll have to hope against hope that the plumbing has been updated sometime in the past century, that the wiring isn't about to burn the entire joint down, that termites haven't been secretly snacking on the floors and supporting beams.

Set-up stories are boring. Get a bunch of hospo folk together and they'll sit around trading war stories like they've just been evacuated in the last helicopter from Saigon, but to the general public they're about as interesting as watching a fly crawl up a wall without even the consolation of a second fly so you can place bets. So I will spare you the details. Suffice to say that if this stuff is interesting it's for nefarious reasons.

My absolute favourite involves one of the industry's more mercurial characters who opened a happening little joint that sparked a huge trend (in what, I won't say—partly to protect his identity and partly because I like being mysterious). He'd work like crazy for six months then take the rest of the year off. One time he'd disappeared to a sunny beach up north and the manager he'd left in charge turned up to work one afternoon to find the rear laneway awash in raw sewage. The incident quickly revealed this most happening of joints had been trading for years with no permits of any kind. Not one. He'd simply found a shop, installed his kitchen and opened his business without any contact with the clipboard carriers. He had plenty of chutzpah but the problem was this: legally (and, let's face it, ethically) a food business needs a grease trap, because flushing this stuff right into the system is toxic and dangerous. But the owner had his tradies tap straight into the sewerage system and, after living on borrowed time, something finally went wrong because on this day there is a river of shit lapping at the back door. His manager rings him frantically. He remains as calm as ever. Eternally chillaxed. 'What you're *not* going to do is not work tonight,' he tells his freaking-out employee. 'What you *are* going to do is go to the safe, take out $2000, call a plumber, hand him the cash, and he'll look after it for you.' There was one important addendum: 'You don't have to pick up any turds.'

It's hard to beat that story. Pope Joan had issues with the ceiling and installing three-phase power but I suspect you just fell asleep halfway through that sentence. No matter how bad things got, however, there was the comfort of knowing they could have turned out so much worse. It's embarrassing to admit but we nearly got suckered into the world of Marcello. Just imagine it. Being beholden to an alarmingly bushy monobrow attached to a short lickspittle Italian with the charm of a dead houseplant. But this is what happens when you are desperate, and the leap from waiter to owner seems so ridiculously . . . quantum.

Among his impressive property portfolio Marcello owned a pub in a godforsaken country town. It was a regional centre, to be polite, but one suffering a chronic drought that pummelled the surrounding landscape into endless fields of brown and an economy on life support. I remember driving there with Ben through never-ending nothing into the sun-bleached heart of nowhere, trying to buoy our spirits against mounting evidence that this was not the place for us. Marcello had promised we could take over the lease of his pub for free if we cleaned the place up. Sounds too good to be true, doesn't it? Would you be surprised to hear it *was* too good to be true? The pub, an ornate monolith that would have been beautiful 150 years ago, turned out to be the hellmouth, or an approximation thereof. It hadn't served a drink in more than a year and its boarded-up windows hid a treasure trove of legless tables, random bags of rubbish and the occasional decomposing small mammal. It smelled of stale beer and death. We swung by the local cops, who laughed bitterly and stroked their moustaches when recalling the time when their Friday and Saturday nightshifts were punctuated by endless summons to the roughest bloodhouse in town, but even then we left thinking: 'We could, couldn't we? Maybe . . .?' What really clinched it for the 'no' vote was seeing a girl who couldn't have been older than fifteen pushing a pram down the main street. She sported a black eye impressive in both its size and shimmering gradients of colour. Skulking along next to her was a boy who couldn't have been older than seventeen. His right hand was in a plaster cast. They were two sides to a story that said everything we needed to know about this town.

It was a lucky escape but some dreams are hard to kill. Enter the milkbar. In some parts of Melbourne it has become easier to get an espresso than to buy a litre of milk, thanks to the conversion of the aforementioned businesses into cafes. If I want to buy a packet of breakfast cereal, I have to jump on my bike, but if I want to eat artisan granola for breakfast there are three places within walking distance that will serve it to me. What can I say? The world is a strange place.

Brunswick locals might remember it as the place with the dummy wearing a gimp mask in the window. It was a decommissioned milkbar, I should have mentioned, now the home of gimp-loving students and, out back, a floating population of New Zealand backpackers apparently making do without a proper kitchen or much of a bathroom. Inside it was like the black hole of Calcutta. I'm no real estate visionary. All I could see was a dank hole where hope went to die and daylight was just a rumour beyond the unrelenting gloom. Everything about it, to me at least, screamed FOR THE LOVE OF GOD, NO! but to their credit Ben and Matt did a fair bit of jumping around in excitement. There was room for a veggie garden out the back, and across a laneway was a little red-brick warehouse where a young fashion designer lived in an amazing bijou nest decorated in layer over layer of beautiful things—a tour appended by the guilty realisation that for once we *were* the wave of gentrification rather than its victim. I had to admire the way she took a sledgehammer the night before we got the keys and smashed the joint back to year zero. Her point was received in the spirit it was intended.

Anyway, Pope Joan opened a disturbingly long time later, after all the nail-biting trials and delays and stuff-ups I won't bore you with, and it was only finally on that first morning when the doors swung open that I was able to say: 'Yes, I *see*. I get it. Well done, fellows.' Even if it wasn't in the family, so to speak, I'd be a placard-carrying fan. It's food that doesn't lecture you. It's just tasty and the animals are treated well, and if you mention this book you can get a free coffee.

Actually, no. News just in from our sponsors. No free coffee. Sorry about that.

I've learned one very important thing through seeing a hospitality business being nurtured as if by a parent rather than the loveless duty of a state-appointed guardian. I expected the customers to be a floating population of faceless people washing in and out each day, as anonymous as the tide, but they're anything but. They're people who live in the 'hood and parents from the local school and those who come by every day and others who trust you for all their birthdays and anniversary dinners. It's totally gratifying in a way that a person who visits a restaurant once or twice to scribble notes and write a judgement before heading off to the next new place never expected it to be.

I won't ever get sick of going to restaurants. I might occasionally sigh and regret that the evening will not be spent curled on the couch in my second-best tracksuit pants (which also happen to be my second-worst) watching minor celebrities renovate South Africa, but when I arrive at my destination and say, 'Table for Biggie Smalls,' it's always with a sense of excitement. I do sometimes wonder, however, if I've had my fill of deconstructions, of clever visual games, of classic menu items like pavlova in inverted commas that basically mean 'Surprise! It's not pavlova at all!' Sometimes I even have the sneaking suspicion that the meal is the sharing and not the science.

Soft, huh? I'm losing my edge. A restaurant reviewer needs to be impervious to sentimentality or basic human emotion, like Steven Seagal in *Under Seige*, or Steven Seagal in *Under Seige 2*. I'm incredibly thankful, then, that whenever I'm about to roll over contentedly and let the world tickle my belly, Pope Joan throws me a timely reminder that people can be truly disgusting, and that the veneer of civilisation that keeps society ticking along hides a phantasmagoria of wrongness. The latest was the Hitchcockian mystery known as: 'Who is leaving green phlegm smeared all over the bathroom wall?' The crack team of PJ staff noticed each incident coincided with the regular visit of a small, neat, late-middle-aged woman with a tight bob and red lipstick. She could have been someone's grandmother. She probably *is* someone's grandmother. And she would have her coffee then stand in the bathroom for five, ten minutes, hacking up enough gobs to coat the wall and declare it a new Pantone colour. She denied everything when confronted about it but she was caught green-handed and banned for life. Disgusting. People like that are the reason the aliens keep flying right past us.

When I was a small child I had a picture book called *Where Does The Butterfly Go When It Rains?* that posed a bunch of questions about where various creatures choose to shelter. You know: The cow goes to the shed. The horse goes to the stable. The chicken goes to the coop. Even then I found it incredibly frustrating that the author failed to answer the title question. In my four-year-old wisdom I reasoned (correctly, I still believe) that if she didn't have the answer she was completely out of line posing it. Now that I'm all grown up, I occasionally lie awake at night pondering a related mystery: where do the waiters go when they get old?

See, my birthdays are ticking by with increasing regularity but waiters somehow stay the same age. Wave after wave head off to join the real world and they're magically replenished. Eternally youthful. It's as if they're a natural resource ready to be plundered and, unlike coal, infinite.

Of those who choose to stick around, some of course go on to open their own places, thereby perpetuating the cycle of life, death and rebirth as outlined in Eastern mysticism and Catholic guilt. But it doesn't happen for everyone. Nor does everyone even want to open their own place. I don't know why; maybe they have no interest in developing stress-related skin conditions. They like floating along shift to shift, year to year, living life like the classic carpark legal disclaimer 'all care—no responsibility'.

Eventually, however, there comes a point when you've worked in restaurants so long you can't do anything else professionally. Same goes for priests and drug dealers. They're all jobs with a high degree of stickiness. Priests retire to the seminary and drug dealers to Surfers Paradise, but waiters? With their bad backs, their shot knees and tendency to blow all their spare cash on eating and drinking, it's not exactly a profession known for its prudent thinking about retirement. So it's got me thinking: other ethnic minorities get their own charitably funded old people's homes, so why not waiters? It'd be a blast. There'll be a blanket ban on playing any Ibiza-related compilation, plenty of slate crockery so everyone feels comfortable, and Bloody Marys served each day at 4 p.m. sharp. Bedrooms will be decorated in a light-industrial style with the odd bit of aerosol art, and dinner will be announced with the familiar *ding ding ding ding* summons of a chef with his larynx surgically removed. There'll be jugs of jus to pour at the table, now in hands unsteady thanks to the tremors of age rather than the misadventures of last night, although misadventures will be tolerated just so long as they don't adversely interact with any legitimate medications.

Ben and I are propped up at the bar of one of those new Italian joints cunningly designed to look like they've been around since the middle of last century. I'm reviewing it; he's along for the free booze. He's also just informed me that he and Matt are opening a new cafe so to keep me from bursting into tears we're workshopping our home for old waiters and workshopping it HARD. Will it have an honour bar or is that self-evidently a bad idea to rival the *Hindenburg*? A proper espresso machine is non-negotiable but what do we do about the inevitable fights between the imported Italian bean crowd and the Fair Trade crew? Perhaps a separate wing for the third-wave coffee wankers, who are guaranteed to annoy the crap out of everyone else. (I recently saw a newspaper print a correction about a young man who had been incorrectly described as a barrister. He was, in fact, a barista—proving that not only do baristas take themselves incredibly seriously, but the person who makes your morning brew is now more esteemed than the person who might save you from jail.)

They've only been open three weeks. All the staff are in the love-in phase. It's kind of sweet, really. You can see a little thrill pass through them every time new customers walk in the door. When they're not cheerily serving people, they bunch together and stare intensely at the meatballs and arancini and polenta arranged under glass at the bar. Someone drops the phrase 'mise-en-scene' while the rest of them nod meaningfully. Must be arts students. I ask the bar chick for her funniest waitering story. She gives me something about a cabbie who shat himself and left his undies on the bathroom floor, whose 'Sorry . . . sorry' as he scurried out alerted them that all was not right. And then in the background, over her right shoulder, it happens. The bar guy, Mr Mise-En-Scene, commits a classic rookie mistake while enthusiastically polishing a Riedel glass. The thing about these rather delicate long-stemmed babies is that if you exert too much pressure the bowl breaks off and the stem becomes a very sharp spear. Straight into Cool Bartender's hand it goes, right into the delicate network of tendons and quite possibly his radial artery, given the rivers of blood spurting everywhere. His consciousness has retreated to a pinprick of light somewhere in the black emptiness of his insensible brain. The only functioning body part is his mouth, repeating, 'Oh god. Oh god.' His co-workers are huddled around him but instead of making the usual overtures telling him he's going to be okay they're all freaked, too, so even with the 5 per cent of his cerebral cortex functioning normally the message trickles through that he's fucked. He redoubles his wailing. They bend him over the sink and try to pull the glass out of his hand—every onlooker is wincing in sympathy—but the cries are getting louder, and the blood is spilling out harder, and he's going white with a clammy tinge of green. Ben and I exchange a glance. I'm picking up what he's putting down. It's a glance that says: 'We just witnessed the death of romance.' And: 'They have so much to learn.' And: 'Were we ever so young?'

Off to hospital you go, my lad. Take your wounded paw as a sign that you're better off finishing your uni degree and getting a job where the sharpest thing you encounter is a stapler. Take it as a hint from the gods that things are much sweeter on the other side of the bar. As for us, we're out of here. Off home, but in truth we're not really going anywhere. We're here for life. Because there will always be another one. And another one. Always onwards. Ever on.

Acknowledgements

No woman is an island and clearly no book is either. A multitude of people aided and abetted the writing of this memoir, from helping dust off long-buried memories to giving the author a kick up the bum when she most needed it.

Firstly, to my beloved Ben, without whom none of this would have been possible—thanks, dude. Words fail me, but I reckon you know.

To Jenny Dubecki, a tower of strength, capability and justified eye rolling. Without you our entire domestic set-up would collapse into rubble. You deserve not only a gold medal but silver and bronze, too (and Mum, I'm really sorry about Chapter 12).

My agent Michael Lynch, without whom I couldn't say the words 'my agent', and Jane Palfreyman and Sarah Baker from Allen & Unwin, who were so kind to this little manuscript I almost fell over in shock.

Michael Harden, Hilary McNevin and Roslyn Grundy—you rock. As do you, Janne Apelgren and Nina Rousseau.

Thanks for the moral support and encouragement to Nina Dubecki, Olivia Hill-Douglas and Marcus Sharp, Toby Hemming and Lara Johnston and my girls Sally Jeremiah, Emma Pullen, Chrisi Shorland and Susie Staples.

To Matt Wilkinson and Sharlee Gibb: there's no one I'd rather be on the runaway hospitality train with than you guys. (Sharlee, if they decide to open another cafe we have to kill them, okay?)

Additional thanks for the generous sharing of wisdom and anecdotes goes to Roger Fowler, Erez Gordon, Chris Lucas, Myffy Rigby, Stuart Neil, Jeff Salt, Rosanne Hyland, Paul McGough, Angie Giannakodakis, Kate Foster, Matteo Pignatelli, Harry Gill, Kathi Jennings, Tony Eldred and Andrea Murphy. If there's anyone I've forgotten I apologise. I love youse all.